Clarity for Lawyers

THIRD EDITION

Other titles available from Law Society Publishing:

How to Grow your Firm
Robin Dicks

Lexcel Client Care Toolkit (3rd edn)
Vicky Ling and Fiona Westwood

Niche Marketing for the Legal Sector
David Monk

Profitability and Law Firm Management (3rd edn)
Andrew Otterburn

Titles from Law Society Publishing can be ordered from all good bookshops or direct (telephone 0370 850 1422, email **lawsociety@prolog.uk.com** or visit our online shop at **bookshop.lawsociety.org.uk**).

Clarity for Lawyers

Effective legal language

THIRD EDITION

Mark Adler and Daphne Perry

The Law Society

Crown copyright material is reproduced with the permission of the Controller of Her Majesty's Stationery Office

ISBN-13: 978-1-78446-048-8

First published in 1990
2nd edition 2007

This third edition published in 2017 by the Law Society
113 Chancery Lane, London WC2A 1PL

Typeset by Columns Design XML Ltd, Reading
Printed by Hobbs the Printers Ltd, Totton, Hants

The paper used for the text pages of this book is FSC® certified. FSC (the Forest Stewardship Council®) is an international network to promote responsible management of the world's forests.

Contents

Foreword

The first edition of this book was published in 1990, and it reflected what was then a relatively new development, namely a move away from unnecessarily obscure, complex and technical language in legal documents – what is pejoratively known as 'legalese'. It is perhaps worth briefly considering why legalese developed in the first place and why it is only in the past 30 years or so that there has been a concerted effort to try and make lawyers speak and write more simply and clearly.

Nine hundred years ago, the law was written and conducted mostly in Latin and Anglo-Norman (a mixture of Old English and French with a smattering of other languages). This was partly because the law was based on Roman, Ecclesiastical and Norman principles. It was also partly due to the fact that Anglo-Norman (or French) was the language of the educated and noble classes, and Latin was used in religious circles, which is where many of those involved in the law came from. English started to replace Anglo-Norman and French in normal discourse in the 13th century, but Latin still hangs on in there. And occasionally the law even clings on to Anglo-Norman – thus, 'La Reyne (or le Roy) le vault' is how the monarch's assent to a statute is recorded in Parliament even in the 21st century.

I do not think it was merely tradition which drove the retention of Latin and Norman French. In a common law system, where judges decide much of the law, so that lawyers and judges habitually refer to what was said in earlier judgments and legal arguments, it was presumably convenient to stick to the language in which those judgments and arguments were expressed. However, there was, I strongly suspect, an additional factor, namely the desire of lawyers to ensure that their expertise seemed even greater and that the law was more unattainable to the average person than it really was. The desire to make one's profession or calling seem as mysterious and complex as possible was by no means limited to the legal profession, or indeed to the professions: the number of guilds whose expertise was thought to involve a 'mystery' can be seen even today in the full names of many of the City of London Livery Companies.

By the beginning of the 16th century, legal documents and discourse (including judgments) were routinely being written and conducted in English. However, as lawyers began to argue cases and draft documents in English, the legacy of using foreign languages and the legacy of maintaining mystery both served to ensure that lawyers maintained an unnecessary degree of strangeness and complexity in their language. Strangeness includes idiosyncratic writing, unusual words and foreign expressions; complexity includes complicated sentences, circumlocution and inordinate length. That has tended to continue and it remains the position to the present day.

The interests of lawyers in preserving the mystique of their calling is no doubt part of the explanation for the current complex state of much legal language. But there are other explanations. Lawyers and judges must always try to be as precise in what they say as they can be, so legal language will inevitably sacrifice elegance for clarity. Nuance and implication may be the hallmark of many good writers, but lawyers should generally avoid them. Further, certain expressions will have a clear and established meaning in the law, often as a result of judges' decisions, but also as a matter of accepted convention among those practising in the relevant field. So, however poor or inapt the language of the expression may be, a cautious lawyer may well include it in a document or submission because he or she knows how it will be understood. Lawyers, like most people, tend to suffer from the belief that 'more is better', and natural caution, a hallmark of a good lawyer, carries with it a tendency to cross every 't' and dot every 'i'. All this has resulted in many documents, legal submissions and judgments being too long. The introduction of IT has tended to reinforce this problem because previous documents of the same sort (e.g. an earlier lease) can easily be used as a template for a document which a lawyer is drafting. And there is no doubt that the advent of IT has added to the length of documents.

So, why is this changing now? I suspect that it is due to a number of factors, which are probably connected. First, since the 1960s there has been a general falling away in what has been called the 'respect agenda'. Those who previously expected, and normally got, respect because of their position in society, have been finding over the past 50 years that much of the respect is gradually being stripped away. This can be seen as having both advantages and disadvantages, but for present purposes, the important thing is that the effect of this development is a greater tendency to challenge accepted norms in many areas of life. And that includes questioning the need for legalese. Secondly, there has been the growth, some might say the explosion, of the consumer society. The focus on the consumer rather than on the supplier in the legal world has meant that clients and others are more ready to expect, sometimes to demand, that documents are written in language that they can understand. Lawyers are now writing as much for clients as for each other.

Thirdly, there has been a very significant increase in the number of people in the legal profession, just as in many other more privileged occupations. Although social mobility remains a very serious problem in this country, this inevitably means that there are many more lawyers who come from non-professional backgrounds, many more lawyers who were the first generation of their families to have gone to university. I suspect that this has led to a greater preparedness to challenge norms, conventions and habits which would have been accepted without question in previous generations. Finally, the internet has taken away much of the mystique associated with many aspects of life. Medical practitioners, like lawyers, are often surprised by the expert and up-to-date information that patients or clients have acquired simply by searching through specialist websites.

None of this should obscure the fact that the reduction or, even better, the removal of legalese from legal documents and legal discussion is to be welcomed. It is appropriate that the reason for this is simple and can be expressed in one sentence: it should be less hard to draft, as well as easier to understand, a document or an oral statement, if it is expressed in language which is as ordinary and simple as possible. I say 'less hard' rather than 'easier', because composing documents or legal arguments well is a real art, and even to the good and experienced drafter it is never easy.

In all these circumstances, a book on clear drafting for lawyers is to be welcomed, and a good book on the topic is to be greatly welcomed. Mark Adler and Daphne Perry have written a good book on the topic, and it is a pleasure to write this foreword to the third edition. The book is engagingly written and well structured. Many parts of the book can be read almost as much for pleasure as for instruction, as they can be regarded as a collection of anecdotes or cautionary tales. That is because the authors very sensibly realise that by far the best way to make their point is by way of examples. Finally, I would venture to suggest that anyone who is engaged in communication, whether in writing or by word of mouth, could profit from reading this book.

David Neuberger
President of the Supreme Court of the United Kingdom
August 2017

Acknowledgements

Mark Adler dedicates this book to his mother, Flora, who spoke sensible English to him in the pram; his father, Bernard, who brought him into the law and let him loose on his practice; and his wife, Jan, who has given him fresh perspectives and wise advice.

Daphne Perry dedicates her part in the book to Mark Adler, for writing the first edition from which she learned plain English, and to Nick Lear, for suggesting she should read it.

So many others have contributed ideas and suggestions over the years that we cannot compile a complete list of the people to whom we are indebted, but we'd particularly like to thank (posthumously, in too many cases):

Professor John E. Adams, Dr Michael Arnheim, Dr Rabeea Assy, Peter Austin, Francis Barlow QC, Francis Bennion, Dr Duncan Berry, Michelle Bevan, Lord Bingham of Cornhill, Dominiek Braet, The British National Corpus, Professor Peter Butt, Sir Edward Caldwell QC, Richard Castle, Paul Clark, Martin Cutts, Dr Robert Eagleson, Editor Software Pty Ltd, Barbro Ehrenberg-Sundin, Chris Elgey, David Elliott, Barrie England, Janet Erasmus QC, Euroclear plc, Mavis Fairhurst, Nicole Fernbach, Dr Helen Fraser, Professor Bryan Garner, Professor Jean-Claude Gémar, Josephine Gibbons, Tamara Gorieli, Jenny Gracie, Stewart Graham, Professor Sidney Greenbaum, John Hightower, Simon Hillson, Myla Kaplan, Professor Joseph Kimble, Clive Kirk, Phillip Knight, Ruth Lawrence, Nick Lear, Marcel Lemmens, Alexandra Marks, Helen McDowell, Professor Kate McLoughlin, Andrew Melling, Dr David Miller, Louise Mills, Paul Milner, Christine Mowat, Lesley Neenan, Justin Nelson, Timothy Norman, Richard Nzerem, Richard Oerton, Rachel Oliphant, Tony Parr, Alison Plouviez, Practical Law Dispute Resolution, James Roberts, William Robins, William Robinson, Professor Robert Rosenthal, Gayl Russell, Jenny Savage, Halina Sierocka , Charles Smith, Dr Clive Mira Smith, Cheryl Stephens, Anita Stueva, Adrian Taylor, Araba Taylor, Professor Peter Tiersma, Professor Nick Trefethen, Anne Trier, Dr Mark Vale, Maria

Cristina Vignolo, Anne Wagner, Rob Waller, John Walton, Kim What-more, Ken Williams, Peter J.G. Williams, Ana Wolchover, David Wolchover, and Professor Richard Wydick.

Introduction

Who is this book for?

Primarily for lawyers and law-makers in England and Wales, from judges and legislators to paralegals and law students.

The earlier editions were welcomed overseas, particularly in common law jurisdictions and even by those using English as a second language. We have continued to write with those readers in mind.

It's also for anyone who writes in, works with, or is interested in legal language. To help non-lawyers, some of the technicalities are explained at www.clarityforlawyers.com, and we'll add to the list on request.

What is it for?

To help lawyers work more effectively and more efficiently, for their own benefit and for that of anyone affected by their work – which is all of us.

To make the law more transparent, so that its benefits and obligations are not lost in a tangle of verbiage.

We have tried to make it more interesting and readable than just a style guide, and we hope that it will sometimes surprise you.

What's new in this edition?

We have added new chapters suggesting a practical approach for those who want to start improving their writing at once (Chapter 8, 'How to start'); outlining what software can do to help improve clarity (Chapter 21, 'Computer aids'); suggesting easy, achievable ways to get user feedback on documents (Chapter 22, 'Testing documents'); and outlining a workshop for teaching lawyers to write more clearly (Appendix A, 'A legal writing workshop'). Parts B ('What is good writing?') and D ('How misunderstandings arise') are also mostly new.

Much that is true of good writing is also relevant to speech, though we have not always spelled this out. But this edition does include more material specifically about speech.

You can find more information about the book at www.clarityforlawyers.com. We intend to add reviews; a forum for discussion, questions, and corrections; and updates.

Mark Adler (MA): As I retired in 2007, a few months after the second edition was published, I was in no position to update it. This was frustrating, because I had used some of my new leisure to read and think about aspects of legal language that I hadn't considered before, and to some extent my views had changed. Daphne resolved the problem by agreeing that we should do the job together. Apart from updating the law and practice, she has contributed much from her own experience and has brought a fresh eye to the text.

Daphne Perry (DP): I was delighted to have a chance to contribute to my favourite textbook and to publish more widely some of the ideas I have developed, first in practice as a commercial litigator and advocate and later in my consultancy, writing, and training work. It is my ambition to make the world a better place by encouraging lawyers to write so that their readers can understand them first time. I hope this book, and my contribution to it, will continue to advance that aim.

Why does it look the way it does?

Ideally, every aspect of its format would reflect the book's recommendations. In reality, there are commercial constraints, particularly as we wanted to keep the price down. Some aspects have not been settled as we write this but we are grateful to Law Society Publishing for their flexibility and for the trouble they are taking to adapt their house style to accommodate us.

Footnotes can be intrusive and annoying, especially when they are merely citations which many readers will not look at, and when citations are mixed up with incidental comments. Where such notes are unavoidable, they have been tidied away as endnotes after each chapter. Comprehensive lists of case citations and publication references are included at the end of the book (see 'Index of cases' and 'Bibliography' respectively).

Part A

What's wrong with legal writing?

Chapter 1

What's wrong with traditional legal writing?

Introduction

Lawyers with keyboards or dictating machines forget they are people; however amiable and unpretentious they are at other times, when they compose the written word a strange personality emerges. Where a human being would say

> The house is ready

a solicitor employs a large staff to say

> We hereby give you notice in accordance with clause 11 of the Contract dated 6th November 2016 the made between Miranda Homes Limited of 157 Bracknell Road South Farnham Hampshire (1) and East Hill Residents Association Limited of 157 Bracknell Road, South Farnham, Hampshire SF4 5GR (2) and James Edward Brownlow & Katherine Elizabeth Brownlow of 81 Landfall Road South Farnham Hampshire (3) that the above property is now constructionally complete.

What persuades solicitors that all this is necessary? The belief that careful drafting will avoid ambiguity? There would have been none; with the address given (as usual) in the heading of the letter, the four-word alternative could not have been misunderstood by the solicitor-recipient. But a more helpful writer could have added:

> You should therefore arrange to complete the purchase by 1st September[, please].

What is wrong with the longer form?

- *Hereby* adds nothing. Could the recipients have argued that *We give you notice ...* did not constitute notice?
- *We give you notice that* is similarly redundant.
- *In accordance with* is wordy; *under* would be neater.
- Nothing is gained by reciting the contract, since it had already been identified by the reference to the house in the heading of the letter.

- So keen was the writer to reproduce the entire contents of the dictionary that he (or she) did not notice the mistaken use of *the* instead of *and* in the second line. This error turns the supposedly precise text into gibberish.
- *Dated 6th November 2016 and made* ... could be expressed more economically: dated *6 November 2016* ...
- *Contract* is a common noun, not a proper one, and does not deserve a capital letter.
- If the names of the parties must be spelled out, the usual *Ltd* would serve.
- Commas are omitted from the first incidence of the Bracknell Road address. This creates ambiguity: is it *157 Bracknell Road, South Farnham* or *157 Bracknell Road South, Farnham*? And if there is a good reason for abandoning punctuation (and the postcode), why are they both restored on the following line?
- The postcode (which the recipient would have checked before exchange of contracts) is no help here.
- The repetition of the address is clumsy and gives the impression that the writer was not aware that it had already been given: *of the same address* could replace the second recital; or (with slight rearrangement) the first could be omitted in favour of *both of* ...
- The use of the numbers *(1)* and *(2)* might be appropriate if it is not otherwise clear who is who (though it always should be – see, for example, the revision on p.86), but it is an affectation in a letter.
- The use of *and* between each of three items in a list is clumsy.
- On the third reference to South Farnham (where both solicitors had their offices) the writer is still assuring the recipient that it is in Hampshire.
- *The above* ... is no more precise than *the* ...; there is no property mentioned below.
- *Constructionally complete* is not a term of art and has no clear meaning. We suspect that it was a slip, perhaps copied from the contract, and that the writer meant practical completion.

Few people read more legal writing than they have to, especially if it's badly written. So it's worth bearing in mind Armstrong and Terrell's warning (2015):

> Our starting point has been a painful psychological fact about how readers, especially readers who are habitually skeptical, approach a document. At every level, from its very beginning all the way down into the innards of its paragraphs, they are constantly asking annoying questions: Why am I reading this? Where are we going? Why are we going there?

But even if the reader perseveres, and is able to unravel the language, the message itself may well be flawed. Justice Samuel Alito of the US Supreme Court thinks that (Garner, 2011):

there is a clear relationship between good, clear writing and good, clear thinking. And if you don't have one, it's very hard to have the other.

Throughout this book we suggest clearer, more concise, and, we hope, more effective alternatives to pieces of traditional drafting. You might find that we – like everyone else – make mistakes. But that does not mean it is wrong to write more clearly; any error can (and is more likely to) be corrected within the guidelines we are proposing. If you spot one, or have any other criticism, please post it on the book's website at www.clarity forlawyers.com.

So what is wrong with traditional legal writing? In summary:

- It wastes everyone's time.
- It wastes everyone's money.
- It reduces lawyers' earnings.
- It holds up commerce and people's lives.
- It is imprecise.
- It causes unnecessary and sometimes expensive mistakes.
- It often fails to achieve the writer's purpose.
- It alienates clients, their advisers, and the public.
- It alienates many judges.
- It sounds archaic.
- It shuts people out of their own business.
- It undermines the rule of law.
- It is often itself unlawful.
- It can be unprofessional.
- It is inhuman.
- And it's as dull as lead (and almost as indigestible).

If you are convinced, you might want to go straight to Part C where we start to discuss the writing habits that can make legal writing more effective. Or, for argument and examples in support of the bulleted assertions and an explanation of what we are trying to do, please read straight on.

Legalese wastes time

Legalese takes longer to read. This is partly because there is more of it, but there are other reasons; several factors make it more time-consuming, word for word. These are the:

- unbroken layout;
- long and convoluted sentences;
- more difficult words; and
- absence of punctuation.

Take this example from a commercial lease, written by a committee of lawyers who had no homes to go to:

> Not to use or permit or suffer to be used the demised premises or any part thereof or any buildings or erections at any time hereafter erected thereon or on any part thereof as and for all or any of the purposes of a brewery or a club (whether proprietary or members) or a public house or other licensed premises or otherwise for the preparation manufacture supply distribution or sale whether wholesale or retail and whether for consumption on or off the premises of all or any alcoholic liquors of any description and not without the previous consent in writing of the Landlord to carry on or permit upon the demised premises any trade business or occupation other than that of a retail shop for the sale of X.

They could have said just:

> Not to make or sell alcoholic drinks in the shop or (without the landlord's written consent) to use it except for the retail sale of X.

(We explain the omission of *not to use or permit* on p.106.) The irony is that the drafters must have started with something like the shorter version in mind. What did the client want? That the premises be used as a shop, with the landlord having a reasonable say in what was sold – but on no account strong drink. Why then did the drafters so painstakingly construct that elaborate waffle? The tenant's solicitor would only have to decode it. So, also, would the parties and their advisers each time a query arose over the years and whenever the lease was sold or mortgaged.

The late Dr Robert Eagleson, an Australian linguist and legal drafting consultant, once said (in correspondence) that he hadn't managed to devise a suitable test

> … but from experience I think it is pretty certain that legalese takes longer to write.
>
> Public servants ('civil servants' in the UK) often begin with a plain version and then redraft into a longer version meaning the same.
>
> Lawyers tend to do the same. No one begins with a grammatically correct 300-word sentence. They begin with many short ones and then merge. To get everything in the right order takes time.

Getting all the right content in the right order takes not only time but experience, skill, thought, and care. An efficient shortcut is to copy what the writer (or someone else) has written before. Using a precedent also reduces the risk of overlooking what others have already considered, although it introduces other, less obvious, risks. Unfortunately, most precedents are still in traditional style, but when it's time to add or update a precedent, a clearer style will be a lasting asset.

Research reported by the Law Reform Commission of Victoria (1987, para.106) shows that plain English (a concept we discuss in Chapter 4)

6

increases the speed with which lawyers read documents and solve problems interpreting legislation. Those findings have since been duplicated, notably by Martin Cutts' research reported in *Lucid Law* (2000).

> **DP**: In 2014, I ran a timed trial on a two-page letter asking a court manager to preserve documents for an appeal. A small group of postgraduate legal writing students read the letter and answered questions testing their understanding. The students given the original version took about 30 per cent longer to finish answering than those looking at the version rewritten according to the principles in this book. The students looking at the rewritten version also gave more accurate answers. This was not an isolated example; I often run less precisely measured tests on shorter documents, and routinely find a noticeable difference in reading time.

The reader of a traditional text has a harder task than the writer, who (ideally) knows the intended meaning.

The 158-word original sentence below took Mark Adler some four minutes to read and understand, a rate of about 40 words a minute. The 54-word plainer version that follows it omitted unnecessary and some irrational detail and should take about 20 seconds, a rate of 165 words a minute. What slowed him down so much in the original? He had to:

- Force himself to read to the end, dragging his mind back to the text when it wandered.
- Concentrate hard on what he was reading.
- Search for cross-references and skim them for their gist.
- Break the text down into its parts, so that he could put subordinate clauses to one side as he worked out the structure of the whole and extracted the essence of the meaning.
- Read each part more than once.
- Reassure himself that he correctly understood it (though a thorough check would have taken much longer).

Original (158 words)

If at any time when the aggregate of the Initial Percentage and any Portioned Percentage (as hereinafter defined) acquired by the Leaseholder pursuant to the provisions of Clause 2 and the Fourth Schedule hereto is less than 100 % there has been a disposal of the Lease otherwise than in the circumstances detailed in Clause 3(15)(b) hereof and the Landlord by notice in writing served upon the Leaseholder within two months after receipt of notice of the disposal pursuant to Clause 3(16) hereof so requires the Leaseholder shall pay to the Landlord on demand the Market Value of the Relevant Percentage as defined in and ascertained in accordance with the provisions of the Fourth Schedule hereto as if the Leaseholder had served upon the Landlord on the date of the disposal a notice pursuant to Paragraph 2(1) of the Fourth Schedule hereto stating his intention to acquire such Portioned Percentage as would thereafter reduce the Relevant Percentage to nil

Revision (54 words)

The tenant must buy the landlord's remaining share of the lease, using the valuation machinery in clause x and paying the price on demand, if:

(1) The ownership of the lease changes in breach of clause 3(15)(b); and
(2) Within two months of receiving notice of the change, the landlord gives the tenant notice to buy.

That example was taken from a document 20 pages long, with about 360 words to a page. Scaling up from the extract, it would take about three hours to read in full, though in practice the sanity breaks will extend that time. Then it must be explained to the client, ideally in writing – another long and tedious job. If the revision reduces the 7,200 words of the original pro rata to 2,500 words, it should take about 15 minutes to read, and leave only points of law to explain to clients (who can read the document for themselves).

Any change in writing habits takes time – whether to simplify a legalistic style or to complicate a simple one (as some writers do on joining the profession). So, at least in the short term, writing clearly saves more time for the reader than it does for the writer. But in Chapter 8 and Appendix A we suggest a practical approach for busy professionals to improve their style without disrupting their workflow. Meanwhile, lawyers should demand, and help develop, clear and simple precedents. They might begin by focusing on those 'high stakes' documents which will most benefit the clients, the firm, and the writer. Improvements might make extra work in the short term for users familiar with the old version, but will guard against the dangers of skimming.

In the longer term, it will become quicker to write the initial draft. Any time saved can be reallocated to think more about what readers will need and to check and improve the draft.

Legalese wastes money

Just as time is wasted, so is money.

Lawyers spending 12 times as many hours as should be necessary on a job are likely to charge up to 12 times as much as they might; more if they think the complexity justifies a higher rate. To give some idea of the burden this imposes on all but the wealthiest clients, a solicitor charging 'only' £225 an hour – and some charge much more – will save a client earning £25,000 a year about two working days' income for every hour's work no longer necessary. Cutting the time taken to carry out the work can make the lawyer's services more affordable for the client and profitable for the lawyer. Even on work charged at an hourly rate, there is commercial pressure to keep fees in proportion to the value of the transaction and unbillable hours may have to be written off. Lawyers working for a fixed fee must reduce their profit or quote more to allow for wasted time. Moreover, our experience has been that clearly written documents attract fewer amendments and so reduce both the cost of negotiations and the delay to the clients' business while they are conducted.

Time and money are also wasted in dealing with queries about unclear text, and in correcting errors arising from it. For example, the UK Parliament's Public Accounts Committee reported that (UK PAC, 2010):

> Feedback from advisors had revealed that a letter [HM Revenue and Customs] sends out each year to people joining Income Tax Self Assessment was confusing. By changing the letter it had eliminated 88,000 calls which would save the Department £447,000 a year.

And in 2015, HM Courts & Tribunals Service was receiving 500,000 applications a year to reduce court fees and rejecting up to 70 per cent, even though most applicants did qualify, because the applicants had misunderstood the form or sent the wrong evidence. Faulty applications dropped once it simplified the application process, changed the form, and reduced the guidance from 37 pages to 12, improving the outcome for applicants and saving work for court staff.[1]

For many more examples, see *Writing for Dollars, Writing to Please* (Kimble, 2012).

Legalese reduces lawyers' earnings

Cynics might argue that lawyers don't *want* to reduce their fees (and some lawyers agree with them). But lawyers who know how to save time and fees on a transaction can still earn as much. If they spend a quarter of the time on a job they can double their hourly rates yet still halve their bill. They will be paid twice as much for each hour worked, and sooner than they otherwise would have been. They can move more quickly to the next job, represent more clients while charging each one less (so reducing the need to work unprofitably), and impress each client with their speed and efficiency.

If they do run out of genuine work – or choose to take less on – they can go home at a reasonable time and relax at weekends, having earned good money for a skilful job. There might come a utopian time when all our precedents are clearly written and fewer lawyers will be needed; if so, let the least talented aspiring newcomers choose a career more useful than stoking fog.

In the meantime, law firms keen to secure these savings might start by clarifying their own most-used documents. Those that rely on the forms and precedents produced by legal publishers should call for these to be improved.

Legalese holds up commerce and people's lives

Traditional writing also slows everyone down in another way. Apart from increasing the number of hours devoted to a job, it extends the time before the work is finished. The recipient of a short, clear document is likely to deal with it promptly, perhaps immediately. But a busy lawyer receiving 60 pages of gobbledigook is likely to put it to one side and to leave it there for as long as possible. They dread spending three hours on a 15-minute job (using the comparison on pp.7–8) and give it low priority, perhaps forgetting it until the dissatisfied client complains.

And while the lawyers put off the long, dull job they can't get around to, the client's property is standing empty (if it's a lease they are negotiating): the landlord is losing rent while continuing to pay the outgoings; the tenant's business cannot open; neighbouring businesses and the local community suffer from a less vibrant district; and the landlord's prospects on neighbouring rent reviews are diminished. Meanwhile, neither client is satisfied with its lawyer, or with the quality of service provided.

> **MA:** Contrast the case of a landlord who telephoned me one afternoon about an empty shop. A prospective tenant had arranged to view it the following day, and the landlord asked me if I could meanwhile email a draft lease to each of them. I typed the proposed details into the standard lease for that trading estate and sent it to them, inviting the tenant to pass it to his solicitor. Next morning, I later heard, the tenant approved the shop, signed the lease (which was clearly written and intended to be fair to both parties) with immediate effect, and took possession.

Legalese is imprecise

The main excuse for the impenetrability of traditional legal writing is that the wording has been honed by the courts over many years and is necessary if the document is to have the extraordinary precision required of such a complex subject. But this is nonsense.

The two strands of this argument are logically separate. Neither is valid.

Sometimes the argument is presented as though the years of litigation have so carefully defined the terms that it would now be dangerous to depart from them, as the new language would then have to be litigated from scratch. On other occasions the argument is presented as though the language was intrinsically precise. Of course, these two hypotheses are incompatible: if the language was intrinsically precise it would never have needed the litigation.

The late Professor David Mellinkoff's law dictionary devoted, he said, more than 200 pages to summaries (summaries!) of conflicting judicial rulings on the meaning of 'accident'. Does that mean that the word is now precise (but wasn't after the penultimate ruling)? Or that it is now much more precise than it used to be, but still needs some litigation, which your client offers to fund? In *The Language of the Law* (1963) Mellinkoff selects a few examples, including these (at p.377; we have omitted the meticulous case references):

> If you reach forward to stop a heavy crate from falling, and get a heart attack, that's an accident. But if you reach upward to stop heavy planks from falling, and get a heart attack, that's no accident. A sunstroke is usually an *accident*, but it is anyone's guess whether sunstroke is an injury by *accidental means*. If there is any doubt in your mind about what an *accident* is, just remember that if Mr Schwartz picks his nose and it bleeds, that's an *accident* ...
>
> Without perceptible benefit, courts have repeated for years the lay definitions of *accident*, and are not even agreed that it has any technical meaning.

A moment's thought undermines the honing argument even without recourse to the details. Every case is decided on its own facts, and the decision will reflect the evidence (so far as it was admissible) of the circumstances surrounding this particular use of the word, and in particular of the parties' intentions. But how often do lawyers using an expression check its meaning in a legal dictionary? As close to never as makes no difference. And how often do they then read the judgments cited? *Absolutely* never. Even if they did, and they tailored their language to reflect all these (often inconsistent) cases, it would not protect them from a judge who disagreed with an earlier decision, nor from one who knows that meaning varies from place to place and from time to time.

'Tried and tested: the myth behind the cliché' (Adler, 1996) looked at these arguments in more detail, comparing the wording of a selection of repairing covenants and the results of the disputes they provoked. It appeared that it was not the *wording* that had become customary, but only the *style*. The wording was different in every case.

But could there be anything in the suggestion that legal language is intrinsically more precise, even if absolute precision is an unattainable ideal?

Look at how that language is constructed:

- Take as many sentences as possible.
- Replace the full stops that separate them with conjunctions to make one super-sentence.
- Remove the rest of the punctuation (to mask the relationship between different parts of the super-sentence).
- Move what used to be one sentence into the middle of what used to be another, and repeat the process as often as you like (to make it difficult to see where one idea ends and the next begins).
- Change the word order to one less familiar to non-lawyers.
- Replace modern words with archaic alternatives.

- List all the specific items you can think of instead of (or as well as) using a general word to cover them all (but don't worry if the list is incomplete, or if it includes items that should not be there).
- Pad out the result with as many synonyms and other unnecessary words as possible.

Forgive us for doubting the sanity of anyone who thinks this is a recipe for precision. But if you still feel nervous about leaving the asylum may we refer you to a more detailed exposition in 'Alphabet soup' (Adler, 1993)?

Legalese causes mistakes

Mistakes are inevitable. Everybody makes them, especially when working under pressure. But just as a traditional document takes even longer to understand than its unnecessary length would lead us to expect, so will it contain proportionately more mistakes. But it goes beyond that: legalese breeds extra errors that could be avoided by clear expression.

This example comes from the terms for supplies of goods or services, offered on its website by one of the 50 biggest UK law firms:

> Without prejudice to any other right or remedy we may have, we reserve the right to set off any amount owing at any time by you to us, whether under this Agreement or any other agreement which may exist from time to time between us, against any amount payable by you to us under this Agreement.

The sentence is long and confusing – to writers and proofreaders as well as the people to whom it is addressed. The idea seems to be that the law firm (but not the supplier) can deduct debts owed under other contracts. In fact, the clause is meaningless because, by repeating the words *by you to us*, it says the law firm can set off the supplier's debts against the supplier's debts.

The harder it is to extract the meaning from text, the easier it becomes to overlook a possible problem. The mistake everyone fears is *not* typed as *now*, or missed out altogether. That could have been the problem in this clause, which the House of Lords called 'half-baked', in a contract to develop land and then lease it:

> Upon the proper issue of the certificate of practical completion referred to in clause 3(a) hereof the landlords will forthwith grant and the tenant shall forthwith accept and execute a counterpart of the lease provided that if for any reason due to the wilful default of the tenant the development shall remain uncompleted on the 29th day of September 1983 the lease shall forthwith be granted and completed as aforesaid but without prejudice to the provisions of clause 3 hereof.

If taken literally, the proviso gave the tenant a good result (a lease of the property) if it acted very badly (failed through 'wilful default' to complete the development). After three and a half years of litigation, the House of

Lords corrected the mistake through a piece of creative interpretation (*Alghussein Establishment* v. *Eton College* (1988)).

Creative interpretation (and rectification) can still correct a mistake in some cases, but not all. Consider this clause fixing the service charge in the lease of a holiday chalet in a caravan park (*Arnold* v. *Britton* (2015)):

> To pay to the Lessor without any deduction in addition to the said rent a proportionate part of the expenses and outgoings incurred by the Lessor in the repair maintenance renewal and the provision of services hereinafter set out the yearly sum of Ninety Pounds and value added tax (if any) for the first three years of the term hereby granted increasing thereafter by Ten Pounds per Hundred for every subsequent three year period or part thereof.

Sixty-nine chalets were let on these or similar terms; some chalets had annual rather than triennial increases. The service charge started at £90 in the first year, and in the last year of at least one term would reach £1,025,004 regardless of the actual cost to the landlord of providing the services. After four years of litigation, the Supreme Court expressed sympathy for the tenants for increases it described as 'alarming' but supported the landlord's interpretation. Lord Neuberger, giving the main judgment, said:

> I accept that the less clear [the words] are, or, to put it another way, the worse their drafting, the more ready the court can properly be to depart from their natural meaning.

Nevertheless, this clause was not bad enough to justify a creative interpretation. It was only bad enough to help disguise the bad bargain the tenants were making.

These mistakes can have savage consequences for solicitors as well as for the clients, since they are likely to be sued for negligence (or worse, if they have deliberately helped to create a misleading document).

Consider also a vital witness whose statement includes a mistake created by the solicitor and thrown up only during cross-examination. If the case turned on the witness's reliability and this witness was made to look careless or a liar, how would the damage be repaired?

Mistakes are bound to increase with both the length and complexity of a sentence, as writers bite off more than they or their readers can chew. Why do lawyers go to such lengths to create unnecessary trouble for their clients and themselves?

Legalese doesn't achieve the writer's purpose

This is a third way in which legalese wastes time. Lawyers write to communicate, not to show off. If the reader does not understand, what should have been said will remain effectively unsaid. To communicate, you must adapt to the reader. It is no good sending a television signal to a radio receiver.

13

If one litigator writes to another *We reserve the right to bring a Part 20 claim against [X]*, the meaning will be clear. But if the recipient passes on the message untranslated, the client will be no wiser, and perhaps ask for an explanation, interrupting the solicitor's other work and adding (unfairly) to the bill. Or perhaps they will just shrug their shoulders and put up with ignorance – a common reaction. So, what should the solicitor have said? *The defendants are threatening to add to this litigation their own claim against [X].*

Formal agreements frequently – we are tempted to say 'usually' – contain provisions that the parties to it did not intend, do not know are there, and accordingly ignore. Too often this applies to their solicitors as well.

A lease (which a client wanted to buy) defined the boundary between the flat (for whose repair she would be responsible) and the rest of the building above and below (for which the landlord was responsible) by reference to the floor timbers and the joists on which they rested. But the floors were concrete. So who pays for their repair? And who pays the legal costs of arguing about it? This and other (equally unnecessary) defects made the lease unmortgageable – except to the many lenders whose solicitors didn't notice – and the buyer very reluctantly withdrew, disappointing both parties.

A more expensive example occurred in the transfer of housing stock, with its associated staff, from a local authority to a company. The deal was complex, and there was an unfortunate misunderstanding over its terms. The company and both lawyers thought the local authority would make up a deficit in the staff pension fund. The local authority negotiator thought the opposite. Here is the clause dealing with the point:

> 14.10.2 In relation to the Transferring Employees and the Support Service Employees [DDC] shall make payments to the appropriate administering authority or the administrators of the Superannuation Scheme for immediate credit to the Scheme as are necessary to ensure that all liabilities in respect of the benefits accrued by (1) the Transferring Employees up to the Completion Date and (2) the Support Services Employees up to the Transfer Date are fully funded based upon the actuarial assumptions used for the 2007 actuarial valuation. For the avoidance of doubt, this means funded to the extent necessary to ensure that there shall be no liability on [DDH] to make any contributions to the Superannuation Scheme in relation to the cost of funding the accrued benefits in relation to the period of time up to the Completion Date in respect of the Transferring Employees (and the Transfer Date in respect of the Support Services Employees) and until such payments are made by [DDC] shall indemnify [DDH] against all costs proceedings damages expenses and Support Services Employees' liabilities and claims of whatever nature in respect of the Transferring Employees and the Support Service Employees said accrued benefits. [DDC] shall be responsible for corresponding with the Superannuation Scheme's actuary in relation to the certification by the Superannuation Scheme's actuary as is mentioned above and shall bear the costs incurred in relation to the obtaining of the said actuarial valuation.

The Court of Appeal, after four years of litigation, said this clause was 'clear' – that is, it could have only one meaning. It meant the local authority must pay the deficit, as certified by the actuary, which was £2.4 million (*Daventry District Council* v. *Daventry & District Housing* (2011)). Nevertheless, the demand had come as a shock to the local authority. Reading and approving the contract had done nothing to correct their misunderstanding of the deal they were about to make.

There is no point in imposing obligations in such language that they are not understood either by those responsible for obeying or those responsible for enforcing them. Unfortunately, many solicitors prepare documents, often with onerous clauses, without consulting their clients. They just copy a precedent that they (or someone else) have used in the past. Similarly, many solicitors do not explain the incoming documents to their clients. Often neither party to a contract knows what the solicitors have arranged. The resulting document does not represent the bargain made by the clients and its provisions are innocently ignored – until there is a problem.

Another consequence is that the bargain is not properly thought through. For example, many disputes have arisen because the co-owners of a house were not asked by the solicitor acting on the purchase to decide what would happen if one died or if they separated.

Legalese alienates clients, their advisers, and the public

Even if no tangible harm follows, the client may well resent being addressed in unfamiliar language. The Solicitors Complaints Bureau reported privately for the first edition of this book that about nine referrals out of 10 arose out of nothing more than a breakdown in communications. Some of these were cases in which the client could not understand what the solicitor had said. This example did not go to the Bureau, but the baffled client did ask another solicitor to translate the letter for her:

> I have been looking into the situation relating to the term of the Lease in the light of indications given with regard to the X Housing Association's standard Form of Covenant. As you know, no Deed of Covenant was required from you at the time of your acquisition, but it appears that arrangements were in hand at one time for the term granted by the Lease which you have acquired to be extended to 999 years. At present you have a term in excess of 70 years remaining on the Lease which is perfectly satisfactory, and if you were to consider moving during the course of the next few years you would have no difficulty in disposing of the Lease. Ultimately, however, difficulties can arise and it may be to your advantage to consider taking a Variation to extend the term. I have now received confirmation that the X Housing Association will be willing to agree such an arrangement, but any such Variation will probably entail the introduction of the need for a Deed of Covenant to be provided by the Purchasers at the time of assignment of the Lease. Please give the matter some consideration and let me know your requirements. I anticipate that you will be expected to bear the costs of obtaining such a Variation.
>
> I await hearing from you both with regard to the above and with your cheque as previously requested.

Far too many solicitors write like this, apparently unaware of the blank incomprehension with which their letter is met. Among the faults:

- The long paragraph is hard on the reader; it looks (and is) too boring to read, and many will start to skim, or give up, before they reach the end, as you probably did.
- There are many words and phrases that might not be understood by a lay reader. These, and the many inappropriate capital letters, distance the writer from the reader by using alien language, throwing away a chance to show that the writer understands the reader's needs.
- The writer had not organised his or her thoughts; the text rambles from point to point and it is not always clear (even to another solicitor) what was intended.
- The style is dull and repetitive.
- It omits the following important information that the client would need to make the decision for which her solicitor is asking:

    - how many years it will be before the value of the lease is affected;
    - how badly it will be affected;
    - how much it will cost to put right;
    - what commitments will be expected from a future purchaser;
    - what sort of 'requirements' the solicitor thought the client might have.

Our interpretation of what the writer was trying to say is:

> Your lease has just over 70 years to run. At the moment that is long enough but in [an unspecified time] it will become difficult to sell.
>
> The Housing Association is willing to extend the lease [to 999 years?] to solve this problem for you, but you will probably have to pay their [unspecified] costs and agree to [unspecified] terms.
>
> Please tell me if you want to accept (and may I remind you to let me have a cheque at the same time?).

If the letter had been written like this it would have taken less time to dictate, type and check; whatever time *was* used would not have been wasted by the client's incomprehension; the involvement of a second solicitor would have been unnecessary; and the writer might have noticed and filled the gaps.

Not all solicitors escape so easily. In an article in the *Law Society Gazette* (25 April 1990), Mavis Fairhurst, the Solicitors Complaints Bureau's press officer, wrote:

> Communication is often a key to a complaint, which on examination very often reveals a misunderstanding or no understanding at all. Who can blame the octogenarian's confusion when she saw a substantial part of a compensation claim clawed back by legal aid? The file revealed that the solicitor had explained the situation thus: 'I am afraid that the Law Society's statutory charge will attach

16

to part of this money but given the defendant's alleged impecuniosity I think it unlikely that you will obtain more if we proceed.'

Some lawyers excuse their traditional style as necessary to impress clients, some of whom they imagine prefer it. But neither of us has come across such a client outside a lawyer's dreams.

Adler (1991) reports research into the public's understanding of and reaction to lawyers' writing style. He reproduced a letter written by a supposedly prestigious solicitor to his client's wife to set divorce proceedings in motion and to suggest a particular division of the assets. The letter was not badly written by the normal standards of the profession, but was chosen to show how inadequate those standards were and to avoid the suggestion that the example was unrepresentative. It was superficially easy to understand, though closer analysis revealed problems likely to be overlooked. With the original recipient's permission, and after changing the names, the letter was sent to 150 clients with a questionnaire, first asking them if they understood it and then asking what they understood by various expressions and proposals in the letter.

Of the 77 who answered, only 28 were confident that they understood it all. All 77 had previous experience of the law, and many were university graduates or had run their own businesses (which gave them advantages over the particular wife to whom the original had been sent). Putting that aside – and ignoring the substantial effect of stress on the comprehension of the unrepresented wife whose marriage was crumbling – a one-in-three chance of understanding the letter was poor odds. But the truth was worse than that: the closer questioning that followed the enquiry *Did you understand the letter?* revealed that every one of the 28 who thought they understood was wrong: not one of the 77 respondents had understood the letter accurately; many had made multiple errors, and some of these were catastrophic.

At the end of the questionnaire the respondents were asked what they thought of the style. Here are a few of the answers:

'Stuffy as well as unclear.'
'Just a general woolliness!'
'Completely uninformative. Very badly drafted. Does not request the wife to obtain independent advice. Could lead to considerable difficulties in future.'
'Sly ...'
'Prolix.'
'It is verbose without containing the necessary information.'
'Sentences too long and riddled with legal jargon and seemingly unnecessary stuff like "the said sum".'
'The style is appalling – definitely dictated, definitely not read before despatch and arrogant.'
'Letter drafted as to deliberately mislead.'
'Important omissions ... Future litigation seems almost invited. [The style is] pompous, platitudinous, cliché-ridden.'

Listen to that contempt! Not one of the respondents had a good word for the writer.

Let us not try to impress our clients by confusing or belittling them. Let us impress them (as a by-product, without trying) with our effectiveness, our integrity, and our humanity.

Legalese alienates many judges

At the *Just Language* conference in Vancouver, Andrew Sims, a Canadian chairman of industrial tribunals, presented a paper 'Writing when your audience is a judge'. The summary in *Clarity* 26 (Dec 1992) quotes these points:

- Counsel often bury their good points in dross ... [though Sims was referring to make-weight arguments rather than verbiage].
- Judges work under time constraints, and are generally short of time. They spend huge amounts of time reading rubbish, and they dislike it. They are almost universally irritated by dross. They would much rather devote that time to hearing the next case, or go fishing.
- A few judges prefer traditional language, but even they do not find against lawyers because they understand their arguments ...
- The judge will read the statement of claim first. It should be crisp and memorable.

Less anecdotally, Professor Kimble reports:

> In 1987, a colleague and I sent a survey to 300 judges and 500 lawyers in Michigan. We received responses from 425. We asked readers simply to check off their preference for the A or B version of six different paragraphs from various legal documents. One version of each paragraph was in plain language and the other in traditional legal style. Neither the survey itself nor the cover letter referred to 'legalese' or 'plain English'. Rather, the cover letter said the survey was part of an effort to 'test language trends in the legal profession.'
>
> The same study was then repeated in three other states – Florida, Louisiana, and Texas. In Louisiana and Texas, only judges were surveyed. All told, 1,462 judges and lawyers returned the survey. And in all four states, they preferred the plain language versions by margins running from 80% to 86%.

This is quoted from p.135 of *Writing for Dollars, Writing to Please* (Kimble, 2012), but a fuller report was published in *Strike Three for Legalese*, in Kimble's anthology *Lifting the Fog of Legalese* (2006). To clarify the results (in a private email) he extracted the figures for judges alone:

> The judges in all four states preferred the plain language versions by 82% to 86%.

Professor Kimble also quotes Benson and Kessler's 1987 study involving

> ... 10 judges and 33 research attorneys at the California Court of Appeal in Los Angeles ...

... By statistically significant margins, the readers rated the passages in legalese to be 'substantively weaker and less persuasive than the plain English versions.' What's more, they inferred that the writers of the plain-language versions came from more prestigious law firms.

These are two of 15 studies of legal writing listed in Kimble (2012) under the heading *Pleasing and Persuading Readers*.

We know of no equivalent British research, but at its 10th anniversary celebration in 1993 Clarity's aim of eliminating legalese in favour of plain language was supported by subsequent law lords Bingham and Nicholls (then Master of the Rolls and Vice-Chancellor of the Chancery Division), Sir Stephen Brown (then President of the Family Division), and an array of other judges. Earlier Lord Justice Staughton, who became Clarity's first patron, had criticised the use of flowery, archaic phrases in an article in *Counsel*, telling lawyers to use direct language, whether in drafting affidavits or addressing the court; it is not necessary, he said, to *crave leave* or refer to *this Honourable Court* (Staughton, 1987).

Retired Supreme Court Justice Lord Hope of Craighead described the Scottish Independence Referendum Bill as

at first sight, a simple and compelling document, as the noble Lord, Lord Elis-Thomas, said. It is brilliantly drafted, readable by everyone, including primary schoolchildren, and is something that anyone who cares to read it will at once understand. All the bits that one would expect to find are there ...[2]

In recent years, the English courts have been plagued by lengthy court documents. In *Standard Bank* v. *Via Mat* (2013) Lord Justice Aikens called overlong pleadings and skeletons 'the bane of commercial litigation'. Many judgments[3] have complained of long documents, threatening or imposing costs penalties, without noticeable effect. Lawyers, asked why they ignore these pleas, seem to be more afraid of leaving out something they might need than of annoying the judge. Judges, asked why they don't reject these documents when submitted, say they don't want to delay proceedings and drive up the costs by doing so.

Judges occasionally strike out a court document as too long, obscure or confused to be any use. For example, in *Tchenguiz* (2015) a Commercial Court judge struck out a 94-page statement of case which contained 'large tracts of unnecessary narrative and rhetoric' and took over 60 pages to get to the point. He gave the claimant 21 days to serve a replacement half the length. And he ordered that, even if the defendants lost, they would not have to pay the claimant's costs of producing the first, prolix statement of the claim. In *Hague Plant* (2014) the judge and Court of Appeal both refused permission to introduce a 65-page 'rambling narrative' as a re-re-amended statement of claim. The document failed to comply with the primary requirement of a pleading, namely that it should include a concise statement of the facts upon which the claimant relies, so as to clarify rather than obscure the issues.

The court expressly identified the document's form and style as the problem, rather than the allegations it contained. However, only the worst documents, in the biggest disputes, are rejected. More often, difficult language, structure, and layout go unchallenged (or are eventually clarified).

Judges have also expressed a preference for plain English in legislation. Lord Brightman, another law lord, moving an amendment to clause 1(6) of the National Health Service (Private Finance) Bill in the House of Lords, said:

> I believe that plain English should be used in the drafting of Acts of Parliament. My amendment does nothing except turn a subsection of the Bill into plain English.

He pointed out that some of the detail given in the original was obvious, and suggested changing

> Nothing in this section affects the validity of any agreement made by a National Health Service trust if the agreement has not been certified under this section; but would have been an externally financed development agreement for the purposes of this section if it had been so certified.

to

> The validity of an agreement which meets the conditions set out in subsection (3) cannot be challenged merely because it has not been issued with a certificate under this section.

which was the wording of the *Notes on Clauses*.

Another sometime law lord, Lord Simon of Glaisdale, supported the amendment, adding:

> We have simply no right to legislate in a manner that is incomprehensible to the people to whom the legislation is addressed and who are primarily concerned, particularly if the matter can be put in lucid and plain terms.

And Lord Renton QC, a former recorder, added (to background acclamation):[4]

> [I]nstead of sticking to the simple language of the *Notes on Clauses*, the draftsman very often thinks that he has to elaborate it in what he considers to be more legal English, and defeats his own purpose in doing so.
>
> I stand open to correction, but I believe that this is the first time that an amendment has been tabled in identical language to that contained in the *Notes on Clauses* ... Lord Brightman ... has perhaps introduced a useful precedent.

Their point was taken, and further editing reduced the enacted version to

The fact that an agreement made by a National Health Service trust has not been certified under this section does not affect its validity.

Lord Denning, when Master of the Rolls, told the future Lord Renton's committee on the Preparation of Legislation:

If you were seeking to see what different principles should be applied, the first would be to recommend simpler language and shorter sentences. The sentence which goes into 10 lines is unnecessary. It could be split up into shorter ones anyway, and couched in simpler language. Simplicity and clarity of language are essential.

Lord Neuberger has repeatedly called for greater clarity. In his 2011 lecture to the Judicial Studies Board he said:

Clarity is not just important where legislation is concerned. If the law is to be properly accessible, then the courts are under the same duty of accessibility as is placed on the legislature – above all in a common law system, where, albeit within bounds, the judiciary make and develop the law, as well as interpret it. Oscar Wilde said that truth is 'rarely pure and never simple', and the same may be said of the law. But that is no excuse for judges producing judgments that are readable by few, and comprehendible by fewer still. Indeed, the increasing complexity of the law imposes a greater obligation than ever on judges to make themselves clear.

He went on to link clarity in judgments to the rule of law, and advised the Judicial Studies Board to train judges in the skill of writing judgments.

In relation to contracts, a similar point was made from the bench by the then Lord Justice Saville (with the agreement of Lord Justice Beldam and Sir Thomas Bingham MR) in *Trafalgar House* (1994) when he concluded:

I would only add a suggestion both to those who seek and to those who provide securities for the performance of commercial obligations. They would save much time and money if in future they heeded what Lord Atkin had said so many years ago and set out their bargain in plain modern English without resorting to ancient forms which were doubtless designed for legal reasons which no longer exist.

In *Bank of Credit and Commerce* v. *Munawar Ali* (2001) (a case about a contract to settle an employee's claims against the bank) Lord Hoffmann said (at para.38):

The modern English tradition, while still erring on the side of caution, is to avoid the grosser excesses of verbiage and trust to the judges to use common sense to get the message. I think that this tendency should be encouraged.

In *Solicitors Regulation Authority* v. *Chan* (2015) the High Court criticised charges of professional misconduct brought against a solicitor. The court quoted two of the charges:

- a 92-word sentence beginning 'They failed, alternatively facilitated, permitted or acquiesced in a failure';
- a 114-word sentence ending 'they breached all, alternatively any, of Principles 2, 3, 4, 5 and/or 6 of the Principles'.

Lord Justice Davis criticised the regulator for lumping together allegations:

> with a plethora of 'alternativelys', 'further or alternativelys' and 'and/ors' and with reference to a variety of different rules, principles and outcomes, into one convoluted and rolled-up charge.

Even if the accused solicitor could understand it, it must have made the disciplinary tribunal's task more difficult, the court said.

If the matter remains in doubt, look at the language of the Civil Procedure Rules, and at the substance of rule 16.4(1), which begins (our italics):

> Particulars of claim must include –
>
> (a)   a *concise* statement of the facts on which the claimant relies;

Perhaps a future amendment will take this further, requiring all court documents to be clear and concise.

Legalese sounds archaic

Much of what passes for legal language may have originally been in common use but has long been abandoned by the rest of the population and is now derelict. Take this example from a 21st century commercial lease:

> … to execute all such works and do all such things as under or by virtue of any Legislation are or shall be directed or necessary to be executed …

This sounds much like the *Book of Common Prayer* (1662):

> … to deliberate of, and to do all such Things, as, being made plain by them, and assented to by Us, shall concern the settled Continuance of the …

Our proposals have nothing to do with the date. On the contrary, we have a horror of fashion. To do something because this is the 21st century or because everyone else is doing it, and to stop because others stop, is to court mediocrity and error. Lawyers who model themselves on the subordinate members of a flock of sheep demean the profession and discourage progress. It is affectation that we object to: the pretentious, ostentatious use of artificial language, whether because it is the latest fashion or because it is obsolete.

Long sentences, passive verbs, capital letters for common nouns, and archaic words or sentence structures give a Dickensian tone, and increasingly few law firms want to adopt a *Bleak House* image. Most prefer to think of themselves as approachable and human and try to address clients in the clients' own language. These firms should avoid old habits that undermine this business aim, especially if their marketing claims that *we don't speak legalese; we talk business* or that *we favour plain English over legal jargon*. In their conversations with clients, no doubt these lawyers do talk business; the challenge is to match this in their writing.

We believe that traditional legal writing survives simply because it is traditional. Lawyers value precedent and continuity, and are often suspicious of change. Beginners learn by copying their seniors, who learned by copying the previous generation. We think this gives a false sense of security, and that the perceived safety of copying previous generations harms the present relationship between lawyer and client.

Legalese shuts people out of their own business

> The conquistadors ... legalised their invasion by reading out their new rights to the natives in a language they could not understand. No matter. They had heard the phrases, and were now subjects of the Spanish king and beneficiaries of his capacious protection. They were also, if they now rebelled, traitors rather than enemy combatants.[5]

A political point: people are entitled to know their rights and obligations. This should be as obvious as their entitlement to make informed judgments about their medical treatment, but many lawyers still write as though it doesn't matter if their clients (or other interested parties) cannot understand the documents that bind them.

And as we suggested on pp.13–15, there is no sense in granting rights or imposing obligations in such a way that neither party is aware of their existence.

New Zealand's Law Commission and Parliamentary Counsel Office put it this way in a joint report in 2007:[6]

> It is a fundamental precept of any legal system that the law must be accessible to the public. Ignorance of the law is no excuse because everyone is presumed to know the law. That presumption would be insupportable if the law were not available and accessible to all. The state also has an interest in the law's accessibility. It needs the law to be effective, and it cannot be if the public do not know what it is.
> ...
> It seems once to have been supposed that law was the preserve of lawyers and Judges, and that legislation was drafted with them as the primary audience. It is now much better understood that Acts of Parliament (and regulations too) are consulted and used by a large number of people who are not lawyers and have no legal training. Many people refer to legislation in their jobs. People who work in the registries of universities and other educational institutions make constant reference to education legislation; employers and trade union officials need to be well versed in employment legislation; the staff of many government departments, many of whom are not legally trained, work closely with the legislation

that their departments administer; the staff of local authorities need to access the large quantity of local government legislation; and company officers need to consult company and financial reporting legislation. At other times ordinary people refer to Acts of Parliament to find the answers to problems that affect them in their personal lives: difficulties with a neighbour may lead to them consulting the Fencing Act 1978; domestic difficulties may lead to them consulting our family and relationship legislation.

Our oblique language excludes clients from their proper part in the decision-making. Lawyers should be acting as guides to their clients, which means the clients must be able to follow.

Apart from the clients' right to make the decisions, they should be part of the team. Usually they will know their case better than their lawyers do and it is important that they should be able to correct mistakes, remedy oversights, and contribute suggestions. It is essential that those affected can read and correct the drafts before their opponents can benefit from the mistakes, and of course before signing a statement of truth.

> **MA:** In my 35 years of preparing statements of case and evidence, it was only in the most trivial circumstances that I was ever able to treat the first draft as the completed document. However careful I was, I expected in distilling detailed instructions into a coherent and hopefully persuasive story to put the occasional wrong shade of meaning (if not an outright mistake) into the client's or a witness's mouth, and sometimes I missed a point altogether.

Lay people reading lawyers' prose usually do not understand it. They may resign themselves to ignorance, thinking themselves foolish or the writer pompous; they may ask for it to be repeated, rephrased, or explained; or they may ask someone else – a friend, another lawyer, a Citizens Advice Bureau, or (if really upset) their lawyer's disciplinary body – what their adviser is trying to tell them.

Fortunately, the courts do sometimes penalise lawyers as well as doctors for the dismissive attitude that assumes that the client or patient can safely leave it to the professional.

For example, in *Houlahan* v. *Australian and New Zealand Banking Group* (1992) Mr Justice Higgins granted a declaration to Mr and Mrs Houlahan limiting their liability under an unlimited liability guarantee to A$10,000, the amount they thought they were underwriting. He said:

> I am satisfied … that none of the persons present had any real knowledge of the nature and effect of the guarantee document that was then being executed. It was even impossible for counsel appearing in the case to construe even the first clause of it when asked.
> There are 'explanatory' side notes to each separate clause of the document. The first is 'Extent of Guarantee'. There is opposite that note a single sentence of 57 lines in length couched in incomprehensible legal gobbledy-gook. That is, it

must be conceded, the most extreme example. However, many of the other clauses would be understood only by a commercial lawyer with the time and patience to read them carefully.

I am also satisfied that the plaintiffs signed the 'Guarantee' without reading it or fully understanding its import. They would have been little wiser had they attempted the exercise …

Another complicating factor is that on the rear page of the 'Guarantee', a statement appears, acknowledged by the signature of each plaintiff, in the following terms

'I HEREBY ACKNOWLEDGE that I have carefully read and understand the purport of the within Guarantee. And I hereby request the Bank to make such advances to the within-mentioned Customer as the Bank may from time to time think proper.'

It is obvious, of course, that the statement was false insofar as it asserted that the plaintiffs had read or understood the document they had signed. The officers of the defendant, however, knew the statement to be false. Indeed, neither of those officers could have truthfully signed such an acknowledgement.

It seems to me, therefore, that it is not useful or necessary to attempt to construe the guarantee document or any part of it. It can be regarded as having no more effect than an acknowledgement of an intention on the part of the plaintiffs, accepted by the defendant, to guarantee the repayment of an overdraft of $10,000.00 …

In Russia, a customer with a sense of humour struck back. Receiving an unsolicited offer of a credit card, he scanned the bank's form of agreement into his computer and changed the small print so that he would have unlimited free credit and a remedy if the bank ended the agreement. The bank accepted his signed version unchecked and their later action for recovery failed. The customer then raised the stakes, bringing his own action for 24 million rubles (£470,000); that and the bank's counter-claim for fraud were settled by mutual withdrawal (*Agarkov* v. *Tinkoff* (2013)).

In an English family-court case, His Honour Judge Jeremy Lea was reported by *The Daily Telegraph* (2 August 2015) as discounting a social worker's adverse report because it used jargon that the litigants were unlikely to have understood, although he does credit its author with knowing what she meant. One passage from the report reads:

I do not intend to address the couple's relationship suffice it to say it is imbued with ambivalence: both having many commonalities emanating from their histories that create what could be a long lasting connection or alternative relationship that are a reflection of this.

Judge Lea is quoted as saying:[7]

I may be accused of linguistic pedantry … [but] [t]here is a serious point here. My reason for criticising [the social worker's] report in this way is not solely borne out of my concern that such reports should be so written as to be readily understood but because I have to question whether [the social worker] was able to communicate orally with [the woman offering to care for the children]. Did [the woman] fully understand what was being asked of her or said to her?

Legalese undermines the rule of law

In a short but devastating attack on the complexity of excessive detail, Manning (1982) took as his example what he called 'the [US] Treasury's proposed 110 single-spaced pages of densely complex regulations', elaborating on s.385 of the Internal Revenue Code. His primary argument was that these regulations – even if well written – could not *in principle* reduce doubt and litigation about their subject-matter (an argument we discuss in Chapter 23 ('Vagueness')). But the evils of what he calls 'hyperlexis' are exacerbated by the poor quality of this 'dismal … draft', which had taken 'thirteen years of labor and debate'. (This entire exercise was only to distinguish *debt* from *equity*, which were – and may still be – differently taxed.) Manning concludes:

> I have no doubt that one evidence of public disgust with this situation lies in the sharp increase in nonpayment of taxes by the people of the United States – a portent of the terrible cost, not only in money, but more important, in decline of civic responsibility, and ascendancy of contempt for the law, in the mind of the public at large …
>
> The functioning of the whole legal system depends upon keeping it understandable. Law unenforced is worse than no law at all. Enforcement against noncompliance is not possible without general voluntary compliance.
>
> As professionals, we lawyers ought to be in the forefront of a movement for radical simplification of our legal system and our laws. We should be in the forefront of a movement to repeal unenforceable and unenforced provisions. We should continuously insist that the aggregate of our law be kept within the capacity – the narrowly limited capacity – of our legal institutions to implement the law in a manner that is fair, effective and swift.

Lord Bingham (2010) identified the rule of law as the

> principle … that all persons and authorities within the state, whether public or private, should be bound by and entitled to the benefit of laws publicly made, taking effect (generally) in the future and publicly administered by the courts

and he goes on to suggest eight component principles, the first of which is that

> The law must be accessible and so far as possible intelligible, clear and predictable.

Under the heading of that principle he blames first 'the torrent of legislation' and the speed and lack of thought with which it is enacted for the inability of anyone – including the most senior judges – first to find and then to understand the law. He gives the example of *R* v. *Chambers* (2008). This prosecution for smuggling tobacco led to a conviction, a £66,000 fine (or two years in prison if the fine was not paid), and an appeal which the Court of Appeal was about to dismiss when someone discovered that the smuggling regulations had been amended in 2001 so that they no longer applied to tobacco. As he allowed the appeal, Lord Justice Toulson said:

> there is no comprehensive statute law database with hyperlinks which would enable an intelligent person, by using a search engine, to find out all the legislation on a particular topic. This means that the courts are in many cases unable to discover what the law is …

But, Lord Bingham adds, judge-made law contributes to the problem:

> The length, elaboration and prolixity of some common law judgments … can in themselves have the effect of making the law to some extent inaccessible.

He gives as an example litigation about whether someone whose tenancy of their home has ended can rely on article 8 of the European Convention on Human Rights to resist eviction by the local authority.

> In the House [of Lords] alone, the question has been addressed in fifteen separate reasoned judgments running to more than 500 paragraphs and more than 180 pages of printed law report. Even after this immense outpouring of effort it may be doubted whether the relevant law is entirely clear, or for that matter finally settled.
>
> When the last of these three cases was before the Court of Appeal, that court, having struggled to give loyal effect to what the majority of the House of Lords had up to then decided (and, as the House was later to hold, reached the wrong answer), made a plea for a single judgment setting out the ruling of the majority. This would allow those who disagreed to say so, and give their reasons for doing so, but (it was thought) give clear and more intelligible guidance to lower courts on the law to be applied.[8]

European law has stirred more stodge into the brew. Apart from its being another source of traditional legal prose, it brings the inevitable problems arising from:

- Political compromise between 28 countries with even more different nationalisms and cultures;
- The fusion of civil and common law, with their different traditions and incompatible concepts;
- The authoritative statement of European law in 24 languages, none of which has priority over any other when the law is interpreted, each suited only to its own legal systems;
- Translation and interpreting during legal proceedings; and
- The imposition of the result on to the national law of each country.

We discuss the difficulties of translation in Chapter 29 ('Translating and interpreting').

Legalese is often itself unlawful

Section 68 of the Consumer Rights Act 2015 provides that:

(1)   A trader must ensure that a written term of a consumer contract, or a consumer notice in writing, is transparent.

(2)   A consumer notice is transparent for the purposes of subsection (1) if it is expressed in plain and intelligible language and it is legible.

And there is a similar provision for guarantees in s.30.

Trader and *consumer* are defined, but *plain* and *intelligible* are not. (We discuss the difficulties of defining *plain* in Chapter 4 ('What is plain language?').)

These clauses go slightly further than regulation 7 of the Unfair Terms in Consumer Contracts Regulations 1999 (which replaced a similar rule in the 1994 regulations) by making clear, if it wasn't already, that a document must be legible as well as intelligible.

The regulations and the Act implemented European Directive 93/13/EEC. It is ironic that, while introducing a huge volume of opaque legislation and judgments into our law, the EU has also been the source of our strongest legislative requirement for transparency in contracts.

The Competition and Markets Authority, the Act's chief enforcer, has said that a contract term is not transparent just because it makes grammatical sense. It must enable the consumer

> to evaluate, on the basis of clear, intelligible criteria, the economic consequences for him which derive from [the term].[9]

So, a long and confusing clause should not qualify as transparent, even if (after careful reading and analysis) it turns out to have just one possible meaning.

What is the penalty for lack of transparency? First, a contract term that lacks transparency is to be interpreted strictly against the trader. This won't affect traders much, since the courts can already, if they choose, interpret any term as strictly as the justice of the case requires. Transparent terms may be more likely to pass the fairness test. (Most terms of a consumer contract are invalid if unfair, except for prominent terms fixing the price or the product. A consumer who knew this rule could challenge an unfair term and perhaps escape its effect.) But the main danger for traders who write opaque terms into their contracts is the risk of regulatory action. In practice, as the regulators focus their enforcement efforts where they will do the most good, this risk is greater for larger traders, for terms affecting many transactions, and for the most unfair terms. The Office of Fair Trading published reports of substandard clauses it had forced traders to remove or rewrite under the previous regulations (as did the Financial Conduct Authority[10]);

the Competition and Markets Authority has re-published the OFT's reports but has not yet added any new ones of its own.[11]

One offender carefully aimed at its own foot by inserting in its contracts a declaration, to be signed by the consumer, agreeing that the contract was fair and written in plain intelligible language. Of course this was itself unfair, since the company would only ever need to rely on the declaration in cases where it was untrue. The OFT extracted from the company an under-taking to remove the clause.

The effect of this legislation has been noticeable in many (but not enough) banking and insurance documents, and in other consumer contracts from big business. Otherwise, it is still widely ignored.

The EU's official guide for its own legislative drafters[12] begins:

1.1.   The drafting of a legal act must be:

- clear, easy to understand and unambiguous;
- simple and concise, avoiding unnecessary elements;
- precise, leaving no uncertainty in the mind of the reader.

Another legal requirement for clarity relates to rules of court procedure. The Civil Procedure Act 1997 introduced a novel provision, that the Civil Procedure Rules should be both simple and simply expressed. Since then, similar provisions have appeared in relation to rules of procedure for family cases, criminal cases, tribunals, and the Supreme Court. However, there is no absolute duty to make the rules simple; no standards have been pub-lished by which simplicity is to be measured; and no consequence is provided for rules that are not simple or simply expressed. In practice, unclear rules, after causing years of uncertainty, litigation, and legal costs, are eventually criticised in court and then rewritten. For example, the rules on serving claims in part 6 of the Civil Procedure Rules 1998 were clarified by the Court of Appeal in *Collier* v. *Williams* (2006) and rewritten in 2008. The problem of unclear rules is now particularly urgent as increasing numbers of litigants struggle to use the courts unaided (since they cannot get legal aid to pay for a lawyer). Sir James Munby, President of the Family Division, said the Family Procedure Rules 2010 were 'unreadable by litigants in person and ... largely unread by lawyers'.[13]

Legalese can be unprofessional

The Solicitors Regulation Authority's *Trainee Information Pack*[14] calls for budding solicitors to be taught to:

- understand the need to refine their communication skills so that they can present oral and written communication in a way that achieves its purpose and is appropriate to the recipient ...
- select appropriate methods of communication

- express ideas concisely, clearly and logically
- use appropriate language
- use correct grammar, syntax and punctuation
- pay attention to detail by proof-reading, checking the format and numbering of documents, cross-referencing and using consistent terminology
- listen actively and speak effectively.

Strangely, the solicitors' *Code of Conduct* does not explicitly call on them to exercise these skills once they are qualified, although it does demand that clients are kept informed, that their needs and circumstances are taken into account, and that they are in a position to make informed decisions,[15] none of which conditions will be satisfied if the clients don't understand.

Legalese is inhuman

> **MA:** I once had a note from a client with whom I'd been on visiting terms when we were neighbours. I'd since moved, and she was too infirm to travel, so she asked a local solicitor to take over her affairs. He produced something for her to sign and send me. Had I been in his position, I would have suggested a personal note something like this:
>
> > Dear Mark
> >
> > I hope you won't be offended but your new office is too far for me to come so I've asked Mr X at Y & Co to … So I'd be grateful if you could send him any papers you are holding for me.
> >
> > Thanks for all you've done in the past (etc). Look in if you're ever back this way.
> >
> > Kind regards
>
> That would have reflected the tone of our relationship and ensured that I would have remembered her with warmth. Instead he wrote (and she signed):
>
> > To whom it may concern:
> >
> > I hereby authorise and request you to …
>
> What had I done to offend her? Nothing, he assured me. I was merely a victim of the solicitor's thoughtless standard style, suitable for everyone and all occasions (or rather, none). But I never felt inclined to visit again.

Legalese bores everyone

Reading legalese is like wading through quicksand, to the extent that no one – however well-qualified as a lawyer – is inclined to read it 'properly or at all'.

Unless you have been reading every word of the examples, and are sorry when you reach the end of each one, we need say no more.

Endnotes

1   **mojdigital.blog.gov.uk/2015/07/29/helping-people-with-court-fees**   and **mojdigital.blog.gov.uk/2016/03/21/help-with-fees-doing-the-hard-work-so-you-dont-have-to**.
2   *Hansard*, 24 June 2014: column 1219.
3   *Commercial Management (Investments) Ltd* v. *Mitchell Design and Construct Ltd* [2016] EWHC 76 (TCC); *Weatherford Global Products* v. *Hydropath Holdings Ltd* [2014] EWHC 2725; *Tchenguiz* v. *Director of the Serious Fraud Office* [2014] EWCA Civ 1333; *Inplayer Ltd* v. *Thorogood* [2014] EWCA Civ 1511; *Ben Nevis (Holdings) Ltd* v. *HMRC* [2013] EWCA Civ 578; *Standard Bank Plc* v. *Via Mat International Ltd* [2013] EWCA Civ 490; *Khader* v. *Aziz* [2010] EWCA Civ 716; *Midgulf International Ltd* v. *Groupe Chimique Tunisien* [2010] EWCA Civ 66; *Tombstone Ltd* v. *Raja* [2008] EWCA Civ 1444; *In re X and Y (Bundles)* [2008] EWHC 2058 (Fam).
4   These quotations are taken from *Hansard*, 26 June 1997, column 647.
5   Michael Wood, 'Living Dead Man'; a review of *Operation Massacre* by Rodolfo Walsh, translated by Daniella Gitlin, in the *London Review of Books* (7 November 2013).
6   New Zealand Law Commission in conjunction with Parliamentary Counsel Office: *Presentation of New Zealand Statute Law* (2007) – paras 1 and 11 (**www.lawcom.govt.nz/sites/default/files/projectAvailableFormats/NZLC%20IP2.pdf**).
7   **www.telegraph.co.uk/news/health/news/11779197/Social-workers-report-may-as-well-have-been-in-foreign-language-Judge-says.html** (last accessed 3 August 2015).
8   The three cases were *Harrow LBC* v. *Qazi* [2003]; *Kay* v. *Lambeth LBC* [2006]; and *Doherty* v. *Birmingham City Council* [2008].
9   'Unfair contract terms guidance: Guidance on the unfair terms provisions in the Consumer Rights Act 2015', para.2.45, quoting the European Court of Justice (31 July 2015, CMA37).
10   See **www.fca.org.uk/firms/unfair-contract-terms/library**.
11   See Annex A ('Historic examples of fair and unfair terms') and Annex B ('New elements of unfair terms law') at **www.gov.uk/government/publications/unfair-contract-terms-cma37**.
12   'Joint Practical Guide of the European Parliament, the Council and the Commission for the persons involved in the drafting of European Union legislation' (European Union, 2015) (see **eur-lex.europa.eu/content/techleg/EN-legislative-drafting-guide.pdf**).
13   See **www.familylaw.co.uk/news_and_comment/the-president-s-address-at-the-annual-dinner-of-the-family-law-bar-association-26-february-2016#.WN9TOVKB0gE**.
14   **www.sra.org.uk/trainees/resources/trainee-information-pack.page**.
15   **www.sra.org.uk/solicitors/handbook/code/part2/content.page**.

Part B

What is good writing?

Chapter 2

The legal writer's aims

To say that writing is good is not to attribute any particular objective quality to it but merely to express approval. As the *Oxford English Dictionary* summarises it, 'good' is 'a term of general or indefinite commendation'. And we commend language if it does what we want of it.

Lawyers, their clients, novelists, poets, preachers, politicians, comedians, Scrabble-players, and others all want different things of language. So different standards apply, and the meaning of *good* varies accordingly. For example, David Wolchover, a barrister and a scholarly legal author, writes the most complex social letters – about what he did on holiday – that must be mulled over for days to extract the meaning. It is appropriate for him to write like this in fun, but he would not dream of addressing a court that way: he would get little thanks if a week after his client had been convicted one of the jury suddenly understood the irrebuttable argument for the defence. And his textbooks are written in yet another style, aimed at a different audience and with a different purpose.

This book is concerned only with lawyers' language, whether it is addressed to other lawyers or to laypeople.

Most people, whether lawyers or not, want legal language to convey meaning from one person to others accurately and as precisely and efficiently as possible. Lawyers in particular often have a fourth requirement: that their language should persuade. Unlike the traditionalists, we (the authors) believe that plain language is compatible with, and even improves, all four of these qualities, subject to the reservations in Part C. All four are important, and there is some overlap between them:

- **Accuracy** is essential, for obvious reasons. We agree with the traditionalists about this, but – as we argue throughout this book – traditional language is often *in*accurate.
- Absolute **precision** may be the ideal but is in practice impossible, thought and language being inherently *im*precise and varying from one person to another. And when it is impossible to legislate precisely for all possibilities, flexibility is required. We discuss this in detail in Part C.
- By '**efficiency**' we mean the transfer of meaning from one person to another with the minimum effort by writer and readers. The benefits discussed in Chapter 1 will normally justify, for the writer as well as for

PART B: WHAT IS GOOD WRITING?

readers, the initial investment of time and effort needed to improve traditional precedents.

- Accuracy and precision help to **persuade**, at least if the persuasion is fair and honest. And understanding is essential, unless the audience surrenders its critical faculties and is blinded by faith. We deal with persuasion in Chapter 19.

Chapter 3

Who says what's right?

It is widely believed that one shouldn't:

- start a sentence with *And* or *But*, or finish one with a preposition;
- say *me and John are ...*, or *between you and I*;
- use *agenda* or *they* as if they were singular rather than plural; or
- split an infinitive (for example, *to run*) by writing *to quickly run*.

But where do these rules come from, if they are rules at all? Should we be bound by them and, if so, why? Who made them, and with what mandate?

All languages constantly evolve, even supposedly dead ones while they remain in use (as Latin does) (Mattila, 2013). Their grammar and pronunciation change; new words are added; existing words adopt new meanings; other words become archaic and eventually obsolete. This can happen rapidly, particularly in the modern world, and considerable change occurs even within a normal lifetime. Some mid-20th century English already sounds dated, especially to the young; as you travel back through time, the versions used by Shakespeare, Chaucer, and the Anglo-Saxons become increasingly like a different language (which it certainly is when you reach the Germanic dialects brought over by invaders in the first millennium). No version is 'right', any more than an ice-age wolf was the correct version of a dog.

In this constant flux, useful distinctions are sometimes lost and each generation nostalgically regrets the passing of its own familiar forms. But language is free and democratic so, overall, over time, useful changes tend to last, sooner or later becoming familiar enough to be accepted as part of the standard language (or of the local dialect). If innovations don't work, people are less likely to adopt them. But nothing is perfect, even people, so change is not always for the better. Our tendency to copy each other – as essential for language as it is for other forms of development – can be misapplied to copy the follies of those with whom we identify. It can also produce changes which are for neither better nor worse.

For example, most of us over 50 were taught to use *I* when we were the subject of the sentence and *me* when we were the object, or following a preposition. So *Me and Daphne wrote this* jars on us in the same way that *Me wrote this* would on most English-speakers, and neither Daphne nor I would use it even in the most informal speech. But whether we say *I wrote* or *me wrote*, the meaning is clear from the word order, so this distinction between subject and object might well dwindle until one day it disappears. If it does, those whose teachers grew up without it will accept *Me and Daphne wrote this* as natural and correct. The rule might become 'Use *I* when you are the only subject of the sentence; otherwise use *me*'. This seems to be the rule applied by many speakers today, although it will probably be some time before it becomes acceptable in formal writing, if it ever does. (*Me and Daphne* seems wrong to us for another reason. In our youth courtesy required us to put *you* first (*You and John will go*) and ourselves last (*John and I went*).)

Meanwhile, we wince when we hear *between you and I*, although that too is now both harmless and common and might in time become universally acceptable.

The same distinction between *who* and *whom* is further along the path towards obsolescence. *Whom are you looking for?* sounds archaic (that is, somewhere between formal and obsolete), while *For whom are you looking?* and *To whom it may concern* sound right to us (if formal). *For who the bell tolls* and *To who it may concern* still sound wrong, presumably because *whom* is so familiar in these phrases. Familiarity dictates the rule.

The all-purpose pronoun *you* has completed this journey. It is now correct as the subject or object, and as singular or plural, even in the most formal documents. The *thee, thou*, and *ye* forms are obsolete except in certain special circumstances.

One person's rule can seem arbitrary and pointless to others. A consultant with many years' experience as drafting counsel to the US Senate disapproved (in a 2014 LinkedIn discussion) of the possessive apostrophe-s in statutes. His view that this was unacceptably informal didn't change even when he was shown the introductory words of the Administration of Estates Act 1925 (as a random example of long-accepted British formality):

> Be it enacted by the King's most Excellent Majesty, by and with the advice and consent of the Lords Spiritual and Temporal, and Commons, in this present Parliament assembled, and by the authority of the same, as follows :–

He and his colleagues, he said, would have replaced *the King's most Excellent Majesty* with *the most Excellent Majesty of the King*. He wasn't joking. None of the other legislative drafters in the discussion, from around the Commonwealth, agreed with him. But it is easier to laugh at this view than to realise that we all have strong opinions about the correctness of arbitrary rules that seem absurd to others.

The prohibition against splitting infinitives is widely attributed to the fact that infinitives were never split in classical Latin (although this couldn't have been a rule because Latin infinitives, as a single word, were unsplittable, so the question would not have arisen). In any event, we're not speaking Latin (or even a language descended from Latin) and might ask by what authority (and for what purpose) a rule from one language may be imposed on another, especially one with a different structure to which the rule is unsuited. In English, the result of applying it can be clumsy or ambiguous. Fowler (1926) comments

> that such reminders of a tyrannous convention as 'in not combining to forbid flatly hostilities' are far more abnormal than the abnormality they evade. We will split infinitives sooner than be ambiguous or artificial; more than that, we will freely admit that sufficient recasting will get rid of any s[plit] i[nfinitive] without involving either of those faults, and yet reserve to ourselves the right of deciding in each case whether recasting is worth while.

It may be that the rule-deniers' residual disinclination to split the infinitive arises from the general principle, which we endorse, that it is usually better to keep different parts of the same thing together than to sprinkle them around the document. But *usually* is not *always*.

Linguistic evolution works in some ways much like biological evolution. Gradual change is both inevitable and useful; 'monstrous' change – change that is too great to function in an unchanged environment – leads to extinction.

As with biological evolution, if a language is to function it requires a high degree of stability. Communication requires a great deal of consensus about grammar and the meaning of words: stability is essential if we are to understand each other. But we also need some flexibility if the language is to develop and adapt to changing circumstances. Even in a precedent-based legal system, flexibility and innovation are necessary, and even legal language mutates more than we are taught.

Language constantly absorbs new words, whether made up (*telephone, radar*) or adopted from other languages (*court, sheriff, bungalow*), and new meanings for old words (*science, computer, liberal, wicked*). These are soon learned by context or explanation. Similarly, the grammatical conventions of the past (*you* as the plural of *thou*) are replaced by the grammatical conventions of the future (the disappearing *m* of *whom*), heedless of the outrage shouted into the wind by drowning Canutes.

If English is your first language, you learned it first by copying what you heard around you. Formal education then began, from teachers without specialist knowledge, when you were too young to question authority. Children are taught that dictionaries, grammar, and usage guides prescribe the correct usage, and that rules are there to be obeyed. Later, we might learn that they merely describe customary usage. Most dictionaries include whatever words are used, and define them as they are used, regardless of the editors' approval.

Questioning the finer points of the language comes later, if at all, but is necessary if we are to write as well as possible. Writing is an art, and creative art is better than writing by numbers. All the supposed rules quoted in the first paragraph of this chapter are routinely flouted without any consequent breakdown in communication. But they are condemned as wrong by purists (or pedants, depending on your view). So are these rules mere snobbery? Are they rules at all?

This is what Sir Ernest Gowers' (1965) edition of Fowler (as only one authoritative example) says about some of them:

> That it is a solecism to begin a sentence with *and* is a faintly lingering superstition. The OED gives examples ranging from the 10th to the 19th century; the Bible is full of them.
>
> For the superstition about beginning a sentence with *but* see [*and*].
>
> Those who lay down the universal principle that final prepositions are 'inelegant' are unconsciously trying to deprive the English language of a valuable idiomatic resource, which has been used freely by all our greatest writers except those whose instinct for English idiom has been overpowered by notions of correctness derived from Latin standards. The legitimacy of the prepositional ending in literary English must be uncompromisingly maintained … Follow no arbitrary rule …

He acknowledged the convenience of the singular *they,* and its established use (at least colloquially), but criticised it as ungrammatical. For a discussion of the present position, see p.68.

Similarly, it makes no sense to say that the modern style is right and legalese wrong. Rather, we are arguing that the practical guidelines we give in Part C should be adopted, and so become standard, because they work more efficiently than legalese. They too will, inevitably and on the whole usefully, evolve.

Lawyers – and others – want to appear educated, and lawyers in particular need to be perceived as competent writers. This requirement usefully discourages pointless innovation but sadly also discourages improvements and useful forms thought to be wrong. The last category includes the initial *And* and *But*, the concluding preposition, and the split infinitive. The balance between the desire to write as well as possible and the fear of appearing uneducated will depend on the audience and on the writer's confidence.

Sir Geoffrey Bowman, when First Parliamentary Counsel, explained (2006) why the Office of the Parliamentary Counsel then had no style manual:[1]

> All Bills are different. All ideas for legislation need analysis and creative ideas from the drafter, and you cannot predict where the iterative process will lead you. The nature of legislation is unusual because its object is limited. This means that the drafter operates in a stark and precise literary environment, where he is denied some of the techniques available to other authors. In using the techniques that are available to him, there is no automatic solution and everything requires

judgment. Language and techniques change all the time, and I hope they always will. In short, legislative drafting is more an art than a precise science.

However, he added that

we are beginning to incorporate guidance on modern drafting techniques. But this amounts only to suggestions, and nothing is prescribed.

Our approach to legal language is not, in our view, unduly radical. Although it differs greatly from traditional legalese it does so only in that it brings legal language back from that extreme towards standard English. More surprisingly, it brings it back towards the comparatively plain English of some earlier lawyers (as we argue in the last section of Chapter 5). We recommend usage that we think makes legal writing more effective and elegant, regardless of any contrary tradition. So we take a robust attitude to harmful rules, but where the uncontroversial form is as good as the controversial we choose the uncontroversial.

Endnote

1   The current guidance is at **www.gov.uk/government/collections/the-office-of-the-parliamentary-counsel-guidance**.

Chapter 4

What is plain language?

What it is

It is customary in anglophone countries to describe the alternative to legalese as *plain English*. *Plain language* is less parochial, reflecting the worldwide appeal of the movement and in Britain the existence of minority languages. But when referring only to English the terms are interchangeable. So, what is it?

Robert Eagleson (1990) kept fairly close to the popular meaning by describing plain English as:

> [T]he opposite of gobbledegook and of confusing and incomprehensible language. Plain English is clear, straightforward expression, using only as many words as are necessary. It is language that avoids obscurity, inflated vocabulary and convoluted construction. It is not baby talk, nor is it a simplified version of ... language.
>
> Writers of plain English let their audience concentrate on the message instead of being distracted by complicated language. They make sure their audience understands the message easily. This means that writers of plain English must vary the way they write their documents according to the composition of their audience. For instance, a document can contain a number of technical words and still be plain. The following extract from a scientific paper is plain to its particular audience:
>
> 'An interesting description of the filamentous gills of lepidopterous larvae is given by Welsh (1922), who finds that each gill filament contains a tracheal branch from the main lateral trunk of the tracheal system, and that the inner surface of the gill is covered by innumerable tracheoles lying parallel with one another. Nearly five hundred gill filaments may be present on a single individual of *Nymphula obscuralis* ...'

But confusion has arisen because many of its proponents have stuffed other criteria of good writing into their definition of *plain language*, stipulating good document organisation, legible typography, and attractive layout. Others have added criteria which have nothing to do with language at all: conceptual simplicity and honesty. These extra recommendations are commendable in themselves but it is unnecessary and counter-productive to include them in the definition.

People unaware of the stuffed definitions of plain language naturally misunderstand what those proponents are offering, and this has contributed to the serious but often unjust criticism that plain writers oversimplify, and so distort, legal concepts. We reply to that criticism in Chapter 5. Here we will try to untangle the confusion.

The great irony is that by taking the definition away from the popular understanding of the term, the plain language experts break their own rule against using unexplained jargon: their phrase *plain language* is not plain language.

But that is not the only difficulty. Even if this problem is resolved, ambiguity would still arise from the multiple common meanings of the word *plain*. Among the meanings listed in the *Shorter Oxford English Dictionary* (1973 revision) are those:

- Describing objective characteristics:

    - flat, level, even
    - free from obstructions or interruptions
    - unembellished, not ornate
    - of simple composition; not elaborate

- Describing their effect on people:

    - open, clear; evident, obvious
    - manifest
    - simple, readily understood
    - not complicated; simple

- With positive connotations:

    - free from evasion or subterfuge, straightforward, direct
    - unaffected

- With negative connotations:

    - ill-favoured, ugly

- With connotations dependent on the reader:

    - ordinary, simple, unsophisticated; such as characterises ordinary people
    - not distinguished by rank or position
    - homely
    - simple in dress or habits; frugal.

And, of course, all these concepts have fuzzy boundaries. So it's no wonder that the plain language movement has been accused of over-simplifying.

The International Plain Language Working Group has proposed this as a definition (Cheek, 2010):

> A communication is in plain language if its wording, structure, and design are so clear that the intended readers can easily find what they need, understand what they find, and use that information.

This goes part of the way towards resolving the difficulties, but:

- The 'if' should be 'if and only if', to exclude the possibility that this is only one type of plain language. (Compare this definition with *A dog is a mammal with four legs and a tail*.)
- It does not make clear whether *easily* is intended to govern *understand* and *use* as well as *find*. (It probably does but an academic definition, as this is supposed to be, should be rigorous.)

And more importantly:

- It suggests that if the intended readers have no use for the information the language is not plain.

What it isn't

A language

It does not help to speak of plain language as if it were a language or dialect in its own right, akin to what is wrongly called pidgin, and perhaps as an artificial language like Esperanto. It is not a language with a particular vocabulary and grammar. It is a relationship between the way a language is used and its audience. Saying that a document is plain doesn't identify any objective characteristics of the document (unlike *This table is made of wood*). Category errors like this reveal muddled thought. And false assumptions lead to false conclusions. (Adler, May–Jun 2011.)

The use of short words

It follows, as Dr Eagleson pointed out above, that plain language should not be identified with the use of short words. An example of unplain 'plain English' appeared some years ago in a standard form of bank deed, which defined *you* as *we/us* and *we/us* as *you*. It was difficult to understand; *lender* and *borrower* would have been much plainer. Using *you* has its place, for example in a leaflet addressed to consumers explaining their rights. But when two or more parties sign an agreement, which one is *you*? We give more examples of imprecise 'plain' words in Part C.

Honest language

It has been suggested that if information is misleading it cannot be plain and that accuracy and frankness are therefore essential components of plain language. This is a seductive idea, but the untruthful denial *I didn't do it* is expressed in language that anybody would call plain.

Nevertheless, as George Orwell (1946) pointed out:

> The great enemy of clear language is insincerity. When there is a gap between one's real and one's declared aims, one turns as it were instinctively to long words and exhausted idioms, like a cuttlefish spurting out ink.

Conceptual simplicity

Another controversial difficulty is whether text should be considered plain if it sets out in the plainest possible language ideas so complex that they are still difficult to understand. We say that it should, and discuss the problem in the next chapter.

The be-all and end-all of good writing

Plainness is an important element of good legal language, but it is only one element.

A practical shortcut

Plain and *plain language* are useful shorthand if they are used in the sense in which they are generally understood – to mean familiar vocabulary and uncomplicated syntax.

But we suggest reducing the misconceptions by avoiding the expressions *plain language* and *plain English* as far as our habits of thought and language permit. Let us instead focus on good writing in general. It is unimportant where the arbitrary semantic line between the different aspects is drawn.

As a rule of thumb for working lawyers rather than as a definition, we suggest that legal writing is plain enough if its intended readers can, with as little effort as the difficulty of the ideas permits, read, understand, and if necessary act on it. Here we use *plain* in the generally-understood sense of plain language; whether it is good in any wider sense is a separate matter.

To ensure that a document meets this usability standard we should observe how users read the document and we should test their understanding. We discuss this in Chapter 22 ('Testing documents').

In summary, we recommend the approach of A.J.G. Mackay, a 19th century Scottish sheriff who wrote in the *Law Quarterly Review* (1887, p.326):

> Good drafting says in the plainest language, with the simplest, fewest, and fittest words, precisely what it means.

45

Chapter 5

Lawyers' concerns about plain language

An overview

People do all sorts of strange things without question, so long as someone once told them to. Christopher Robin avoided the cracks in the pavement in case the bears ate him. And sometimes people do inconvenient things just to impress the neighbours, like wearing platform shoes. The main purpose of this book is to persuade lawyers to abandon the bizarre tradition of treating incomprehensibility as a virtue.

Adler (1993) looked at lawyers' motives. He sent four versions of a lease assignment to a selection of lawyers in England and Wales. Versions A and B were traditionally written; C and D were plainer. A was more traditional than B, and D was more radical than C. Minor deliberate mistakes were planted in the texts. They were accompanied by a questionnaire designed to show:

- whether respondents thought they supported plain English in principle and used it in practice; and
- how accurate those opinions were.

Of the 55 lawyers who answered, only one denied supporting the use of plain English in the law. To the question 'Do you use plain English?' an implausible 93 per cent answered 'yes' or 'maybe', although their other answers often suggested they were mistaken.

Table 5.1 sets out their perceived disadvantages of plain English.

Table 5.1

Reason	Number so answering
Fear of error, ambiguity, or unpredictable effect	24
Belief that judges disapprove	14
Harder or slower to write (at least at first)	14
Dislike style; insufficient gravitas	8
Harder or slower to read	7
Unfamiliar, loss of tradition	6
Harder to take instructions	4
Contrary to expectation of other lawyers	3
Generally less efficient	3
More expensive	2
Legalese justifies fees	2
Restrained by employers	1
Disliked by clients	1

Perhaps it was unfair to satirise the most common of these beliefs as being *The more clearly I write the more likely I am to be misunderstood.*

Of course, you have to be careful. Skill with the language is not enough: you must also know the law.

A plain English enthusiast might easily dismiss as unnecessary the traditional phrase *whether formally demanded or not* from the forfeiture clause imposed on tenants who do not pay their rent; but the firm's insurance premiums would increase after the client's action for possession failed because the rent had not been demanded between sunrise and sunset.

Even when knowledge of the law is not necessary it is helpful: if you know that a provision is implied – or ineffective – by law then you can leave it out. For example:

- There is no need in an instrument (any formal legal document) to specify *calendar month*; s.61 of the Law of Property Act 1925 defines *month* as a calendar month unless a contrary intention appears.
- A lease need not say that the landlord's consent to assignment, where required, may not be unreasonably withheld: s.19 of the Landlord and Tenant Act 1927 already provides that.

On the other hand, you might feel that it is useful to include something not strictly necessary as an aid to readers unfamiliar with the law. In that case include it; but there's no point in doing so in language they won't understand.

All drafters inevitably take risks. Any lawyer, however skilled, takes a chance when drafting a new document or even using an existing precedent in new circumstances. Some possibility or rule of law might be overlooked. This applies whatever the style, but with traditional drafting there is more chance of making or missing a mistake buried in obscure language. Clear drafting calls for rigorous thought about what the writer needs to say as well as how best to say it, and translating legalese into clear language often exposes errors long overlooked. But whatever the text's history, writers can keep better track of their needles if there is no haystack. And if the writer does not notice a mistake, anyone checking the draft has a good chance of spotting it before the damage is done.

There remains the danger that a writer who does not know the purpose of a particular form of words might create a problem by omitting them. In fact, the risks are much less than sometimes feared. We have tried to illustrate that much of what passes for thoroughness and care in traditional legal drafting is neither thorough nor careful. A lot of it is pomposity or just a failure to adapt a precedent, through carelessness, haste, or lack of skill or confidence.

It is worth taking the care needed to reduce this risk to a minimum, otherwise drafters will never remove the barnacles that grow on a standard document whenever someone has a bright idea for a new clause. When solicitors installed computers from the late 1970s onwards, words burst forth from them and buried the surroundings, like Vesuvius on a bad day. It is worth remembering that word processors do not just copy, amend, and re-format blocks of text but they delete them too. It is no excuse for including a paragraph, sentence, or word that we do not know the effect of excluding it. Lawyers are paid large sums to know. And without that knowledge they cannot explain the document to their clients, nor be sure it does what is wanted. It is worth finding out, and then you will know for all future times.

Some of the books listed at the end of this one will help this process, notably Mellinkoff (1963), Garner (2011), Butt (2013), and Duckworth & Spyrou (1995).

We have tried throughout this book to show why lawyers' fears are misconceived, but two call for specific attention here. The first, not raised by any of the 1993 respondents but since expressed by Bennion (2007) and Assy (2011), does have some merit. The other is the fear of novelty.

Literal understanding is not the same as understanding the law: the danger to the public

Bennion and Assy each argue that because few, if any, plainly written documents set out a full statement of the law, a lay person might under-stand the literal meaning of plainly-written legislation but misunderstand the legal effect, and they may not realise that they need legal advice. (Despite this, they both favour clarity to the extent that this danger permits, and Assy in particular opposes legalese.)

This concern applies to any document imposing the law or creating rights or duties enforceable by law. These include not only statutes and secondary legislation but also (for example) court orders and judgments, rules governing organisations, contracts, trust instruments, and wills. Neither Bennion nor Assy suggest that documents *explaining* the law should not be as clear as possible – as they must be if clients are to understand their lawyers' advice.

The Bennion-Assy risk is real, and is exacerbated by the inherent vagueness and ambiguities of even the plainest language (as discussed in Part D). But we believe that any difficulties arising from that risk are far outweighed by the benefits discussed in Chapter 1. In balancing the risk against the benefits we should take into account that:

- Legal advice is often unavailable or impracticable, because of cost or inconvenience.
- Whether or not they need legal advice, non-lawyers do read legislation. In the UK, two million separate users a month visited the free-to-access legislation at www.legislation.gov.uk in 2012–13. Research by the National Archives, which runs the site, has shown that 60 per cent of these users are non-lawyers who need to use legislation for work; for example, a police officer, a local council official or a personnel manager. Another substantial category of users was members of the public seeking to enforce their own rights or those of a friend or relative (Bertlin, 2014).
- As the examples in this book and others like it show, even lawyers routinely misunderstand legalese and can benefit from the changes we suggest.

It is better to devote what expert advice *is* available to substantive problems than to waste time and money creating and then untangling avoidable complexity. We suggest these questions (and the relationship between them) for research:

- Are the following facts widely known?

    - The law is complicated by details and exceptions;
    - Several years of study and practical training (not principally spent learning the jargon) are required before a lawyer is qualified;
    - Some lawyers then specialise in narrow fields; and
    - All lawyers accumulate experience over their lifetimes.

- If so, would lay people with a legal question:

    - Enquire about the likely cost, or assume it would be too much?
    - Take professional advice – if the cost and inconvenience are acceptable – rather than rely on their own reading of a particular document?

If, as we believe, the answers to the first four questions are 'yes', it reduces the Bennion-Assy risk. But either way it leaves unsolved the need to ensure

– as far as practicable – that lay users of a seemingly plain document know when there is a legal question that they should be asking. We suggest these precautions:

- Consider how your reader will use the document. Warn about, and perhaps explain, any dangers you identify; where appropriate, recommend legal advice.
- Avoid misleading simplification; accuracy and comprehensiveness are more important than brevity. For instance, you might keep your clients out of trouble by expanding repossession clauses along these lines:

   > If the conditions imposed by law are satisfied, the landlord may enter the flat, so ending this lease …

- Keep a record of queries, and if possible test user understanding, to see what problems still arise, and edit your precedent to avoid them.
- Generally publicise the need for, and the advantages of, legal advice, with guidance as to when it should be sought.

For a fuller discussion online, see Adler (2008, Feb 2011, 2013).

Is plain legal language otherwise safe?

We hope we have shown in Chapter 1 that traditional legal language is inefficient, conceals mistakes, and harms client relations.

> **DP:** A will writer once drafted a will for me. Among many points, I questioned a convoluted clause describing various people who could never be appointed to replace a trustee under the will. I asked why the clause appeared to describe me, since I would already be dead. The reply was that this clause came from a well-respected precedent book. I had another firm write the will.

Yet although lawyers are mostly literate, intelligent, and averse to risk, they continue to use precedents written in traditional style, and to write afresh in that style themselves. It feels safe, even though it is not: reliance on someone else's precedent is a weak defence to a negligence claim.

Lord Justice Rix discussed this question in relation to contracts, in his speech to Clarity (Rix, 2006). He concluded:

> Like our homes, and our clothes, and everything about us, there is a constant need for maintenance and refurbishment. You cannot rely on the old for ever; you cannot keep on patching; from time to time you have to have a proper overhaul. That is what plain English is about. And if you do not carry out that overhaul, then the risk of simply carrying on in the old way is greater than the risk of undertaking the new. And if the work is done with care and intelligence, the risk of error which might involve a claim of negligence is likely to be small. And it is

there in any event: and is perhaps all the greater where you follow unthinkingly in an old path, rather than rethink everything in a fundamental and intelligent way.

Is plain legal language new?

Lord Justice Denning once said (in *Packer* v. *Packer* (1954)) about a point of law:

> What is the argument on the other side? Only this, that no case has been found in which it has been done before. That argument does not appeal to me in the least. If we never do anything which has not been done before, we shall never get anywhere. The law will stand still while the rest of the world goes on: and that will be bad for both.

The same could be said about improving legal writing. But anyone worried by change and by the loss of tradition might be reassured to some extent by the surprisingly long – though occasional – history of plain legal language, in Britain and elsewhere. This could fill a book of its own but we offer just a few examples. They are chosen for their style rather than their content, as some, in or presaging the civil law tradition, are too vague for modern common law lawyers; but the extra detail could have been added in the same plain style.

The Code of Hammurabi, from the 18th century BCE, contains 282 clauses. The language of clause 5 is typical, although it has almost twice the code's average word-count:

> If a judge try a case, reach a decision, and present his judgment in writing; if later error shall appear in his decision, and it be through his own fault, then he shall pay twelve times the fine set by him in the case, and he shall be publicly removed from the judge's bench, and never again shall he sit there to render judgement.[1]

Moses also benefited from the incentive to brevity arising from the need to carve each letter in stone. His *Torah* (literally, *Law*) is believed by some traditionalists to be the perfect word of God, and to contain no superfluous words. For example, the eighth commandment, two short words in the original, can fairly be translated as *Do not steal*. The *Thou shalt not steal* of the King James version sounds stilted to us but was written in the formal vernacular of the time. The Theft Act 1968 necessarily opts for greater precision but remains succinct and jargon-free (with the constituent parts separately defined):

> A person is guilty of theft if he dishonestly appropriates property belonging to another with the intention of permanently depriving the other of it.

The Napoleonic Penal Code of 1810 is also (apart from *frauduleusement*) clear and to the point. Article 379 defined theft:

Quiconque a soustrait frauduleusement une chose qui ne lui appartient pas, est coupable de vol. (Whoever wrongfully takes something which does not belong to them is guilty of theft.)

By 2016 this had been trimmed without change of substance to article 311:

Le vol est la soustraction frauduleuse de la chose d'autrui. (Theft is the wrongful removal of another's property.)

Mattila (2013, p.128) quotes the sixth century CE Byzantine Emperor Justinian's instructions that the Roman laws then being codified were to be *accurate* and *concise*.

The waves of Germanic-language speakers who crossed the North Sea to fill the vacuum after the Romans left Britain had a tradition of plain law (and, having resisted the Romans and Christianity, no Latin). Their language replaced rather than merged with that of the Celts (Ostler, 2005, pp.311–14) and the Normans had not yet imported the French influence. Anglo-Saxon wills used everyday English vocabulary built into simple sentences, although some Latin terms did filter in once the church arrived (Mattila, 2013). A typical Anglo-Saxon will, showing the original language and a modern transcript, can be downloaded from www.adler.demon. co.uk/saxon.docx.

The occasional initiatives to simplify English legal language in the centuries after the Norman invasion have been well documented by Mellinkoff (1963) and others, so we'll move on.

Mattila (2013, p.128) reports of 18th century legal German that:

The celebrated Prussian code ... is one of the principal monuments of the history of the German language in general. This code is characterised by the clarity of the language and by the fact that it avoids loanwords ... It also appears that one of the architects of the code ... especially counselled lawyers not to add too many subordinate clauses within sentences: they are a sign of 'deficient thinking'. The [code] provided a model for later codes in Austria, Germany, and Switzerland ...

Care over proper usage of legal language radiated from German-speaking countries to other corners of Europe [including Russia].

Although the Office of the Parliamentary Counsel in England did not adopt a modern-language policy until the 1990s (since when successive first parliamentary counsel have championed it), the Theft Act was far from the earliest example. Here is the opening subclause of the Sale of Goods Act 1893 (which departed from convention by including two sentences):

A contract of sale of goods is a contract whereby the seller transfers or agrees to transfer the property in goods to the buyer for a money consideration, called the price. There may be a contract of sale between one part owner and another.

Professor Reed Dickerson was teaching plain writing to his Indiana University law students in the 1940s. And Anthony Parker, an English solicitor, published plain precedents for wills and conveyancing in 1964 and 1969. A consumer movement in the 1970s encouraged the profession to renounce legalese, and when John Walton, the solicitor for Rugby Borough Council, wrote in the *Law Society Gazette* in 1983 proposing an organisation to this end, he received over 200 letters of support, including one from Lord Denning. 'Most of these,' he reported in Clarity's first newsletter (August 1983) 'have been from lawyers who already believe in the aims of Clarity'.

There has been progress, in legislation and through other initiatives, many of them government sponsored. In 2013 the Cabinet Office launched the 'good law' project, which aims to make legislation more accessible and understandable for UK citizens.[2] Among the other initiatives prompted by this project are:

- collaboration between the Government Digital Service and

    - the Department for the Environment, Food and Rural Affairs, which has been reducing DEFRA's published guidance by over 80 per cent;[3] and
    - the Government Legal Department, which has redesigned the Digital Services contract, reducing its length by more than 40 per cent,[4] and which is now redesigning other standard forms of government contracts to make them easy to use;[5]

- reviews of

    - explanatory notes; and
    - the visual design of legislation; and

- proposals

    - for a drafting tool to allow better collaboration between drafters and legislators; and
    - to simplify various complexities in the structure and wording of legislation,[6] in particular using software to show the structure of our tax system.[7]

In recent decades some law firms have adopted plain language, though with varying degrees of skill. One of the pioneers in the 1980s was Mallesons Stephen Jaques, then with 600 fee earners the largest law firm in Australia. It set up a plain language department of six lawyers to convert the whole practice to plain language, and marketed itself with great commercial success as a plain language firm. Others have followed, in Australia and elsewhere, but disappointingly few, leaving a substantial opportunity for those willing to exploit the gap in the market.

Endnotes

1 Taken from L.W. King's translation at **avalon.law.yale.edu/ancient/hamframe.asp**.
2 **www.gov.uk/government/collections/good-law**.
3 **quarterly.blog.gov.uk/2015/09/10/clearing-the-thicket**.
4 **digitalmarketplace.blog.gov.uk/2015/09/03/creating-simpler-clearer-contracts-for-the-digital-services-framework**.
5 **digitalmarketplace.blog.gov.uk/2016/07/14/working-together-to-design-government-contracts-for-the-digital-age**.
6 **www.instituteforgovernment.org.uk/blog/7084/guest-blog-good-law-nine-months-on**.
7 **good-law.tumblr.com/post/133133255176/visualising-tax-law**.

Chapter 6

The need for thought

It's almost a little bit meaningless.
BBC Radio 4 speaker (17 December 2013)

Many of our examples reveal a lamentable lack of thought. But the problem is so widespread that we highlight the need to pause and reflect by giving it its own chapter. Legal writing requires thought about *what* is being said (or overlooked) as well as attention to *the way* it is said. Lawyers are well paid to anticipate and avoid problems, not to create them.

The lawyer's real job is not to translate ordinary language into 'legal' language but to think through the scheme you are creating to ensure that it does the job. As Rix LJ (2006) said, always ask 'What if?'

Many lawyers skip the *thought* stage and rely on hand-me-downs. They expect a precedent – or just their favoured form of words – to work, not only in general but for the case in hand. They are often under pressure and do not have time to check the detail each time; that responsibility is delegated silently, retrospectively, and ineffectively to whoever developed the precedent. And the provenance is often casual; the lawyer may have come across the document without knowing who wrote it or what the original client's instructions were.

This lack of thought and perspective – and the consequent poor drafting – are sadly familiar. But the pressure to skimp in this way is relieved as plain language reduces our workload.

Here is a rather strange, though common, example of pointless words camouflaging woolly thought (from the tenant's covenants in a lease):

Twice or oftener in every year to permit the landlord to inspect ...

What does this mean? On the face of it, that the tenant does not have to admit the landlord on the first occasion each year unless he promises to come again. If it obliges the tenant to let the landlord in less than twice, then either 'once or oftener' or 'three times or oftener' would have the same effect.

This example comes from a City of London firm's standard lease:

> At all times during the term to keep the demised premises sufficiently supplied and equipped with such fire fighting and extinguishing apparatus and appliances as may be required by any competent authority and from time to time by the Landlord ...

What is the role of 'sufficiently'? The tenant must either comply with the requirements of the landlord and the authority, or provide adequate protection, the details of which are left to the tenant. This passage tries to impose a combination, which makes poor sense.

Similarly,

> at least more than 3,

which, as has been seen, means

> more than 3

if fractions are possible, but otherwise

> at least 4.

In

> Since dictating, we have now received your letter of the 25th April

now is redundant, and momentarily confusing in that it conflicts with the continuing-past sense of *since*.

Commendable caution in avoiding prejudice (and sometimes litigation) can be undermined by the careless labelling of events as allegations. For example, the report of

> a ... challenge ... to the Presidential power to conclude international agreements that allegedly interfere with constitutionally guaranteed rights

implies a challenge to the president's supposed power to conclude questionable agreements rather than to his supposedly illegitimate exercise of an unquestioned power. And a report that a car *was stopped ... after allegedly travelling at 105mph* makes little sense: if the allegation was false, when was it stopped?

Another recent development is the misuse of *after* for *when*. This can be distracting, as in newspaper reports that someone died after an event that must have killed them instantaneously.

An outstanding example of thoughtless copying is the survival of backsheets in litigation. These were useful in past centuries, when foolscap or larger documents were folded lengthwise and stored in a pile held together with tape. The back of the last page would give such useful information as the nature and date of the document and the names of the parties, on the right-hand side so as to face upwards when the document was folded and taped. But now that we store A4 documents face up, usually in ring binders, this information on the back of the last page merely wastes the time of preparation and page-turning and the extra sheet of paper. Yet it is still routinely photocopied, and ludicrously inserted in the trial bundle at the end of the document, often blank face up. In 2014, backsheets were banned from Chancery court orders,[1] but they are still tolerated elsewhere. Some barristers still like a backsheet on their instructions, because it has always been their custom to *endorse the brief* (note the outcome) on the backsheet, but why can't they do that on the front? A solution has been to allow them a space there marked *Endorsement:* but they have tended to ignore that and add their own backsheet. (*Endorse* originally meant *write on the back* – from the Latin *dorsum* – but is now used more generally to mean *add a note anywhere on the document.*)

And we leave you with:

> **PRIVATE**
> **No trespassing after 6pm**

Endnote

1   'Chancery Masters' Orders: Effective 1st October 2014', extended to judges' orders by 'Chancery Division – production of orders for Master and Judges', 30 December 2014, and now to be found in the *Chancery Guide* (February 2016, last amended August 2017), paras.22.5 and 22.23.

Part C

How to make legal writing more effective

Chapter 7

An overview: three rules of thumb

In any document it is important to retain an overview to keep the detail in context. It is particularly important with legal writing, in which the reader's view of the wood is often impeded by impenetrably dense growth.

So before plunging into the detail we offer (in no particular order) three perspectives of our wood to summarise the theme of this book.

- Ask yourself: *How would I say this if I was not being a lawyer?* (We touched on this on p.3.)
- Write invisibly (so that the reader is focused on what you are saying, and oblivious to how you are saying it). Style distracts from substance.
- Don't meander; go directly from beginning to end in a straight line, except to the extent that you can justify a scenic route. So:

  1. Think what you want to say (and keep it in mind).
  2. Say it unpretentiously and without fuss.
  3. Then stop.
  4. But edit exhaustively.

We have put *stop* before *edit* because we mean that having said what you want to say you should not wander on; it wastes time and signals a lack of confidence. Editing comes next because it is intended to hone the text rather than add to it (although it may prompt you to step back to stage 1 to include a point previously overlooked).

Chapter 8

How to start

There are many ways to improve legal writing and we hope we have covered most of them. But what if you have only a little time to devote to improving this essential skill? Which will give you the best quick results – that is, the most impact for the least effort?

Here we each offer our three favoured suggestions for clarity in legal writing. If you only change one thing as a result of reading this book, you might choose one of these.

DP: Here are my chosen three, in order:

- **Use headings.** Add short, informative and accurate headings. Even a badly written document will then be well organised and signposted for the reader. See Chapter 10 ('Organising your document').
- **Put the main message first.** This focuses the reader's attention where you most want it and creates a framework on which readers can hang the details as they read what follows. For instance, if you are answering a question give the answer before the reasons. This reduces effort for the reader and improves the chance of getting your main message across. Again, see Chapter 10.
- **Keep sentences short.** This is one of the easiest changes, as well as one of the most powerful. Not only are short sentences easier to read, they are also easier to edit and less likely to contain mistakes. See Chapter 17 ('Sentences').

MA: I don't disagree with Daphne's choice, but as I can't say which three I think are the most important I'll add another three that must be near the top of the list:

- **Paragraph for meaning.** There are two techniques here. One is to start a new paragraph when you move on to a new point. The other is to break long paragraphs into indented subparagraphs to guide the reader through complex material. Neither of these need involve any change in wording (except perhaps the occasional link word). You just need additional white space. See Chapter 16 ('Paragraphs').
- **Punctuation.** If you use standard punctuation when you're not being a lawyer, do the same with legal documents, however formal. Properly used

punctuation helps you control a river of words which might otherwise be too wide and fast to navigate. Think of it as a series of lifebelts thrown to drowning readers. See Chapter 12 ('Punctuation').

- **Use your imagination.** Identify any gaps in your instructions. When you read over the document, imagine yourself to be the intended reader and change anything that you think needs changing. Or get someone else to do this. Or both.

If time is precious, we suggest you choose one technique and practise it briefly – a few seconds will sometimes be enough – in every piece of writing you do. Specifically, practise it in every email. For example, suppose you have chosen to work on short sentences. Before you send your next email, look for a sentence that runs over two lines. Change it before you press 'Send'. Then, in your next email, do the same. By the end of the day, you will have spent a few moments each on dozens of emails, making the sentences shorter. Before long, you will find yourself writing with more full stops in the first place, knowing as you write what you will have to change before you send it. In a few weeks, you will have developed a new writing habit that can last the rest of your life. Then you can relax and turn your attention to the next technique on your list.

Ideally, don't stop after these six.

Great Tip

Chapter 9

Be human

Tone

We all respond better to humanity than to its alternatives, whether that be cruelty or just indifference, arrogance, pomposity, or the artificial voice of an automated telephone service programmed with options we don't want.

Lawyers can be cruel, but often this inhumanity is thoughtless rather than intentional. We forget that the legal process – and even a routine solicitor's letter – is likely to be intimidating in itself, and that the recipient of the forbidding notepaper will often be an innocent party. Yet one aggressive firm added **LITIGATION DEPARTMENT** to its letterhead in large bold caps where it was visible through the envelope's window.

The damage will be greater in delicate situations. This letter before action was sent in the 1980s to a distressed woman whose 20-year marriage was collapsing, by a young solicitor who had heard only the husband's side of the story. It is a model of insensitivity:

> We have been consulted by your Husband regarding matrimonial difficulties which you have been experiencing during your marriage ...
>
> We understand that there were arguments culminating in Easter this year when there were considerable difficulties presented when your Parents were invited to stay at the matrimonial home. Our client had already intimated to you that he intended to redecorate the house, and that our client would be unable to accommodate your Parents.
>
> Since Easter we understand that you have not spoken, and that prior to this occasion there were periods of up to 7 days when you did not speak to each other. This was mainly caused by the difficulties that our client has experienced with his Parents-In-Law, and in particular with your Father whom he finds a difficult man to get on with.
>
> Our client has given us other grounds which have led us to advise him that he has sufficient grounds for a Divorce based on your unreasonable behaviour, and we are writing to enquire whether you would agree to allow such a Petition to proceed undefended ...
>
> Despite the small financial contribution that you have made towards the house, and the fact that our client has paid most, if not all, of the bills on the house during the period of your marriage, and that the house is in our client's name, we have advised our client that you may have a small claim for a share in the property, 15 Green Lane. Our client would be prepared to consider making a payment to you to discharge any

interest that you may have in the property, on the basis that this would be in full and final settlement in respect of all claims that you may have against him.

In any event any payment that is to be made will have to be made out of the proceeds of sale of the house, so that any payment would be dependent on obtaining a purchaser at a suitable price.

You are of course aware that Alice is continuing her further education and there is the question of her Grant for the final year of her studies at University. Our client has confirmed to us that he will be prepared to contribute the greater part of her Grant, but that you will be required to pay the sum of £250 towards her final year's expenses. Please confirm that you are willing to do this ...

Even a tactful letter would have been a gross (if sadly necessary) intrusion into an intimate private relationship; this size 20 boot trampling over the wife in her own home must have left her feeling violated. What, in particular, is wrong with it?

- There is no compassion for the recipient (or insight into the husband's shortcomings, which emerge clearly between the lines).
- The constant referral to *our client* makes the letter pompous and remote and the style repetitive. Why not *your husband*, or *Mr Smith*?
- There is irrelevant detail which invites equally irrelevant denial and counter-accusations, increasing the scope of the conflict.
- Yet important information is omitted. The proposal is:

    'If you drop all your other claims, your husband may pay you an unspecified small amount. But then again, he might not.'

    This was too vague for the wife to decide, or even to consider whether she was interested.

So the letter is inefficient as well as being unkind. Far from achieving its purpose, it stimulated opposition. How much better to have begun (after ensuring that the client had warned his wife that the letter was on its way):

Dear Mrs Smith
    I believe you know that your husband has decided to start divorce proceedings. I am sorry that your long marriage has broken down.
    Mr Smith has asked me to represent him and I am writing to you personally as I believe you have not appointed a solicitor ...

For a full revision, see Example A on p.234.

An aggressive tone may be appropriate, but it should be reserved for the proper occasions. And on those occasions let us be as plain in our speech as when we are being polite. *That is untrue* is more persuasive – when supported by reasons – than the inept euphemism *I am surprised to note that ...* Let us call a spade a spade, though as eloquently as possible.

Whether the purpose of your document is to persuade or intimidate, it is more likely to succeed if you treat your reader as a human being. Without that there will be no rapport; in fact, it is unlikely that there will be a reader, since few people have the patience to persevere to the dreary end of an impersonal document and an offensive one may be screwed up and binned in anger.

Here are four pieces of writing from judges who did not let self-importance isolate them from their audience: the litigants waiting anxiously for the result of their case; the lawyers who had argued it; and other lawyers researching the law in the future.

The first two come from judgments of Lord Denning MR in the Court of Appeal (in *Beswick* v. *Beswick* (1966) and *Hinz* v. *Berry* (1970)):

> Peter Beswick was a coal merchant in Eccles, Lancashire. He had no business premises. All he had was a lorry, scales and weights. He used to take the lorry to the yard of the National Coal Board, where he bagged coal and took it round to his customers in the neighbourhood. His nephew, John Joseph Beswick, helped him in the business.
>
> In March 1962, old Peter Beswick and his wife were both aged over 70. He had had his leg amputated and was not in good health. The nephew was anxious to get hold of the business before the old man died. So they went to a solicitor, Mr Ashcroft, who drew up an agreement for them. The business was to be transferred to the nephew: old Peter Beswick was to be employed in it as a consultant for the rest of his life at £6 10s per week. After his death the nephew was to pay to his widow an annuity of £5 per week, which was to come out of the business ...

> It happened on 19th April 1964. It was bluebell time in Kent. Mr and Mrs Hinz, the plaintiff, had been married some ten years, and they had four children, all aged nine and under. The youngest was one. The plaintiff was a remarkable woman. In addition to her own four, she was foster mother to four other children. To add to it, she was two months pregnant with her fifth child.
>
> On this day they drove out in a Bedford Dormobile van from Tonbridge to Canvey Island. They took all the children with them. As they were coming back they turned into a lay-by at Thurnham to have a picnic tea. Mr Hinz was at the back of the Dormobile making the tea. The plaintiff had taken Stephanie, her third child, aged three, across the road to pick bluebells on the opposite side. There came along a Jaguar car out of control driven by Mr Berry, the defendant. A tyre had burst. The Jaguar rushed into this lay-by and crashed into Mr Hinz and the children. Mr Hinz was frightfully injured and died a little later. Nearly all the children were hurt. Blood was streaming from their heads. Mrs Hinz, hearing the crash, turned round and saw this disaster. She ran across the road and did all she could. Her husband was beyond recall. But the children recovered.

By telling the stories in human terms (and in short, comprehensible sentences each of which follows easily from the one before), the judge interests even those unconnected to the case. More immediately, he conveys the subliminal message to the litigants and their lawyers that he cares about the litigants as people, and wants to do justice between them.

This style can be taken too far. More informal and less judicial is this extract from a judgment by Justice Watt, a judge of the Court of Appeal for Ontario. In *R* v. *Flores* (2011), an appeal against a murder conviction, his judgment began:

> [1] They met in a bar in London. Melvin Flores and Cindy MacDonald. Soon, they

became lovers. Then, Cindy got pregnant. Melvin was excited about the prospect of fatherhood. He wanted to get married. Cindy did not share her lover's excitement. She had an abortion.

[2] Cindy made it clear to Melvin that their relationship was over. But Melvin continued his pursuit. He enlisted the assistance of some of Cindy's relatives to convince her to marry him.

[3] Early one morning in June 2006, Melvin Flores closed the book on his relationship with Cindy MacDonald. With a butcher knife left embedded in Cindy's back. Fifty-three blunt force injuries.

Although commendably readable and concise, the style is closer to pulp fiction than judicial reasoning.[1]

DP: I prefer the pulp fiction style to legalese. The tone grates but the message gets straight through.

The third example of good judicial prose is from another Court of Appeal judgment from Lord Denning's friend Lord Scarman (in *Chase International Corporation* v. *Oliver* (1978), unreported, but quoted in Denning (1979, p.221):

The plaintiff and the defendants are adjoining landowners. The plaintiff asserts that he has a right of way over the defendants' land giving access from his land to the public highway. Without this access his land is in fact landlocked, but, for reasons which clearly appear from the narration of the facts already given by my Lords, the plaintiff cannot claim a right of way by necessity. The plaintiff has no grant. He has the benefit of no enforceable contract. He has no prescriptive right. His case has to be that the defendants are estopped by their conduct from denying him a right of access over their land to the public highway. If the plaintiff has any right, it is an equity arising out of the conduct and relationship of the parties. In such a case I think it is now well settled law that the court, having analysed and assessed the conduct and relationship of the parties, has to answer three questions. First, is there an equity established? Secondly, what is the extent of the equity, if one is established? And, thirdly, what is the relief appropriate to satisfy the equity?

Lord Scarman uses many technical expressions, and explains none of them, but that is appropriate in their context. They are genuine technical expressions, useful shorthand in the circumstances, rather than archaic or abstruse words used merely to impress, or because *that's how lawyers write*. And, since he was giving judgment in the Court of Appeal, he can reasonably expect his audience to understand them. (Adler used to ask in seminars who Lord Scarman's primary audience was; some said the lawyers in the case, others the litigants, but there was general agreement that the lawyers would have explained the technicalities to the litigants at an earlier stage of the proceedings.) Moreover, the meaning is not obscured by convoluted grammar:

- The judge's 192 words are divided into 12 sentences (averaging 16 words each).
- Each sentence is a clear step in a lucid argument.
- Only two sentences are interrupted by subordinate clauses.
- The subordinate clauses are not too long, are clearly flagged by a comma at each end, and are restricted to one per sentence.
- Of some 25 verbs, only three are passive, each of those with good reason.
- Each subject is close to its verb (and almost all are immediately followed by their verb).

Compare that to this fragment written by a far less eminent lawyer:

> Provided always ... that the Lessor shall be entitled at its absolute discretion to vary the proportion of the Service Costs payable by the Lessee as defined in clause 1(n) in the event of rights being granted pursuant to the terms of paragraph 5 of the Fifth Schedule hereto Provided that such variation shall not result in the said Service Charge proportion being increased.

An informal tone is not necessarily better than a formal one. The expected degree of formality varies from one culture (and subculture) to another, and according to circumstances. But a neutral tone, neither elaborate nor over-familiar, often works. If in doubt, it is safer to start formal and loosen up as you get to know your reader than to risk giving offence.

Political correctness

Gender

Men often do not realise how irritating women find the customary assumption that everyone is a man. The traditional lawyer's answer is that *the masculine includes the feminine,* a long-established convention expressly applied to some documents by s.61 of the Law of Property Act 1925 and s.6 of the Interpretation Act 1978. But that misses the point.

Some writers overlook the possibility of confusion and consider the offence unimportant. One judge changed her mind about that on finding that jurors only began to elect forewomen when she started instructing them to elect a fore*person* instead of a fore*man.*[2]

There is no completely satisfactory third person singular pronoun when the sex must be left open. *S/he* is unpronounceable, and *he or she* is cumbersome, especially if used more than once. Neither form can be repeated without destroying the flow of the document and both are inadequate when the party to which they refer may be a company. *They, them* and *their* are useful and it is often worth switching to the plural to take advantage of its inconspicuous neutrality.

Some of us use *they* as singular, and Robert Eagleson and a few colleagues (1996) traced this use back to the 14th century, with examples from Shakespeare, the King James Bible, Fielding, Thackeray, George Bernard Shaw, and others. Some people find it annoying and it can be confusing if a distinction is needed between singular and plural, but tests conducted in Australia showed its unconscious and natural vernacular use. For example, of the 95 people asked to complete the sentence

Somebody showed her the way, didn't … ?

87 per cent used *they*. We expect the same would apply in Britain; this exchange seems natural:

A: Who was that on the phone?
B: I don't know; I missed it.
A: No matter; if it's important they'll ring again.

… and not easy to improve on, though perhaps *whoever it was will ring again* would do.

Sex-based nouns are also a problem. How do we refer to the draftsman without assuming, often wrongly, that the work was done by a man? We recommend the neutral *writer* or *drafter* (now increasingly common). Or you can recast the sentence, so that

There is a temptation for the draftsman to allow

becomes

There is a temptation when drafting to allow

and

The draftsman and his client

becomes

The drafting solicitor and the client.

Person is not much help. It is, paradoxically, impersonal in tone, especially in its plural form *persons*, although the customary plural *people* sounds natural in any tone.

Discriminatory forms of speech are not limited to those that can be blamed on the constraints of the language.

One common and particularly offensive habit, easily avoided, is the reference to women as *girls*, happily much less common than when this chapter was first written. (The same goes for referring to a female employee as *Your young lady*.) It is as unnecessary and as demeaning as to call a grown

69

man *boy*, a device to remind the socially despised of their imagined inferiority. Similarly, women should not be referred to by their first names when a man would be *Mr ...*, or initials and surname.

It used to be the norm to address any firm as *Dear Sirs*, a survival from the days when the bosses were always male. *Dear Ms Wylie*, addressed to the individual handling the case, solves the problem and improves the tone. Where a personal letter is not practical, try *Dear Sir or Madam* (one way round or the other), or *Dear [Firmname]*.

In some jurisdictions, legislative counsel have used gender-neutral language for years, so there is no excuse for practitioners to rule it out as impracticable. David Elliott, a legislative drafter who has practised in England, New Zealand, and Canada, wrote in 'Gender-neutral drafting in Canada' (1990):

> Sex-neutral legislative language is not just a fad. It is being used in several Canadian jurisdictions ...
>
> Having been required to use gender-neutral language in New Zealand for nearly two years, I came to live with it. Despite early reservations, I now feel quite comfortable with gender-neutral drafting, and find the constant masculine reference in some Canadian legislation and most legal documents objectionable.

The underlying rule is simple: to address everyone (whatever your views on their status) without giving offence. It may not always be easy to put this into practice, but it is worth trying. Miller & Swift (1995) and Doyle (1995) are full of useful ideas, as is the UK Office of the Parliamentary Counsel's guidance for drafting legislation.[3]

The folly of euphemism

If everyone is to be treated with respect, language must not demean the members of any group (or any individual), not just women.

But in a 1994 *Clarity* editorial, 'The folly of euphemism', Adler wrote:

> According to *The Daily Telegraph*, the Labour Party passed a resolution last week 'to re-integrate special needs children into mainstream education'. On the face of it, this means that children who need special treatment won't get it ...
>
> What are special needs? Vegetarian meals? Instruction in their native literature for foreign pupils? Advanced mathematics for a prodigy?
>
> We should not use vague words to avoid the negative content of precise ones. It is pointless because the vague words either do not carry the writer's meaning (if the reader does not understand the code) or carry the negative meaning anyway (if the reader does understand).
>
> Every so often the delicate wordsmiths concoct a new euphemism. We guess, or are taught, its real meaning. But once the new word (or more often, the new clumsy phrase) is generally understood, it has outlived its purpose, and is replaced in its turn. So we have artifically fast obsolescence. We replaced 'backward children' with 'educationally sub-normal', moved on to 'ESN', and through 'children with learning difficulties'. This last is more precise than

'special needs children', but does it include bright children too bored to concentrate, and intelligent dyslexics?

There is no point in telling your readers that someone has difficulties requiring special treatment if you do not say what the difficulties are or what treatment you recommend.

On reflection, there *is* a point: to signal respect, and we cannot offer an all-purpose answer. There is sometimes a conflict between tact and accuracy, and any judgement on the balance will depend on individual circumstances. By all means be as diplomatic as possible, but be aware of the scope for misunderstanding.

It is a pity that the desire to avoid giving offence sometimes leads to wordy and vague writing. Unfortunately, the political correctness movement has made itself absurd by imagining offence where none could reasonably be taken, and by tying us in linguistic knots to avoid it. In one psychiatric centre it was a sacking offence to wish a Christian *client* a *Happy Christmas*, leading bemused patients greeted with the mandatory *Happy midwinter festival* to wonder about role reversal. Another local council wanted to ban the word *brainstorming* to avoid offending *people with epilepsy*; the suggested alternative was *thought showers* – a double euphemism, since no storm could fail to take offence at being described as a shower.

Abstraction (how examples help)

Perhaps this heading speaks for itself. But in case not ...

Concrete thought is easier than abstract thought.

The use of examples

David Elliott began 'The arguments in favour of using examples in legislation' (1993):

> Whenever people read a text they bring to it all their accumulated knowledge. That knowledge is used to help understand the text. Research (and a moment of personal reflection) tells us that one way in which people interpret texts is by thinking through a series of examples to see what impact the text has on the example.
>
> If we have a limited background knowledge about the subject matter of a text it is that much more difficult to understand. It is through the internal processing of examples that we develop a keener understanding of what the text means.

Over the last few decades, examples have become increasingly popular with legislative counsel. Francis Bennion used them to particularly good effect in the Consumer Credit Act 1974, where they formed a nine-page schedule illustrating the many novel concepts the Act introduced. Here is one instance. Section 11 provides that:

71

(1) A restricted-use credit agreement is a regulated consumer credit agreement–

    (a) to finance a transaction between the debtor and the creditor, whether forming part of that agreement or not, or

    (b) to finance a transaction between the debtor and a person (the 'supplier') other than the creditor, or

    (c) to refinance any existing indebtedness of the debtor's, whether to the creditor or another person,

and 'restricted-use credit' shall be construed accordingly.

(2) An unrestricted-use credit agreement is a regulated consumer credit agreement not falling within subsection (1), and 'unrestricted-use credit' shall be construed accordingly.

(3) An agreement does not fall within subsection (1) if the credit is in fact provided in such a way as to leave the debtor free to use it as he chooses, even though certain uses would contravene that or any other agreement.

(4) An agreement may fall within subsection (1)(b) although the identity of the supplier is unknown at the time the agreement is made.

This is explained by example 12 in Schedule 2:

Facts: The N Bank agrees to lend O (an individual) £2,000 to buy a car from P. To make sure the loan is used as intended, the N Bank stipulates that the money must be paid by it direct to P.

Analysis: The agreement is a consumer credit agreement by virtue of section 8(2). Since it falls within section 11(1)(b), it is a restricted-use credit agreement, P being the supplier. If the N Bank had not stipulated for direct payment to the supplier, section 11(3) would have operated and made the agreement into one for unrestricted-use credit.

Examples can be equally helpful in private documents. This is taken from a rent review clause in a shared ownership lease:

6. (A) On each rent review date the basic rent will change in line with the change in the RPI [a defined term] over a period similar to that between the starting date and the review dates, using the last figures published [X] weeks before the rent review date.

Example

Suppose: the number of weeks specified in subclause (A) is 3;

        the rent is reviewed on 1 February 1999 after 5 years;

        on 1 February 1999 the latest RPI figure is 310 (published 15 January 1999) and the one before that had been 300 (published 15 December 1998);

        the RPI figure published 15 December 1993 was 195 and that published 15 January 1994 was 200.

Then:	the January 1999 RPI figure cannot be used because it is published less than 3 weeks before the review date, so the December 1998 figure is taken;
	as the period between reviews is 5 years, the December 1998 figure must be compared with that of December 1993;
So:	The basic rent increases in 1999 to 300/195ths of its existing level (that is, by 105/195ths or about 54 %).

The use of analogy

While examples illustrate a generality that is difficult to imagine by replacing the general terms with something specific (and so imaginable), analogies illustrate the unfamiliar by comparison with something familiar. For example, on p.37 we used the similarities between the biological evolution of dogs and the linguistic evolution of modern English to show the absurdity of venerating earlier versions of the language merely because they came before.

Analogy is a useful device as long as everyone remembers that great similarity is consistent with material difference. Language might bark and bite but it doesn't eat.

Endnotes

1 For more examples of Justice Watt's style see **www.theglobeandmail.com/ news/national/ontario/the-judge-who-writes-like-a-paperback-novelist/ article1937791** (*The [Toronto] Globe and Mail*, 10 March 2011). For a comparison of Judge Watt's style with Lord Denning's see Adler (Mar 2011).
2 This is taken from the report in *Clarity 26* (Dec 1992) of Lynn Smith's presentation at the *Just Language* conference. Ms Smith was Dean of Law at the University of British Columbia.
3 Office of the Parliamentary Counsel 'Drafting Guidance' (2017) section 2.1 (see **www.gov.uk/government/uploads/system/uploads/attachment_data/ file/622457/drafting_guidance_june_2017.pdf**).

Chapter 10

Organising your document

The need for organisation

The usual advice is to plan your work before you start. You need to think not only what you are going to say, and how you are going to say it, but in what order.

> **MA:** I have never had the patience for this. I usually know pretty much what I want to say and in what tone, and I prefer to start writing than to plan the document meticulously in advance. But the structure evolves as I go: planning is deferred rather than skipped, and I edit thoroughly while I write and again at the end. If I am stuck or struggling, I find it helps to summarise each paragraph already written to ensure a logical progression, and then to re-write and re-arrange the main text as necessary. Often my ideas change during this process, or I think of new points. Sometimes I realise that I have started on the wrong tack, though perhaps only when I find I cannot make a convincing case. This may not be unusual. One law lord mentioned at a Clarity function that when he was writing the deciding speech in a particular appeal (the other members of the appeal committee being split 2–2) he wrote the first five drafts giving victory to one party before changing his mind and with it the result of the case.

But Dr Betty Flowers[1] offers a different approach. She divides the writing process into four stages, each requiring the adoption of a distinct personality: the enthusiastic, brainstorming, creative madman; the organising architect; the workmanlike carpenter; and the reviewing judge.

> **DP:** Like Mark, I'm too impatient to plan every document. But I always use the madman, the architect, the carpenter, and the judge on difficult documents. They are the perfect antidote to writer's block. Planning is helpful, but when procrastination threatens I find the most effective cure is the carpenter's task – to write a draft on every point in the plan without editing. Personally, I make it my aim to finish writing a bad draft before I stop work in the evening. Then I sleep on it. I am convinced that my brain continues working on the document in my sleep – my favourite way to work. In the morning, I edit (now working as the judge). Editing is so much easier than creating new text. Some of my most successful documents began as a bad draft that no one ever saw.

We suspect that many lawyers sign off their documents without having planned them at any stage. They may know what they are going to say, but they have a standard tone for all purposes and the parts of the document come out in the order they think of things.

Look at this extract from a disorganised will (which survived the testator):

1. I revoke all former Wills heretofore made by me

2. (a) I appoint ABC … and DEF … to be executors and trustees of this my Will
   (b) The expression 'my trustees' whenever used in this will shall mean my executors and the trustees or trustee for the time being whether original or substituted or added

3. I wish to be cremated

4. I give to my wife GH if she survives me by one month my property known as Number 12 Downs Drive Dorking aforesaid or failing which any other property where I live at my death together with all my chattels in and about my said property …

5. If my said wife survives me I give the following cash legacies to the following persons:

   (a) Unto each of the said ABC and DEF the sum of one hundred thousand pounds
   (b) Unto IJK … ninety thousand pounds

6. (a) Subject to the payment or discharge of my funeral testamentary and administration expenses and debts and other liabilities and legacies I give all my property and assets of every kind and wherever situated to my said wife absolutely if she survives me by one month
   (b) If my said wife dies before me or survives me by less than one month or if the said gift to her fails for any other reason or if my said wife and I die in the same disaster in circumstances rendering it uncertain which of us survived the other clauses 7 to 10 hereof shall take effect

7. I give free of inheritance tax unto the said IJK the sum of ninety thousand pounds
   …

This organisational chaos reflects the solicitor's disorganised mind and failure to think through the consequences of the draft:

- Paragraph 4 applies if the testator's wife survives him by a month, giving her the matrimonial home (or, in ill-defined circumstances, another property instead).
- Paragraph 5 also applies if the wife survives him (though this time she need only survive by a moment), and gives cash legacies, including IJK's £90,000.
- Paragraph 6(a) gives the wife the residue if she survives him (this time by a month again), partly duplicating paragraph 4.

- Paragaph 6(b) introduces clauses 7 to 10, which apply only if the wife dies before the testator or within a month after his death. So these clauses would have been better placed as subclauses of 6(b).
- Paragraph 7 mistakenly gives IJK a second £90,000 (or a third, if the surviving wife does not replace her mirror will to correct the error).

Headings

The best way to improve organisation, whether in planning, writing, or editing, is to add headings, which also help the reader by improving structure and signposting the content.

Writers and readers alike need bifocals, to give a good aerial view of the wood as well as detailed attention to individual trees and their branches and twigs.

> **MA:** It was only as I reviewed this chapter for the third edition that it occurred to me that the expression *You can't see the wood for the trees* was ambiguous. I had always understood 'wood' in the sense of *a small group of trees* but it could refer to the material of which the trees consist, which changes the focus.

To help us grapple with the detail and structure of this book we each used a large screen to display a whole page of the text on one side and a draft of the contents page, amended as we worked, on the other. For writers using Microsoft Word, its navigation pane offers even more help. Any text to which you apply a heading style appears there and is automatically updated as you work. As its name suggests, you can use the navigation pane to flit around the document from one section to another. You can also reorganise the document by dragging a section in the navigation pane.

Here is a different will:

Cancellation of previous wills

1   I revoke [or cancel] any earlier wills.

Funeral

2   I wish to be cremated.

Interpretation

3   A   'Glenda' is my wife Glenda Googleheim.
    B   'Alice' is Alice Tate of …
    C   'Deborah' is Deborah Oldcourt of …
    D   'Irene' is Irene Smithson of …

4   'Survive(s) me' is to be read as 'survive(s) me by 30 days (calculated from 00.01 am on the day following my death)'.

Administration

5   I appoint Alice and Deborah my executors.

6   A   My executors are to have all the investment and management powers of an outright owner, except that they must act for the benefit of the beneficiaries.
    B   No executor will be liable for anything done or overlooked in good faith.
    C   Professional executors may charge their usual fees.

Gifts

7   If Glenda survives me I give:

    A   £75,000 each to Alice and Deborah.
    B   £90,000 to Irene.
    C   The rest of my property to Glenda.

Alternative arrangements

8   If either Alice or Deborah does not accept the executorship, or has to be replaced …

9   If Glenda does not survive me I give:

    A   …

10 Any part (or the whole) of any gift which is not taken by the person to whom it is given is to be treated as though that person did not survive me. This will apply if a gift is forfeited or renounced, or if a precondition of the gift is unsatisfied.

It would be equally valid to dispense with the *Alternative arrangements* heading, moving clause 8 to *Administration* and clauses 9 and 10 to *Gifts*.

Would the organisation of this will be improved by moving the interpretation section to the end, a common place for a glossary in non-legal documents? A lawyer familiar with wills would expect to see it at the beginning. Which will be more convenient for the executors of this will? Does the detail delay them in getting to the point as they look for their instructions? Or will they find it convenient to have the beneficiaries' full names and addresses on the front page as they proceed? Perhaps it makes no difference in a short document, where the headings will direct all readers straight to the information they need.

Headings must accurately reflect their contents, and both headings and contents must be mutually exclusive and comprehensive. This will ensure that you cover each possibility (omitting nothing), and that you do so once only (avoiding repetition and inconsistency). This simple rule will protect you from the negligent muddle of the disorganised will example.

But applying the rule requires careful thought. How will the reader use the information in the document? The answer should dictate how you divide and signpost its contents. To explain this we have built on Professor Kimble's analogy of sorting washing:

- As *whites* and *coloureds* must be washed separately you begin by sorting them into different piles. This is the equivalent of leaving white property and coloured property to different beneficiaries, and of heading clause 1 *Whites* and clause 2 *Coloureds*.
- Then you come to something grey. What do you do with it? This depends on how you want it washed.

    - If you want it to go in the machine with the coloureds you can leave the headings as they are, or (perhaps, to avoid doubt) change the second to *Greys and other colours*.
    - If you want it washed with the whites, accuracy requires a change in the headings to *Whites and greys* and *Other colours*. But this would not meet the user's needs. It would tell the inexperienced launderer to put a deep charcoal T-shirt, full of dye and likely to run, into the whites wash, while leaving a pale pink blouse in the *Other colours* wash, at risk from darker items. *Light* and *Dark* might be better headings.
    - For the sake of this example, let's suppose you wash the greys separately. Then you will need three headings: *Whites*, *Light colours*, and *Dark colours*. (Some might say that white is also a colour; that may be so, but it is not relevant to the launderer.)

- Now you find a red woollen pullover.

    - Lawyers of the old school might put it into *Dark colours* (even if it's bright red?) and restock their wardrobes from the proceeds of their professional indemnity insurance.
    - More thoughtful drafters will not only keep red woollens separate but will realise that the whole document must be restructured, giving:

        1 Machine wash

        A *Whites*
        B *Light colours*
        C *Dark colours*

        2 Hand wash

        A *Red woollens*
        B ...

- Next comes a suit that needs dry-cleaning. Its colour is irrelevant.

- The tradition is to tack on a third category, so our main headings are now:

  1   Machine
  2   Hand
  3   Dry cleaning

- But that overlooks the fact that the reader will do both machine- and hand-washing at home, but must take the dry cleaning to a shop. To reflect this, we suggest:

  1   Washing at home

      A   Machine

         1   Whites
         2   Light colours
         3   Dark colours

      B   Hand

         1   Red woollens
         2   ...

  2   Dry cleaning

- If you hand wash at home, but take dry cleaning and machine-washables to the launderette, the structure should change to reflect this.
- Putting the laundry away afterwards requires a different set of headings to reflect the different functions. If you are dealing with that in the same document you will have to push the existing headings down another step, so that you have, perhaps:

1   Cleaning

    A   Washing at home

       1   Machine

          a   Whites
          b   Light colours
          c   Dark colours

       2   Hand

          a   Red woollens
          b   ...

    B   Dry cleaning

2   Putting away

    A   Bill's room

       1   Drawers

> *a*   *Socks*
> *b*   …
>
> 2   **Wardrobe**
>
> **B**   **Muriel's room**
>
> 1   *Drawers*
> 2   *Wardrobe*

Contrast this orderly approach with that quoted by Steven Pinker (1998):

> Jorge Luis Borges writes of a Chinese encyclopedia that divided animals into: (a) those that belong to the Emperor, (b) embalmed ones, (c) those that are trained, (d) suckling pigs, (e) mermaids, (f) fabulous ones, (g) stray dogs, (h) those that are included in this classification, (i) those that tremble as if they were mad, (j) innumerable ones, (k) those drawn with a very fine camel's hair brush, (l) others, (m) those that have just broken a flower vase, (n) those that resemble flies from a distance.

Eileen Kavanagh (2005–06) tells us that Justice Voelker, when drafting his opinions in the Michigan Supreme Court,

> often wrote a topic sentence at the top of each … page … and then filled out the paragraph. As he neared a final draft, and in the copy sent to his closest colleagues for comments, he wrote one paragraph on each page, then edited that paragraph, including deciding where it would go.

He retired from the law to became a full-time writer soon after Otto Preminger bought the film rights to his novel *Anatomy of a Murder*, which was based on a case in which he had been defence counsel.

Starting with the most important information

As the usual function of a document is to install your thoughts into your reader's brain, the structure should reflect the reader's priorities. This usually involves putting your conclusion at the beginning:

> I suggest you do nothing

or

> It is probably worth suing X.

After this, you give the detail. Readers know from the beginning where your argument is leading, and can defer or dispense with the detail if they wish. Even if they do want to read it all at once, the 'initial ending' enables them to put the detail into context, and meanwhile satisfies their curiosity. Readers anxious to know where they stand do not enjoy suspense.

This approach is still unusual in legal writing. It is more common to see lawyers state the facts, the law, their reasons, and only then their conclusions. This approach saves the writer thought and effort but at the readers' expense. Lawyers who want to give good client service or to persuade their readers to do as they ask would do well to adapt their organisation to the readers' needs.

In an account of his time on a jury, journalist Trevor Grove (1998, p.257) explains that it is difficult to remember and assess the evidence without knowing the point that counsel is trying to establish and before being told the law that the jurors are to apply to it. He quotes an unnamed federal judge writing (in an unspecified 1960 article in the *American Bar Association Journal*):

> What manner of mind can go back over a stream of conflicting statements of alleged facts, recall the intonations, the demeanour, or even the existence of the witnesses, and retrospectively fit all these recollections into a pattern of evaluation and judgement given him for the first time after the events?

Lawyers sometimes worry that, if they put the answer first, readers will not bother to read the full message. However, in their own reading, they are quite happy to look first wherever they hope to find the answer, moving on afterwards to the rest of the document. So, on receiving an anxiously-awaited written judgment, they turn immediately to the last page.

You can defeat the reader's insubordinate disinclination to be tortured by suspense by hiding the conclusion in the middle. In *B (a child)* (2016) the UK Supreme Court disclosed the outcome on page 18 of 35, where it is tucked away in the fourth line of subsection (c) of the fifth section (*Habitual residence*) before the sixth and seventh sections (*Nationality* and *The dissenting judgments*). The main judgment then ends on page 21. The traditional clear note *Appeal allowed*, even on page 35, would have been helpful. Better is the habit of the UK Employment Appeal Tribunal (and some judges in other courts) of starting each decision with a short summary of the question and the answer.

Putting the most important information first helps writers achieve their aims. In any writing, you have the reader's attention (if at all) at the beginning. We can improve communication by putting what particularly needs the reader's attention into the spotlight that's already focused at the top of the document, before that attention wanders.

The same principle applies to the start of a chapter, section, paragraph, and even sentence. Writers often want to emphasise a point in case the reader misses it. They should place it at the top of the document, or create a new start (a new section or paragraph) where it can come first. Don't waste this valuable space with throat-clearing expressions like *It is worth noting that* or with inessential or low-priority information. You will be more likely to grab the reader's attention and more likely to retain it long enough to slip in the duller material later if you need to. And you are less likely to clutter your document with highlighted words mid-text.

The next most important place is the end of a document, section, paragraph, or sentence. A reader bored in the middle might skip to it, and a dutiful reader will be more likely to remember the last thing mentioned. Material buried in the middle is the most likely to be overlooked – another reason to use short sentences and plenty of section headings.

Endnote

1   See **www.ut-ie.com/b/b_flowers.html**.

Chapter 11

Format

White space and typeface

Indentation and spacing between lines combine to make a simple but useful way of helping the reader. Large blocks of text are daunting. Even readers who persevere can inadvertently skip a section (especially when the same phrase appears repeatedly).

Look at this example:

> The Guarantor in consideration of the Vendor making the foregoing assignment at the request of the Guarantor hereby covenants with the Vendor that the Purchaser will at all times hereafter duly pay the rent reserved by the Lease the service charges (if any) and all other payments and costs thereby provided for and will duly observe and perform all the covenants on the part of the Lessee and conditions therein contained and that the Guarantor will at all times hereafter duly observe and perform all covenants on the part of the Guarantor with the Landlord of the property and will at all times hereafter pay and make good to the Vendor on demand all losses costs damages and expenses occasioned to the Vendor by the non-payment of the said rents service charges or other payments or the breach non-observance or non-performance of any of the said covenants and conditions or any breach of the Purchaser's covenants as to payments observance and performance and for indemnity expressed in this assignment and notwithstanding any termination of the obligations of the Purchaser or any successors in title of the Purchaser by reason of disclaimer by any Trustee in bankruptcy or liquidator or the winding-up of the Purchaser or any successor in title of the Purchaser being a Corporation IT IS HEREBY AGREED AND DECLARED that any neglect forbearance or indulgence of the Vendor in enforcing or giving time to the Purchaser (or any Trustee in bankruptcy receiver or liquidator of the Purchaser) for any payments or observance or performance of any obligation shall not in any way release the Guarantor in respect of the Guarantor's liability under this present clause

Can any of us be sure that the original was not longer, and that nothing was missed in the copying? This passage has many more faults than its layout, but see how it can be improved, without altering the wording, just by careful spacing:

> The Guarantor in consideration of the Vendor making the foregoing assignment at the request of the Guarantor hereby covenants with the Vendor

that the Purchaser will at all times hereafter

duly pay

the rent reserved by the Lease
the service charges (if any) and
all other payments and costs thereby provided for

and will duly observe and perform all the covenants on the part of the Lessee and conditions therein contained and

that the Guarantor will at all times hereafter

duly observe and perform all covenants on the part of the Guarantor with the Landlord of the property and
[will at all times hereafter] pay and make good to the Vendor on demand all losses costs damages and expenses occasioned to the Vendor by

the non-payment of the said rents service charges or other payments
or
the breach non-observance or non-performance of

any of the said covenants and conditions or
any breach of the Purchaser's covenants as to payments observance and performance and for indemnity expressed in this assignment

and notwithstanding

any termination of the obligations of the Purchaser or any successors in title of the Purchaser
by reason of disclaimer by any Trustee in bankruptcy or liquidator or the winding-up of the Purchaser or any successor in title of the Purchaser being a Corporation

IT IS HEREBY AGREED AND DECLARED that

any neglect forbearance or indulgence of the Vendor in enforcing or giving time to the Purchaser (or any Trustee in bankruptcy receiver or liquidator of the Purchaser) for any payments or observance or performance of any obligation
shall not in any way release the Guarantor in respect of the Guarantor's liability under this present clause

Apart from helping the eye and the concentration, layout is a guide to meaning. If used correctly, it helps the reader understand. But the reader can be misled into thinking unrelated points are connected if they are included in the same sentence or paragraph, or if they are similarly indented. We had difficulty deciding how to set out the lines from *and notwithstanding* onwards because it is not clear from the original whether *and notwithstanding … being a Corporation* belongs to what went before (and should have been followed by a full stop) or whether the writer meant that *notwithstanding X it is agreed that Y*. Either way, *IT IS HEREBY AGREED AND DECLARED* is a subordinate part of the paragraph, rather than the headline its capitalisation suggests.

For a full revision of the whole text, see Example B on p.235.

In the following extract, to which we will return when discussing lists on p.91, the reader is left to guess that *AND ALSO PAYING* is not part of paragraph (d):

> ... YIELDING AND PAYING therefor ...
>
> (a) Such rent to be subject to review on each twenty-first anniversary of the grant hereof and then shall be increased to such sum as is the same percentage of the Review Value of the Building as the rent reserved hereunder is of the First Value of the Building ...
>
> (b) The amount of the rent shall be specified in a notice in writing given by the Lessor to the Lessee ...
>
> (c) The surveyor may be requested to determine all or any of the rents together
>
> (d) The Lessor and the Lessee shall pay the fees of the Surveyor appointed under this clause in equal shares ... AND ALSO PAYING as provided by paragraph 7 of the Sixth Schedule by way of further or additional rent the Lessee's Proportion of the Service Charge

This sign in a county court robing room was misread

```
THIS IS AN OVERFLOW
      WARNING
   NOT TO BE USED
   AS AN ASHTRAY
```

perhaps because the fourth line was clearly part of the same sentence as the third, suggesting subliminally that the second line should be read with the first. It was, after all, not formatted as a heading. But who would use a warning as an ashtray? The court might have been troubled by fewer delinquent advocates if they had rearranged it to something like this

```
         Overflow
Not to be used as an ashtray
```

changing the emphasis according to which part of the message they wanted to stress.

Columns are useful for showing at a glance the connection between groups of words or ideas, notably (but not only) definitions. Compare

> ... made between Miranda Homes (Southern) Limited of 157 Bracknell Road South Farnham Hampshire ('the Vendors') and Easthill Meadows Residents Association Limited of 157 Bracknell Road, South Farnham, Hampshire SF4 5GR ('The Association') (2) and James Edward Brownlow & Katherine Elizabeth Brownlow of 81 Landfall Road South Farnham Hampshire ('the Purchasers') (3)

with

The Vendors	Miranda Homes (Southern) Ltd
	of 157 Bracknell Road, South Farnham, Hampshire
The Association	Easthill Meadows Residents Association Ltd
	of the same address
The Purchasers	James Edward Brownlow and Katherine Elizabeth Brownlow
	of 81 Landfall Road, South Farnham

Here are a few simple tips for improving the appearance of text. Use a legible font. If you can choose the size of your type, do not make it so small that it is hard on the eye; remember that some readers will have poorer vision than you. Leave plenty of white space around the edges of the page and between paragraphs, none of which should be tediously long; break text down into lists of numbered or bulleted items; always leave a space between items in a list, especially if any one item runs on to a second line. Put headings in bold text and distinguish main headings by bigger text. Indent successively (so that sub-subparagraphs are indented more than subparagraphs). Consider using ragged right-hand margins; they may not look so neat but they do make neighbouring lines easier to distinguish from each other and prevent odd spacing, especially in narrow columns.

If the point is not yet made, here it is in practice:

Here are a few simple tips for improving the appearance of text:

- **Use a legible font**.
- **Vary the size of type**, if you can, but without making it so small that it is hard on the eye; remember that some readers will have poorer vision than you.
- **Leave plenty of white space** around the edges of the page and between paragraphs, none of which should be tediously long.
- **Break text down into lists** of numbered, lettered, or bulleted items.
- **Leave a space between items** in a list, especially if any one item runs on to a second line.
- **Put headings in bold text** and distinguish main headings by bigger text.
- **Indent successively** (so that sub-subparagraphs are indented more than sub-paragraphs).
- **Consider using ragged right-hand margins.** They may not look so neat but they do make neighbouring lines easier to distinguish from each other and prevent odd spacing, especially in narrow columns.

There is some old authority for the view that the court will not take layout into account when construing an ambiguous contract. In *Yorkshire Insurance Co Ltd* v. *Campbell* (1917), where 10 different fonts had been used, Lord Sumner said (using a variant spelling common before computers):

Founts of type have no legal meaning.

That, of course, does not mean that a well-drafted contract should not use layout to help the reader, but in any case Lord Sumner's view might have been different if the layout had been used to show the meaning; in the document before him it was inconsistent and had added to the confusion. In support of the modern practice of using typography, Denning LJ said in *Spurling Ltd* v. *Bradshaw* (1956) that he would not have considered certain onerous clauses to have been incorporated into a contract unless they were highlighted by a pointing red hand.

Sans serif fonts (fonts without serifs, the twiddly bits at the end of letters) are neater, and seem to some to look better in large sizes than fonts with serifs, which are suitable for normal text. The distinction is also useful to distinguish headings (which tend to be larger) from text.

In July 2015, Professor Paul Luna, Professor of Typography and Graphic Communication at the University of Reading, addressed a Clarity meeting on the subject of choosing typefaces and fonts for clear communication. Among the practical points to emerge were these:

- There is no single perfect font for every use and occasion, in every size and style.
- Microsoft put a lot of work into developing modern fonts that work in print and on screen in its 'C-fonts' (such as Calibri and Cambria), included in Microsoft Office.
- To improve legibility, we should pay attention first to line length (not too long), interlinear spacing (not too close) and print size (not too small) before we worry about the appearance of the font.
- To improve a document's impact on the reader, the choice of content, the order in which it is presented and the layout on the page are more important than the choice of font.
- In emails, there is no way to control what the reader sees. Even if you choose Rich Text format, it might not be available on the reader's phone. Your paragraph spacing, bold and italics may be lost, as well as your choice of typeface. So it's silly to do too much detailed formatting of emails.

He also suggested that *The Guardian*'s Egyptian font family works well in print and on screen and in different sizes. This is commercially available at commercialtype.com/typefaces/guardian.

A major heading should use more prominent type than a minor heading, forming a hierarchy from larger to smaller, or from bold to Roman.

> **MA:** This may seem obvious. But I have seen a book that broke this rule, and found that the counter-intuitive format seriously impeded my grasp of the book's structure, making it difficult to navigate and understand.

> **DP:** And I've seen a firm redesign its publications with grey headings and then swiftly change back to a style that restored the headings to visibility.

Indentation and numbering also help navigation, as shown here:

1   Text text text text text text text text text text text text text text text text text text text text text text text text text text text text text text text text text text text text.

   A   Text text text text text text text text text text text text text text text text text text text text text text text text text text text text text text text text text text text text.

      1   Text text text text text text text text text text text text text text text text text text text text text text text text text text text text text text text text.

         a   Text text text text text text text text text text text text text text text text text text text text text text text text text text text text text text.

         b   Text text text text text text text text text text text text text text text text text text text text text text text text text text text text text text.

      2   Text text text text text text text text text text text text text text text text text text text text text text text text text text text text text text text.

   B   Text text text text text text text text text text text text text text text text text text text text text text text text text text text text text text text text text text text text.

Readers can see at a glance where one topic ends and the next begins, more clearly than in the decimal system, which might render this as in the example below. And it avoids the unnecessary complexity of Roman numerals (for example, xxviii for 28).

1.   Text text text text text text text text text text text text text text text text text text text text text text text text text text text text text text text text text text text text.

1.1   Text text text text text text text text text text text text text text text text text text text text text text text text text text text text text text text text text text text text.

1.1.1   Text text text text text text text text text text text text text text text text text text text text text text text text text text text text text text.

1.1.1.1 Text text text text text text text text text text text text text text text text text text text text text text text text text text text text.

1.1.1.2 Text text text text text text text text text text text text text text text text text text text text text text text text text text text text.

1.1.2   Text text text text text text text text text text text text text text text text text text text text text text text text text text text text text text.

1.2   Text text text text text text text text text text text text text text text text text text text text text text text text text text text text text text text text text text text text.

As well as tabs, normal business software can be used to format tables (with invisible gridlines). For example, Rob Waller (2015) of The Simplification Centre formatted an amending provision of legislation like this:

2.5 In section 110 of the Equality Act 2010 (liability of employees and agents), after subsection (5) insert—

5A	A does not contravene this section if A—
	a does not conduct a relevant marriage,
	or b is not present at, does not carry out, or does not otherwise participate in, a relevant marriage,
	or c does not consent to a relevant marriage being conducted, for the reason that the marriage is the marriage of a same sex couple.
5B	Subsection (5A) applies to A only if A is within the meaning of "person" for the purposes of section 2 of the Marriage (Same Sex Couples) Act 2013; and other expressions used in subsection (5A) and section 2 of that Act have the same meanings in that subsection as in that section.

Lists

We use *list* here in the special sense of dividing items vertically

A
B

as opposed to horizontally

A B

Listing is our first tool in understanding a long, difficult paragraph or sentence. We used it to break down Example D on p.237. The technique is widely (but often badly) used.

A good list obeys these rules:

- Each list item must make good sense, in good English, when joined to the introductory words.
- Each item should have the same grammatical structure (which it normally will have if the first rule is obeyed). But some flexibility might be appropriate when the bullets are in whole sentences and independent of the introductory line, as in our own list on p.87.
- Information common to all the list items should if possible appear in the introductory words.
- The format should follow the guidelines in this chapter, with sublists indented and numbers or bullets in their own column, not mixed with text.
- The order in which the items are listed should follow the guidelines in Chapter 10 ('Organising your document').

Here is an example of some common faults:

9. MY TRUSTEES shall have the following powers in relation to my residuary estate in addition to their powers under the general law:

9.1.1 Power to apply any part of the capital …

9.1.2 All powers of sale …

9.2 Power to retain …

9.3 Power to permit …

9.4 In relation to any property movable or immovable which (or the future proceeds of sale of which) forms part of my residuary estate all the powers of leasing …

9.7 To exercise the power of appropriation given by …

9.8 Power to borrow money …

9.12 My Trustees shall have power by deed or deeds to release or restrict the future exercise of any power or discretion conferred on them …

9.13 To exercise any power or discretion vested in my Trustees notwithstanding that one or more of my Trustees may be personally interested in the exercise thereof

What is wrong with this?

- The introductory line, read with each list item, does not form one or more coherent sentences. For example:

    My trustees shall have the following powers …

    9.12 My trustees shall have power … to release …

  should be

    My trustees may …

    9.12 Release …

- The list items are not 'parallel' (that is, they don't share the same grammatical structure):

    9.3   Power to permit …
    9.4   In relation to … all the powers of leasing …

  should be (if the introductory line is *My trustees may*):

    9.3   Permit …
    9.4   Lease [*or, if it is necessary to make clear that the trustees can be landlords but not tenants:* Grant a lease] …

- There is unnecessary repetition. Everything common to all the list items should be removed to the introductory line.
- There are arbitrary differences (*power; all powers; all the powers*).
- The numbering of the first two list items wrongly suggests that they share some characteristic that the others do not have.
- The left margin obscures the numbers.

Improving the language as well as the structure (and bearing in mind that in this case the trust fund *was* the residuary estate), this might become:

    9   My trustees may (even if personally interested in the transaction):

        A   Do anything permitted them under the general law.
        B   Apply any part of the capital …
        C   Retain …
        D   Sell …
        E   Grant a lease of any property …

F   Permit ...
G   Appropriate under ...
H   Borrow money ...
I   Restrict or surrender any of these powers irrevocably [*presumably including this one*].

Numbers should be given for ease of reference, especially if the list is too long to refer conveniently to *the nth bullet*, or if the exact order of priority is important (as in a top 20 list). But, if the number doesn't matter, bullets are less distracting.

Here is the example from p.85 in more detail, with complete sentences in some of the subclauses before the writer absurdly revived the opening sentence in the last two lines:

... YIELDING AND PAYING therefor during the said term the yearly rent for the first twenty-one years thereof of One Hundred and Twenty Five Pounds by equal half yearly payments in advance on the Thirtieth day of June and the Thirty-first day of December in each year the first of such payments being a proportionate payment to be made on the execution hereof calculated from then to the next payment date

(a) Such rent to be subject to review on each twenty-first anniversary of the grant hereof and then shall be increased to such sum as is the same percentage of the Review Value of the Building as the rent reserved hereunder is of the First Value of the Building ...

(b) The amount of the rent shall be specified in a notice in writing given by the Lessor to the Lessee ...

(c) The surveyor may be requested to determine all or any of the rents together

(d) The Lessor and the Lessee shall pay the fees of the Surveyor appointed under this clause in equal shares ... AND ALSO PAYING as provided by paragraph 7 of the Sixth Schedule by way of further or additional rent the Lessee's Proportion of the Service Charge

Had this been formatted (as it should) to show that *AND ALSO PAYING* was a new paragraph and not part of (d) it would have been a slightly neater example of that indigestible meal, a 'clause sandwich', which offends against the drafting principle that you should keep like with like (bread, bread, filling), not move on to a new topic and later meander back to the old one (bread, filling, bread). Clause sandwiches can always be avoided with a little ingenuity, by merging into the introductory line, or moving to a separate clause, any material you are tempted to tack on at the end. To this extent legal drafting is no picnic.

The citizens of Lilliput and their neighbours disagree about whether each item in a list should end with a full stop or a semi-colon. Semi-colons work better if you want to link the items with *and* or *or* and perhaps if you prefer to begin each item with a lower-case letter. Full stops may be easier on the eye, and are perhaps more consistent with an initial capital. But it's not important, and to show even-handedness we have sacrificed consistency to use both forms. Incidentally, in anything but a very short list it is better to make clear in the introductory line whether the list refers to all the items or only some; readers will not then have to wait almost until the end to discover whether the items are linked by *and* or *or*. So we might say:

The buyer must do all of: (= *and*);
The buyer may do any one or more of: (= inclusive *or*);
The buyer may do any one of: (= exclusive *or*); or (if appropriate)
The buyer may do any two of.

Punctuation at the end of a list item might eventually go the way of the comma at the end of each line of an address. But few writers are ready for that yet.

MA: After this paragraph went to press in the 2nd edition I was embarrassed to discover the same Lilliput reference in Bowman (2006). It wasn't attributed because as far as I was aware it was my own metaphor, but in case I'd previously read and forgotten the article I'm putting the matter right.

Algebraic formulae

A logophiliac lawyer might say:

The amount payable shall be such sum as is equivalent to one thousand times the amount equal to twice the area plus the breadth divided by three times the circumference minus the distance

but it would be much easier to see what was intended if it was expressed (after defining the variables so that $a = area$, $b=breadth$, etc) as

$$\text{amount} = 1{,}000 \left(\frac{2a + b}{3c - d} \right)$$

Mathematophobes may disagree that the algebraic format is easier but cannot deny that it avoids all the ambiguities of the verbal one, which could be read (among various other possibilities) as

$$\text{amount} = \left(\frac{1{,}000 \times (2a + b)}{3(c - d)} \right)$$

or

$$\text{amount} = \left(\frac{(1{,}000 \times 2a) + b}{3c} \right) - d$$

Assigning values to the variables and running the calculations through a calculator shows how serious those ambiguities are. If (to assign random values)

$$a=12, b=4, c=15, \text{and } d=7$$

the final amount could be

£736.84
£1,166.67 or
£526.42

depending on which interpretation you adopt.
A chance was described on the radio as

one in a million times a billion

which could be

$$\frac{1}{1m \times 1bn}$$

(if applied to the current human world population, about 170,000 to 1 *against* it happening even to just one person)
or

$$\frac{1}{1m} \times 1bn$$

which is 1,000,000,000,000,000,000,000,000 times more probable (about 1,000 to 1 *in favour* of it happening to any named person).
Drafters can learn from mathematicians' (and computer programmers') rigorous use of format and parentheses to avoid this form of ambiguity.

Graphics

Now that photographs, graphs, and other images can be so easily imported into documents we might as well use them. They will sometimes make the point much more easily and effectively than words. We give an example of graphs' persuasive potential on p.159.

Flowcharts

Flowcharts are familiar and simple to read but lawyers rarely think to create them. A good example is the one published[1] by HMRC in February 2017 to help UK suppliers of digital services work out whether they were affected by new VAT rules.

Steps

These are the verbal equivalent of formulae and flowcharts, and readers unfamiliar or uncomfortable with mathematics will find this format easier to follow.

Here is a simple example:

$$A = \frac{2}{3} \times 16$$

could become:

To find A:

1   Divide 2 by 3.

2   Multiply the result by 16.

Duncan Berry sent this example from the Australian Commonwealth's Social Security Act 1991 (s.1044A):

Step 1   Work out the number of days that, at the time of qualification under section 1035A, remain from the period of 26 weeks referred to in paragraph (c) (counting the day on which that qualification occurs as a whole day).

Step 2   Multiply the result under Step 1 by the amount worked out under the following formula:

$$\frac{\text{Rate of mobility allowance specified in subsection 1044(1)}}{\text{Rate of mobility allowance specified in subsection 1044(1A)}}$$

If the result is not a whole number, round the result down to the next whole number.

Step 3   Subtract the result under Step 2 from the result under Step 1.

Step 4   Subtract the result under Step 3 from the number 182. The result is the number of days in the person's advance payment period.

This is not light reading, but it is much easier to understand than if it had been written in the traditional way as continuous text.

This technique is increasingly used in English criminal trials to help jurors apply the law to the facts. The judge agrees with the parties a written set of 'steps to verdict', a series of simple factual questions in this form:

A. If No, acquit. If yes proceed to B.

B. If No, acquit. If yes proceed to C.

C. Etc.

Endnote

1 whitehall-admin.production.alphagov.co.uk/government/uploads/system/ uploads/attachment_data/file/390300/VAT_MOSS_Flow_chart.pdf.

Chapter 12

Punctuation

Incorrect punctuation, like errors of spelling, grammar, and layout, can confuse. Even when it doesn't, it damages the reader's confidence in the writer and the text, especially when making a first impression. A client who is not in a position to judge the quality of legal advice may notice a misplaced apostrophe or a wrongly-used comma and think worse of the writer. Lawyers are therefore well advised to learn the rules and check their work, especially when writing for a new and critical readership.

This chapter is not intended as a comprehensive review of punctuation; other books exist for that. The most useful rules are outlined in a few pages of Humphries (2003, pp.46–66).

We will just mention here a few problems common among lawyers, and offer this rudimentary rule of thumb to those who think the subject dauntingly technical:

> Punctuation signals pauses of different lengths: a full stop is a long pause; a semi-colon slightly shorter; a comma shorter yet. Listen to the natural pauses when you read your sentence into your mind's ear, and punctuate accordingly.

But beware: punctuation fulfils different and sometimes incompatible functions. In Tom McArthur's (1992) words (noting his reservation *mainly*):

> Until the 18c, punctuation was closely related to spoken delivery, including pauses to take breath, but in more recent times has been based mainly on grammatical structure.

Whether to use it

Nick Wright of Editor Software had this conversation with his solicitor:

> 'I had reservations about only one sentence in the lease.'
>
> 'Oh, yes?' said the solicitor, flattered. 'Which sentence?'
>
> 'The one that begins on page 1 and finishes on page 28.'

Certain documents (notably conveyancing documents and wills) were traditionally written without punctuation. But there is no point in refusing to punctuate.

In earlier times, punctuation was haphazard and it was common for printers to change it to accord with their house style. Consequently, lawyers could not be confident that the punctuation printed in legislation had been enacted, and they interpreted statutes without reference to it. However, this excuse disappeared long ago. Modern legislation is fully punctuated, and the courts consider punctuation when interpreting legislation.[1]

Punctuation plays a part in contract interpretation,[2] although the courts can overlook obvious mistakes.[3] And although the House of Lords confirmed in 1918 that punctuation should be taken into account when interpreting a will[4] this new-fangled idea still hasn't entirely caught on.

> **MA:** In one institutional lease still used countrywide around the turn of the century I had to read four unpunctuated pages twice in a fruitless search for a missing end bracket, which I needed before I could identify the main verb (and with it the nub of the sentence).

> **DP:** When working on this revised edition in 2016, I thought (and some property lawyers told me) that no one drafts documents without punctuation any more. So I asked around, and the first lawyer I spoke to said he had just received an unpunctuated lease from one of the 100 largest UK law firms.

The common justification for omitting punctuation has been that punctuation can mislead. So it can, if it is badly done. So can any other type of botch. Taking this argument to its logical conclusion, we should not write words, either.

Omitting punctuation can also cause problems. An application for summary judgment in a class action between an employer and 75 of its truck drivers turned on whether an Oxford comma (see p.100) had been omitted from legislation. The amount at stake was estimated at over $10 million. The employer won at first instance but then lost on appeal (*O'Connor* v. *Oakhurst Dairy* (2017)). The 29-page appellate judgment begins:[5]

 For want of a comma, we have this case.

The answer is not to leave out the punctuation but to use it correctly, as it is an invaluable guide to meaning. Some care is required to punctuate correctly; much more to write unambiguously without punctuation.

A variant of the non-punctuation policy is to punctuate, not with the usual marks, but with extra spaces to indicate full stops. Occasionally a capital letter is used in the middle of a paragraph to show that a new sentence is beginning. The following example came from a large firm's standard contract:

> The plan attached hereto is a copy extract from the Company's layout plan and is intended to indicate only the approximate position and extent of the plot which will be transferred to the Purchaser As soon as practicable the Company will carry out a survey of the plot and following such survey will if necessary prepare and supply to the Purchaser's solicitors for use with the Transfer an accurate plan based on such survey showing the exact position and extent of the plot to be transferred to the Purchaser The Company hereby expressly reserves the right to substitute (for use with the Transfer) notwithstanding the completion of the sale and purchase the survey plan for the plan attached hereto The Company will take due care in the setting out of the Estate but differences between the plan attached hereto and the plan to be attached to the Transfer may occur and it is hereby expressly agreed and declared that such differences shall not annul the sale nor shall they entitle the Purchaser to any compensation or abatement in the purchase price provided that such differences do not materially affect the value of the Buildings and the property.

We cannot think of any reason to follow such an unusual and barely visible form of punctuation.

Capital letters

In the 18th century, nouns were commonly written with a capital letter. This habit is preserved by 21st century lawyers who pepper their writing with random capitals.

The ordinary rule is that common nouns start with a lower case letter (unless at the beginning of a sentence) and only proper nouns (individual names or titles) take a capital. So we have

solicitor
client
court
judge
contract
will

but

Solicitor General
Staines County Court
Lord Chancellor

If you write about the Court of Appeal, you can call it the Court after the first time – not as a defined term, but just as you might write about Daphne Perry and call her Daphne the second time. The capital C is correct as you are still using part of the name. But if you are writing about the courts generally, or what a hypothetical court might do, then it's not a name but a description, so a small c is correct. The same goes for judges, so it is correct to write that Lord Justice Smith heard the appeal, and that the judge gave his decision the same day. It is not necessary to dignify *judge* with a capital letter, as it is not part of his name or title. Still less do we need to do so for the Defendant, the Case and the Order, any more than we do for the House, the Door, or the Doormat.

Lawyers also use capitals to flag defined words but we dislike this for the reasons given in Chapter 14 ('Definitions').

Another survival from a bygone age is the habit of putting selected words in block capitals. In documents without paragraphs, clauses or punctuation, these indicated key words to help the user navigate the document. Today, in a document divided into numbered clauses arranged under headings, it is a pointless distraction.

But tradition and the lawyers' habit of copying older documents have preserved this ritual. In wills and trusts you may see, mid-sentence, PROVIDED THAT. It also affects commercial contracts. A 200-page construction contract from 2009 began like this:

THIS AGREEMENT is made the ... day of ...

BY AND BETWEEN ... [the parties are then listed]

WHEREAS ... [This is lawyers' code for 'Here are a few paragraphs of background information, whose truth we accept'.]

NOW THIS AGREEMENT WITNESSES as follows:

This has clearly been modernised to the extent of changing 'witnesseth' to 'witnesses'. And the rest of the contract is free from block capitals.

This strange behaviour is damaging, like all legalese, in that it gives the impression that the writer neither knows nor cares what might help the client. The best way to help readers navigate a document is to use headings.

Punctuation after paragraph numbers

One quirk of legal writing is lawyers' tendency to number every paragraph and subparagraph, with various numbering systems ranging from the decimal (1, 1.1, 1.1.1) to Roman numbers: 1, 1(i), 1(ii).

Paragraph numbering is useful for navigation and for ease of reference. But why punctuate the number with a stop, a bracket or a pair of brackets? If clause 1 has two subclauses, it makes sense to call them 1.1 and 1.2, to distinguish them from clauses 11 and 12. But the other stops and brackets that routinely appear around clause numbers are visual clutter and serve no useful function. Thanks to Rob Waller (2015) for making this point and illustrating it in 'Layout for legislation'.

Commas

Commas are often used as a form of parenthesis and must then come in pairs:

> The solicitor, who did not know how to punctuate read a book on grammar.

makes no more sense than

> The solicitor (who did not know how to punctuate read a book on grammar.

Without the closing comma or bracket after *punctuate* readers are condemned to sail the textual oceans, forever searching for the lost punctuation so they can pick up the main thread of the sentence. In such a short passage, they can easily spot the mistake; in a long one it might need extensive research.

O'Connor, mentioned on p.97, turned on the 'Oxford' comma, also known as the 'Harvard' or 'serial' comma. This comma precedes *and,* introducing the last item in a list. Some writing guides, including the guide for those who drafted the legislation in *O'Connor,* condemn this comma but without it there may be ambiguity. (For consistency in this book, we use it regardless of whether there would be ambiguity.) For example:

> A, B or C and D

could mean

> A and [B or C] and D

or

> [A or B or C] and D.

On the other hand, a reference to

> my aunt, Anne Wolchover, and me

leaves open whether Anne is my aunt or someone else, so this would be better phrased, referring to Aunt Anne,

> my aunt (Anne Wolchover) and me

or

> my aunt Anne Wolchover and me

with – if necessary for consistency at the end of a longer list – a comma before *and me;* or, if Anne is not my aunt,

> my aunt Joan, Anne Wolchover, and me

This is not the only circumstance in which a comma can be useful before *and*. In line with the view that a comma represents a brief pause in speech, we use it before *and* and *but* where we would pause momentarily if reading aloud.

The following example might confuse anyone ignorant about wine:

> Even Banks could tell that the wines there were very high end clarets, chiantis and burgundies.

Are chiantis and burgundies *very high end clarets*, or different items in the list? If the former, a colon would have been better than the comma. If the latter, did the list include 'low end' chiantis and 'low end' burgundies, or did *high end* apply to all three?

List format (p.89) can resolve ambiguity better than punctuation, as we show on p.102.

Semi-colons

The main use of a semi-colon is between two sentences, where it signals that the two sentences are connected, without saying how. Commas are sometimes misused instead.

> Commas are sometimes misused. This misleads readers.

and

> Commas are sometimes misused; this misleads readers.

are correct, as is

> Commas are sometimes misused, misleading readers.

But

> Commas are sometimes misused, this misleads readers.

is wrong. It fails to indicate the end of one clause capable of standing on its own, and the start of another.

A helpful and increasingly popular use of semi-colons is to separate long items in a horizontal list, especially if the items already contain commas.

For example:

> The judicial system includes the Supreme Court; the Court of Appeal; the Queen's Bench, Chancery, and Family Divisions of the High Court of Justice; and local county courts.

But list format, where it is appropriate, is the clearest way to separate items:

The judicial system includes:

- the Supreme Court;
- the Court of Appeal;
- the Queen's Bench, Chancery, and Family Divisions of the High Court of Justice; and
- local county courts.

Apostrophes

The phrase *to our respective firm's orders* appeared in a letter from one firm of solicitors to another, as part of proposed terms of settlement. The reply confirmed that money would be held *to our respective firms order*. Of the three possible places for the apostrophe (before the 's', after it, or nowhere), only one was right. Each solicitor chose a different wrong option. This looked bad, but worse consequences followed from a draft judgment awarding legal fees. The judgment was issued but then reversed on appeal as too ambiguous to enforce (*Bradshaw* v. *Boynton* (2013)). The appellate court described the draft as:

apostrophe-challenged, creating ambiguities as to whether the drafter intended references to singular or plural defendants or plaintiffs.

And did this client have an alias?:

My client's names are Anthony Edward Johnson and Elizabeth Bridgette Cairns.

Hyphens

Hyphens can be useful in showing the links between the parts of a phrase that are more closely connected to each other than to the rest of the phrase. It is easy to miss the possible miscue in

There were difficulties in deciding which therapies to include, and how widely differing therapies were to be subject to the same regulatory body.

But when adding a prefix that needs a hyphen to a phrase, rather than to an individual word, it is customary to write, for example, *ex-appellate judge*. However, this suggests that *ex* and *appellate* are more closely linked to each other than either word is to *judge*, implying a trial judge who used to be appellate. Where the reference is to someone who is no longer on the bench, *former appellate judge* avoids this implication though it might still be ambiguous. *Ex-appellate-judge*, though not a generally accepted form, is clearer. The customary form is even more confusing with longer chains, as here:

> Scalia was … more concerned with the objectively realisable-non-objectively realisable spectrum than the general-specific spectrum,

which might be rephrased:

> Scalia was … more concerned with the spectrum between the objectively and the non-objectively realisable than with that between the general and the specific.

Hyphens connecting prefixes to a word (like *e-mail*) are generally dropped once the compound form becomes so familiar as to be recognised as a new word (*email*) – so long as the unhyphenated form will not be confused with another word or pronunciation (*re-form, re-enter*).

Endnotes

or sound eg e-commerce -

1 *Hanlon* v. *The Law Society* [1981] AC 124 (HL).
2 *Reilly* v. *National Insurance and Guarantee Corp Ltd* [2008] EWCA Civ 1460; *Osmium Shipping Corp* v. *Cargill International SA* [2012] EWHC 571 (Comm); *Soufflet Negoce SA* v. *Fedcominvest Europe* [2014] EWHC 2405 (Comm).
3 For example, *Cambridge Antibody Technology* v. *Abbott Biotechnology Ltd* [2004] EWHC 2974 (Pat), paragraph 59.
4 *Houston* v. *Burns* [1918] AC 337 (HL).
5 For more-entertaining examples, see **news.bbc.co.uk/2/hi/uk_news/magazine/ 4583594.stm**.

Chapter 13

Repetition

Repetition has the obvious disadvantage that it lengthens the document. It is also tedious and clumsy, distracting the reader from the sense.

But it causes three more serious difficulties:

- Where a long block of text is repeated, the reader must compare the different incidences carefully to ensure they are the same or to see how they differ, and to work out why it has been repeated.
- A difference may pass unnoticed.
- Unintentional differences are confusing.

Here is a fine example, quoted in a discussion paper 'Legislation, legal rights and plain English', written by Robert Eagleson and published by the Law Reform Commission of Victoria, Australia, in 1986:

> (2) Where, on an application made under subsection (1), the Court is satisfied that a contravention of a provision of Part II has been committed, the Court shall not, in respect of that contravention, make an order or orders under subsection (1) that the Court considers would, or would be likely to, require the expenditure by the person or persons to whom the order or orders is or are directed of an amount that exceeds, or amounts that, in the aggregate, exceed, $50,000.
>
> (3) Where, on an application made under subsection (1), the Court is satisfied that a person has committed, or been involved in, two or more contraventions of the same provision of Part II, being contraventions that appear to the Court to have been of the same nature or a substantially similar nature and to have occurred at or about the same time (whether or not the person has also committed, or been involved in, another contravention or other contraventions of that provision that was or were of a different nature or occurred at a different time), the Court shall not, in respect of the first mentioned contraventions, make an order or orders under subsection (1) that the Court considers would, or would be likely to, require the expenditure by the person or persons to whom the order or orders is or are directed of an amount that exceeds, or of amounts that, in the aggregate, exceed, $50,000.
>
> (4) Where –
>
> (a) on an application made under subsection (1), the Court is satisfied that a person has committed, or been involved in, a contravention or contraventions of a provision of Part II; and
>
> (b) an order has, or orders have, previously been made under subsection (1)

against the person who committed, or against a person who was involved in, that contravention or those contraventions in respect of another contravention or other contraventions of the same provision, being a contravention which, or contraventions each of which, appears to the Court to have been of the same nature as, or of a substantially similar nature to, and to have occurred at or about the same time as, the first-mentioned contravention or contraventions (whether or not an order has, or orders have, also previously been made under subsection (1) against any of those persons in respect of another contravention or other contraventions of that provision that was or were of a different nature or occurred at a different time) –

the Court shall not, in respect of the contravention or contraventions mentioned in paragraph (a), make an order or orders under subsection (1) that the Court considers would be likely to require the expenditure by the person or persons to whom the order or orders is or are directed of an amount that exceeds, or of amounts that, in the aggregate, exceed, the amount (if any) by which $50,000 is greater than the amount, or the sum of the amounts that has or have been or that the Court considers would be or be likely to be, expended in accordance with the previous order or previous orders first mentioned in paragraph (b).

Dr Eagleson offers a revised version, condensing all that by 89 per cent into a remarkable 58 words:

$50,000 is the most that a person or persons may be required to spend by an order or orders under subsection (1) (whether made on one or more occasions) for all contraventions of any one provision of Part II which are of the same or a substantially similar nature and which occurred at or about the same time.

With respect to Dr Eagleson's considerable achievement, both in redrafting and in staying awake while he did so, even this is hardly light reading, and we have had another look at it on p.236 (Example C).

You can avoid repetition by:

- Using lists, as we are doing here.
- Using pronouns to replace names (which is their purpose).
- Using synonyms.
- Rearranging the text in some other way.

These techniques usually simplify and shorten the document, and make it flow better.

A change of word in the right place can be useful. The next example comes from a letter written by solicitors acting for a charity that was trying to uphold a will challenged by the testator's family:

The late Mrs X bequeathed one fourth of her residuary estate to her grandson, who is one of your clients, and our clients feel that they must honour the wishes of the late Mrs X and utilise the rest of the monies for the good cause for which she bequeathed the same. In the circumstances, we do not feel that it is our clients place to suggest figures for a 'split', however if your clients wish to suggest figures, we will of course obtain our clients instructions.

Clients appears five times, and *bequeathed* and *the late Mrs X* are each used twice in one sentence.

That passage could have been written:

> The late Mrs X gave a quarter of her residuary estate to her grandson, and our clients feel that they must honour her wishes and use the rest of the money for the good cause for which she left it. In the circumstances, we do not feel that it is the charity's place to suggest figures for a 'split'; however, if the Johnsons wish to suggest figures, we will of course take instructions.

- The first *the late Mrs X* has been left as it is and the second changed to *her*.
- The first *bequeathed* has been changed to *gave* and the second to *left*.
- The first and fifth *clients* have been omitted altogether as unnecessary; the second has been left as the sole remaining use; the third has been replaced by reference to the clients as *the charity*; and the fourth has been replaced by the clients' name.

But beware possible confusion arising from 'elegant variation' – the use of synonyms to avoid repetition. If this passage had read

> The deceased bequeathed one fourth of her residuary estate to her grandson ... and our clients feel that they must honour the wishes of the late Mrs X ...

the reader is cued to think that Mrs X was someone other than the testator.

Not to do or permit to be done

To avoid repeating the usual formula 'Not to do or permit ...' for each covenant in a lease, you can add that:

> A covenant not to do something is also a covenant not to allow others to do it.

You might think that *permit* requires permission and that *suffer* is wider, in that it includes toleration, but the courts have tended to treat *permit* alone as including intentional toleration. See, for example, *R v. Jasper* (2003) and Atkin LJ's comment in *Berton* v. *Alliance* (1922):

> It is not suggested that there is any difference between (the words) in this context [a lease], and I treat them as having the same meaning.

Garner (2011) dismisses *suffer* in two lines, saying it means to permit or acquiesce in and calling it an archaic use of an ordinary English word. We suggest *allow* as clearly covering both meanings without archaism or redundancy. If your client wants anything wider – for instance, heroic efforts against a stranger – and you think it would be enforceable, it would be wise to spell out the precise obligation.

Chapter 14

Definitions

Definition – the giving of a name – is a useful way to avoid repeating a long phrase.

This is an old device. For example, old leases added in brackets, after the address or description of the property, *hereinafter called 'the Demised Premises'* (now usually abbreviated to *'the Demised Premises'*). It can be useful but is often overdone, with long definition sections common at the beginning of documents. It is even common to find the beginning of a letter to clients interrupted with a defined term for half the nouns, like this:

> This letter relates to the Agreement dated 1 December 2016 ('**the Agreement**') between Firstname Lastname Ltd ('**Firstname**') and Another Companyname Plc ('**Companyname**') for the development and use of certain land ('**the Land**').

It is hard to know which is worst – the constant interruptions, the distracting bold type applied to the least important information in the sentence, or the subtext that shouts *I would rather write like a lawyer than consider your needs as my reader and my client*. Often, these definitions add nothing, because the letter will not mention any other agreement, land, or companies. The writer could have gone on to discuss the agreement between Firstname and Companyname without any possibility of doubt or confusion. Where there is doubt – perhaps as to the extent of the land – this opening sentence, as often happens, left the matter unclear.

Omit unnecessary definitions

We suggest restricting definitions – like all other clauses – to those that pass the purpose test ('What's it for?').

As far as we are aware there are only four functions for a definition:

- To introduce a short name for convenience;
- To introduce an unfamiliar expression;
- To restrict or expand the usual definition; and
- To specify which of more than one commonly accepted definition we intend.

There is no need to define words used in their everyday or obvious sense, as in this absurd definition taken from a licence to assign submitted by the solicitor for an insurance company:

> By the Lease (hereinafter called 'the Lease') ...

It should (but unfortunately doesn't) go without saying that there is no point in including a definition that will not be used or whose meaning is obvious. For example, in a letter about a bank loan, having once written out 'Lloyds TSB Bank plc', it is not necessary to define 'Lloyds' (or if no other bank is involved, 'the bank') before using the short name. And consider whether it is necessary to define a term that will only be used once or twice.

Make defined terms short and meaningful

If a definition is used to create a short name, that name may as well be the shortest convenient. A common form is:

> 'The Demised Premises' means the ground floor and garden at 124 High Street, Swanage, shown edged red on the plan.

But rather than commit yourself to constant repetition of the phrase *the Demised Premises*, why not use just *the premises* or (better, if appropriate) *the flat*, *the shop*, or *the office*? Whichever expression is chosen, it is just a name, and you can call your premises what you like (unless constrained by the land registry's prescribed form to use *property*). We prefer *property* to *premises*; it is more familiar, especially to non-lawyers.

Unusually daft is this definition, taken from a lease offered by the head of the conveyancing department of a central London firm:

> 'The Lessee's proportion' means 2.5 %.

How much simpler life would have been if the definition had been omitted and the writer had just said *2.5%* when that was what was meant. The definition might be justified by the convenience of inserting each tenant's figure only once, but how long would it take to use the software to replace each *'the Lessee's proportion'* with *2.5%*?

And, instead of 'transmission media' – a clumsy, artificial phrase that became fashionable in the 1980s, why not use the (fairly) familiar *conduits*?

Make the definitions coherent

Too often, definitions are long, circular, incoherent, and (despite appearances) incomplete. A lease made in 2009 defined *conduit* as:

any pipe, drain, culvert, sewer, flue, duct, gutter, wire, cable, optic fibre, conduit, channel and other medium for the passage of water, soil, gas, air, smoke, electricity, light, information or other matter and all ancillary equipment or structures.

This apparently comprehensive definition was criticised as inapplicable to a shaft through which the tenant expelled fumes and gas. In practice, nobody denied the tenant's right to use the shaft for its air duct, but the point still featured in litigation and the Court of Appeal in *Balogun* v. *Boyes Sutton* (2017) found it was arguable.

The *Shorter Oxford English Dictionary* already defines *conduit* as 'an artificial channel or pipe for the conveyance of water or other liquids; a tube or trough for receiving and protecting electric wires'. So, in this list *pipe, drain, culvert, sewer, gutter, duct, channel and other medium for the passage of water,* (arguably) *soil, electricity,* and *light* were all redundant, while *conduits* was redundant and circular. As the dictionary does not mention the wires themselves, or gas ducts and information cables, some definition might still be needed, but we could reduce this (depending on the property's construction) to

'Conduits' includes all cables and channels for air, power, and communications.

Drafters are nervous about reducing so long a word string to such a short proposition. But there is no safety in length.

Avoid surprises

As far as possible, names should be used in their ordinary sense. Ideally, the reader should not need to consult the definitions to get the gist of the document.

It avoids the risk of misunderstanding should someone read only the clauses that seem relevant rather than the entire document (as we all must do sometimes if we are to get through the day). For instance, the strangely named Party Wall etc. Act 1996 sets out in the 17 subclauses of s.10 a detailed scheme for resolving disputes using one or more surveyors without warning readers that in a different part of the Act s.20 defines *surveyor* as 'any person not being a party to the matter appointed or selected under section 10...'. Even s.20 does not explicitly warn that no professional training or experience is required: anyone in the world other than the parties to the dispute can be a *surveyor* for this purpose.

It also avoids the need for the Olympic-standard mental gymnastics required to apply these counter-intuitive definitions:[1]

'Unmarried person' means a person who is not married ... 'Married person' includes a de facto spouse but does not include a legally married person who is living separately and apart from the spouse of the person on a permanent basis.

The provisions of sections 43 and 48 shall with such modifications as are necessary extend and apply to and in relation to this Division and, without affecting the generality of the foregoing, in particular with the modifications that –

(a) a reference to eggs or to eggs or egg pulp or to eggs and egg pulp shall be construed as a reference to citrus fruit.

Don't stuff definitions

Never include substantive provisions in definitions (a practice known as 'stuffing' the definition). For example, does defining *the Regulations* as *any rules and/or regulations made from time to time by the Lessor* give the landlord power to make rules?

In *Burford UK Properties* v. *Forte Hotels* (2003) the drafter had tacked on to the clause defining *Net Bedroom Revenue* the words *Provided always that the tenant shall at all times use its best endeavours to maximise the Net Bedroom Revenue*. The Court of Appeal, refreshingly intolerant of such shoddy drafting, supported the trial judge's refusal to accept this as a tenant's covenant.

Identifying defined terms

When a term has been defined, the reader needs to know there is a definition and where to find it.

> **DP:** I once watched two barristers puzzle over a statute. It gave the court power to act – but which court? They looked in every section of the act that seemed relevant to the power, but not at the interpretation section, which defined *court*.

Lawyers normally use initial capitals to flag defined words but we prefer not to. It is not clear that all clients understand this convention. And, since lawyers (obeying the usual rules) begin names and each sentence with a capital letter and (departing from those rules) often add an initial capital to any word that seems official or important, the convention is not obvious or reliable. Of the several words or phrases in this example with initial caps, we suggest that four (*Provided*, *Fifth Schedule*, and, as explained three paragraphs down, *Lessor* and *Lessee*) would not have been defined:

Provided always … that the Lessor shall be entitled at its absolute discretion to vary the proportion of the Service Costs payable by the Lessee as defined in clause 1(n) in the event of rights being granted pursuant to the terms of paragraph 5 of the Fifth Schedule hereto Provided that such variation shall not result in the said Service Charge proportion being increased

Writers sometimes disguise the convention further by using a defined term, with or without an initial capital, in another sense within the same document.

If it is necessary to highlight defined terms we suggest SMALL CAPS, as clear but relatively unobtrusive and still allowing an initial (full size) capital when the ordinary rules demand it. Or, in text to be read on screen, add a distinctively formatted hypertext link to the definition.

Beware the common fallacy of treating these as definitions:

| 'The Landlord' | AB Ltd. |
| 'The Tenant' | CD Ltd. |

This text is intended to identify the original parties; if instead it defines the expressions *landlord* and *tenant*, the definitions become inappropriate when the property changes hands. The error is not cured by adding *and their successors and assigns*, which wrongly includes the original parties after they have been released by the Landlord and Tenant (Covenants) Act 1995. (Moreover, the reference to successors and assigns has been unnecessary since 1926, thanks to ss.78 and 79 of the Law of Property Act 1925.) Where the land registry's prescribed clauses are not used, it is better to have a separate introductory section, *Details*, for the names of the original parties, the address of the property, the date of the document, and so on.

Alternative formats for defined terms

An alternative to definitions in advice and informal documents is to use in-line headings. For example, in the letter quoted at the start of this chapter, supposing it had been necessary to explain the words, and useful to do so before saying anything else, the writer might have begun with something like this:

This letter concerns:

- **Firstname:** Firstname Lastname Ltd.
- **Companyname:** Another Companyname Plc.
- **The agreement:** The Agreement dated 1 December 2016 between Firstname and Companyname.
- **The land:** The land to be developed and used under the Agreement, identified in Schedule 1 of the Agreement.

But we suggest that the information would have been better placed in a glossary at the end:

Terms used in this letter

Firstname	Firstname Lastname Ltd
Companyname	Another Companyname Plc
The agreement	The Agreement dated 1 December 2016 between Firstname and Companyname
The land	The land to be developed and used under the Agreement, identified in Schedule 1 of the Agreement

Use definitions consistently

Once a term is defined it (and any capitalisation) should be used consistently. Detailed safety regulations made by one American county and quoted in Child (1992) relied on these definitions:

Swimming Pool	Any constructed or prefabricated pool used for swimming or bathing over 24' in depth measured between the floor of the pool and the maximum water level.
Swimming Pool (Private)	Shall be defined to include all constructed or assembled pools which are used as a swimming pool in connection with a residence whether single or multi-family and are available for use only to the family of the owner or owners and their private guests or invitees.
Swimming Pool (Public)	Shall be defined to include any constructed or prefabricated pool other than a private pool.

Barbara Child used this example to make the point that since the uncapitalised single word *pool* in the third paragraph was undefined, and its dictionary definition includes *A small shallow collection of any liquid*, the regulations for a public swimming pool could apply to a washing-up bowl.

Check how each defined term works in the text

There should be no need for the expressions *unless the context otherwise requires* and *unless the context otherwise permits*, which we suspect are used more often than the context requires. How often are the (different) consequences of these two alternatives thought through? And how often might there be an argument over whether a different meaning is required (or permitted)? If the writer does not know to what the definition applies, the reader certainly will not. Go through your document (an easy task with the 'find' command); note any instances in which the defined use is inappropriate; and exclude them expressly – ideally by using a different expression.

Extended litigation over a contract for the sale of land delayed completion for several years because the purchase price was defined *for all purposes* as including a deduction which circumstances made it difficult to apply.[2]

Paul Clark (2015) wonders whether the omission of *for all purposes* would have made a difference, but in any case recommends the 'context-variable' option to protect future users of the precedent from the consequences of overlooking the problem.

Where to put the definitions

If you have chosen short, meaningful definitions that contain no surprises, the reader should be able to form a general understanding of the document without first reading the definitions. They can be considered later when checking the details.

In any document, the most important information should come first (as discussed in Chapter 10, 'Organising your document'). When is a definition more important than (say) the commercial terms of a contract or a summary of legal advice? In most books and non-legal documents, the glossary is found at the back. That is where we suggest putting the definitions in legal documents, although readers should be told where to find them. If definitions are well identified and easy to find, there is no reason for them to occupy the prime location at the beginning of the document.

Martin Cutts (2000) wrote this in the margin of the contents page of his Clearer Timeshare Act:

> In the main text, *italic type* signifies the first use of a term defined in section 13, unless that first use occurs in the definition of the term itself.

Then each page of the Act has a list of defined terms in the margin, in alphabetical order.

Endnotes

1   We are grateful to Robert Eagleson for these Australian examples, from the Social Security Act 1947 and the Marketing of Primary Products (Citrus Fruit) Act 1973.
2   *Anglo Continental* v. *Capital Homes (Southern) Ltd* [2009, 2010].

113

Chapter 15

Consistency

Sensible drafters follow the 'consistent terminology' rule, summarised by Butt (2013), quoting E.L. Piesse (1995):

> Never change your language unless you wish to change your meaning, and always change your language if you wish to change your meaning.

This principle is particularly important in formal documents and for technical expressions. You will confuse your readers if you write

The tenant must decorate the outside every five years

and shortly afterwards

Nor may the lessee be a nuisance to the neighbours.

Who, they will ask, is the tenant and who the lessee? One way to ensure consistency is to avoid the repetition by creating a list (as discussed on p.89):

The tenant must:

- Decorate the outside every five years;
- Not be a nuisance to the neighbours.

The swimming pool regulations quoted on p.112 are a fine mess of inconsistency as:

- *Shall be defined to include* [or *mean*] is arbitrarily used or omitted.
- *Any constructed or prefabricated pool* becomes *all constructed or assembled pools* for private (but not public) pools.
- The clumsily named *Swimming Pool (Private)* becomes *private pool*.

The principle of consistent terminology only applies strictly to formal documents to be legally construed. The meaning of words routinely varies with their context. *We*, for example, has an infinite range of meanings, including *you and I*, *we and you*, and any category to which the speaker belongs. In drafting, it is normally reasonable to define a word or rewrite the text to avoid inconsistency. In another context, it might be pedantic and unreasonable to do so.

That reservation aside, consistency is important in everything, not just in the use of words. Even if inconsistency doesn't confuse the reader it can give the impression of unprofessional sloppiness. For example, if items are listed one to a line (as in the tenant's covenants immediately above), you should not haphazardly include two in a single line:

Must not be a nuisance to the neighbours or make structural alterations.

Similarly, if each clause is indented one inch, and the subclauses two inches, a subclause indented only one inch can mislead the reader about its status. For similar examples of inconsistency, see p.89.

Chapter 16

Paragraphs

When should you begin a new paragraph? On p.86, as part of a recommendation for plenty of white space, we said that paragraphs should not be tediously long. Attention deficit disorder is a matter of degree: even obsessive scholars need the occasional break and most of us drift away from long stretches of unbroken text. But this is not to condone the common practice of beginning a new paragraph just to create a rest point and without regard to the content. As:

1. a book is a collection of related chapters;
2. a chapter is a collection of related paragraphs;
3. ...; and
4. a sentence is a group of related words;

so (fitting into the gap in this hierarchy):

3. a paragraph should be a collection of related sentences.

Paragraph breaks are used in two ways that are sometimes incompatible: to signal meaning and to give the reader somewhere to pause. Ideally, both purposes should be served. Interminable paragraphs are hard going, but in legal writing especially it helps readers if paragraph breaks signal a change of subject.

An overlong paragraph can be pruned (deleting redundant words and information) or split into separate paragraphs or subparagraphs. Headings can also signal changes of topic.

It often helps to begin a paragraph with a 'topic sentence'. This keeps the writer focused, and tells the reader what the paragraph is about; the rest of the paragraph should only elaborate on the theme. Different theme; different paragraph.

 And if the writing is to flow (gently carrying the readers downstream), each paragraph – and each sentence – should follow naturally from the one before. That is why it is often useful to begin them with *and*, *but*, or some other conjunction (or, when telling a story, an adverb like *meanwhile* or *later*); it signals the relationship between the two pieces of text.

Chapter 17

Sentences

Length

Perhaps the most important single way to ease understanding is to use short sentences. There is only so much that readers can get their brain around at once. If you are told a seven-digit number you can remember it while you look for some way of retaining it long term; you search for a pattern (say, 246 1234) or for a similarity with something else (perhaps it includes the number of your house, or the year you were born). If you cannot find a mnemonic you will at least have time to look for a pen. But if someone read out a 30-digit number you would not be able to retain it. Following language is similar. You need to grasp each section long enough to understand it as a whole so you can digest it, by summary, mental picture, or otherwise.

Look at this extract from a transfer:

FULL RIGHT AND LIBERTY for the Board and its successors in title:

(a) to retain lay and maintain (which expressions shall without prejudice to the generality thereof include to use and from time to time to repair alter re-lay renew supplement inspect examine test and remove) electric lines under the yellow land including (but not so as to limit the generality of the foregoing grant) through the ducts hereinafter referred to and under the roads (a road including in addition to the carriageway one or more pavements and/or verges where present or intended) and footpaths now or within Eighty years from the date hereof constructed (which expression shall for the purposes hereof shall be deemed to include laid out preparatory to construction whether or not actual construction has commenced) on or over the property including (but not by way of limitation) the roads and footpaths shown on the said plan and the sites thereof before the same are constructed so far as the same lie within the Property all which said roads and footpaths and (if such be the case) the sites of those shown on the said plan before the same are constructed are hereinafter called 'the Estate Roads and Footpaths' TOGETHER WITH FULL RIGHT AND LIBERTY to break up the surface of the yellow land and the Estate Roads and Footpaths so far as may be necessary from time to time for all or any of such purposes

(b) ...

That was not the whole sentence, which would take more years than we have left to type in full. Yet paragraph (a) alone contains 227 words, many of them long. After reading it you do not know what it means. You need to re-read and analyse it, searching for the meaning.

Absurdly long sentences are at the heart of legalese. Who but a lawyer would compose an 1,100-word sentence such as the one reproduced (in Butt, 2013, p.180) from the modern standard mortgage of a major New Zealand bank? But we are improving: an 1853 conveyance consisting mostly of a 6,000-word sentence is reproduced and analysed in Adler (2013–15).

There is, of course, a temptation when drafting to provide for all conceivable circumstances. Up to a point, that is a lawyer's job, although it can be taken to extremes. Yet however many loopholes must be plugged, there is no need to deal with all of them in one sentence. You can stop for breath. As Lady Justice Arden said in her article 'The impact of judicial interpretation on legislative drafting' (2008):

> I would like to start by saying that there is something which I definitely do not find helpful [in legislative drafting], and that is the tendency of some drafters to see how many ideas and concepts they can pack into a single clause. This can lead to great loss of clarity.

Lord Denning was the master of the short sentence. Contrast the 'full right and liberty' example on the previous page with this passage, in which the average sentence length is 13 words. It comes from the chapter on the interpretation of statutes in Denning's *The Discipline of Law,* published in 1979, when he was 80:

> The first case in which there was an opportunity to advocate a new approach to the interpretation of statutes was *Seaford Court Estates Ltd* v. *Asher.* I was a very junior Lord Justice of Appeal of only six months' standing. Lord Greene MR was presiding with Asquith LJ and me. It was a case where the rent of a flat had been increased from £175 a year to £250 a year. The increase was because the landlord agreed to provide the hot water for the flat. The tenant freely agreed to pay the £250 but then tried to get it reduced to £175. He had no merits at all. His argument depended on giving a literal meaning to the word 'burden' in the Rent Act 1920. It was a situation which parliament never foresaw and for which it had made no provision. We reserved judgment for four weeks. I prepared my judgment and showed it to Lord Greene. He agreed with it and said so in his own judgment. Lord Justice Asquith also agreed with it. So it had backing of the first order.

This is beautifully clear. You can understand it without effort as you read. There is no need to study it. One possible criticism is that the sentences are a little too regular in length and in form. This can become tedious after a while. It is easy to parody. Many have done so.

MA: And you can go too far. Elegant word-flow is more important than numbers, especially where those numbers are manipulated to improve your statistics.

Sentences can be shortened in various ways but the most obvious is by reducing the number of ideas expressed in each one. Sometimes this will require the use of a few extra words but that does not matter: brevity is a great aid to comprehension, but it is not an end in itself.

Look at s.27 of the old Matrimonial Causes Act 1965:

> (1) Subject to the following provisions of this section, where an order (in this section referred to as 'the original order') has been made under the last foregoing section, the court, on an application under this section, shall have power by order to discharge or vary the original order or to suspend any provision of it temporarily and to revive the operation of any provision so suspended.

This sentence starts 'Subject to ...', continues 'where ...', adds a definition, then comes to the nub ('the court ... shall have power ...') but breaks that up with yet another subordinate clause ('on an application under this section'). It would be easier to follow if it began with the important point and then dealt separately with the subordinate matters:

> (1) The court has power to vary or cancel an order made under section 26, to suspend any provision, and to revive any suspended part.

Subordinate clauses that seemed to contribute nothing to the sense are omitted but, if they were needed, they could be brought in as following subsections.

For another possible revision, see Example D on p.237.

How short should a sentence be? There is no rule limiting the length of a sentence, but no sentence should be so long that readers must struggle to remember the beginning when they reach the end. At least the structure of the sentence – if not every word – must remain in short-term memory until the reader understands the whole. And you can test the severely limited capacity of short-term memory by seeing how long a series of digits you can remember when hearing or reading it the first time. The 26 characters (including hyphens) '10-20-30-40-50-60-70-80-90' can be memorised in a second, but memorising the alphabet scrambled into random order would take extended effort. Traditional legal writing approaches the scrambled-alphabet end of the spectrum; good writers prefer the comprehensible end.

The following numbers, or others much like them, are widely accepted as a guide (not as a straitjacket):

- Restrict each sentence to one or two ideas.
- Do not allow more than 40 words in any sentence. The gov.uk website follows a shorter limit; its style guide suggests splitting any sentence over 25 words to make the site readable by all users.[1]
- Aim for an average sentence length of about 15–20 words.

It is fair to count paragraph breaks before and after numbered or bulleted points in a list as if they were full stops, since they helps the reader as much.

Style-checking software makes it easy to apply these guidelines (see Chapter 21 ('Computer aids')). Otherwise, we suggest a two-line limit: in most printed formats, if there are no more than two lines of text between each full stop, your maximum and average sentence lengths should be good enough.

Another suggestion relates more to elegance than to clarity (and is therefore subordinate): follow a long sentence with at least one short sentence (to provide variety). But elegant variation in sentence length is not appropriate in a document whose only purpose is to set out rights or duties (for example, a contract or a statute). In these cases the length of each sentence will be more rigidly dictated by the material; moreover, readers are less likely to read from start to finish than to extract the parts relevant to their enquiry, so there is less need for variation.

Those are the principles, but how in practice do you reduce the traditional Leviathans to sentences of acceptable length?

The first, easiest, and most obvious way is to unpick multiple sentences. In the simplest cases you need only add a full stop. For example:

> The Seller will transfer the Property with full title guarantee but the transfer is to contain a provision in the following terms modifying the covenants implied into it by statute: ...

becomes (ignoring other possible improvements)

> The Seller will transfer the Property with full title guarantee.

> But the transfer is to contain a provision in the following terms modifying the covenants implied into it by statute: ...

Sometimes this technique will require some rewording (if only the removal of 'and' between two sentences). For example:

> I APPOINT my Husband ABC of ... and DEF of ... Solicitor and GH of ... ('my Trustees' which where the context so admits shall include the survivor or survivors of them or other the trustees for the time being hereof) to be the Executors and Trustees hereof and if any of my trustees shall predecease me or for any reason be unable or unwilling to act as Executor or Trustee I APPOINT IJK to fill any resulting vacancy as Executor or Trustee

could be reduced (without more serious and badly needed editing) to

> I APPOINT my Husband ABC of ... and DEF of ... Solicitor and GH of ... ('my Trustees' which where the context so admits shall include the survivor or survivors of them or other the trustees for the time being hereof) to be the Executors and Trustees hereof.

> If any of my trustees shall predecease me or for any reason be unable or unwilling to act as Executor or Trustee I APPOINT IJK to fill any resulting vacancy as Executor or Trustee.

A slightly more ambitious improvement would be:

> I APPOINT as Executors and Trustees hereof ('my Trustees' which where the context so admits shall include the survivor or survivors of them or other the trustees for the time being hereof):
>
> 1. my Husband ABC of ...
> 2. DEF of ... Solicitor and
> 3. GH of ...
>
> If any of my trustees shall predecease me or for any reason be unable or unwilling to act as Executor or Trustee I APPOINT IJK to fill any resulting vacancy as Executor or Trustee.

This leaves many faults untouched but allows substantial improvement by minimal change.

Reformatting a long sentence into a bulleted list (or numbered, if someone may need to discuss a list item) breaks the text into manageable parts and communicates the structure of the sentence at a glance. The process also often reveals syntactic ambiguity (see Chapter 24 ('Ambiguity')).

Subordinate clauses buried in the middle of sentences can be extracted to form separate sentences. In the next example, words which can be omitted are struck through, and the underlined words should be shipped off somewhere else.

> The Lessor will ~~at all times during the term~~ <u>(unless such insurance shall be vitiated by an act or default of the Lessee)</u> insure ~~and keep insured~~ all buildings ~~for the time being~~ on the Estate against loss or damage by ~~fire aircraft and other~~ comprehensive risks normally insured against in the case of premises of the same or a similar nature and any other risks which the Lessor shall ~~from time to time~~ in its absolute discretion decide in the full reinstatement value ~~thereof~~ <u>plus Ten per cent for professional fees</u> in some reputable insurance office and shall also insure ~~and keep insured~~ with a reputable insurance company the Third Party Employers and Property Owners Liability in respect of the Estate and shall ~~duly and~~ punctually pay all payments necessary for those purposes and shall produce to the Lessee on demand the policies of ~~such~~ insurance and ~~every~~ receipt for every ~~such~~ payment

Sentences can also be shortened by removing words (of course), though again you may need to reorganise what is left.

Words may be removed if:

- They add nothing to the sense, as in the case of those struck through in these examples:
  - I enclose ~~herewith~~
  - The ~~said~~ building ~~and all structural parts thereof~~
- What they do add does not need saying:
  - I will take instructions ~~from my client~~.

- The defendant was driving his ~~blue Ford motor~~ car ~~registration K623 NOK~~ [*when the only issue is which of the drivers is to blame for the accident*].

- Their meaning can be better expressed by recasting the sentence.

  - Please accept this letter as our Undertaking to ...
    = 'We undertake to', *or* 'We will'
  - The claimant was employed by the defendant as a shop manager at the defendant's premises.
    = 'The defendant employed the claimant to manage its shop'.
  - It is admitted that if, contrary to the Defendant's principal contentions, it be held that the Claimant is entitled to the sum claimed or any sum, it is entitled to interest.
    = 'We concede that the claimant is entitled to interest on any sum found due'.
  - She wrote a number of long letters to me with enclosures and I was slow in getting around to read the correspondence and act as at the time I was involved in dealing with a number of urgent ongoing matters from my case load.
    = 'She kept sending me long letters and other documents, but I was too busy to read them until later'.

See the next chapter for more on removing surplus words.

Organisation

It is easier to read something that comes to the point than something that doesn't. This may seem trite but it is a principle often ignored, applying to sentences as well as to documents as a whole (see p.74).

Take this example, from a pleading settled by counsel:

1. Save that by clause 6 of the said Agreement, the Plaintiff was allowed by the Defendant into possession and occupation of 'the storage area' in order to carry out in a good and workmanlike manner and to the reasonable satisfaction of the Landlord's Surveyor, the works set out in a Section 146 Notice, a copy of which was annexed to the said Agreement and save that by Clause 10 of the said Agreement the Plaintiff was to comply with the said Section 146 Notice and save that by Clause 11 of the said Agreement the Plaintiff was to so comply within three months from the date of the said Agreement, that is, by 3rd September 1987 and that provided the said Notice was complied with within that time the Defendant agreed to grant the Plaintiff a supplementary Lease of the 'storage area', Paragraph 1 of the Statement of Claim is admitted.

It would have been much easier to put the rest of the sentence into perspective (and so to understand it on first reading) if it had started:

Paragraph 1 of the statement of claim is admitted, except:

(A) By clause 6…

(B) By clause 10…

For a full revision, see Example E on p.238.

It is also easier to read something in which like is grouped with like rather than jumbled arbitrarily. On p.116 we suggested a hierarchy in which related words were grouped into sentences, related sentences into paragraphs, paragraphs into chapters, and chapters into books. This sequence is continued upwards in the arrangement of libraries and bookshops. The advantages of order over disorder extend to the words within each sentence.

Take this example from a commercial lease, with the auxiliary and main parts of the same verb separated by 43 words – a parenthesis longer than any complete sentence ought to be:

> (b) To execute at their own expense all such works as are or MAY under or in pursuance of any Act or Acts of Parliament statutory instruments rules orders and regulations for the time being in force relating to planning control and any orders directions or notices made or given thereunder already or hereafter to be passed BE directed or required to be done or executed at any time during the said term upon or in respect of the demised premises or the use thereof or its fixtures and fittings therein whether by the landlord or the tenant thereof and to pay all fines and charges

The two lost parts of the verb are capitalised here but the 15 tenants had no such help. On the contrary, the writer made the readers' task unnecessarily difficult by spinning out the insertion with pointless words.

Some lawyers' sentences begin as though they were coming to the point but then drift off into the bush. The example below, taken from the (Victoria, Australian) Construction Industry Long Service Leave (Amendment) Act 1985, as well as this sentence, which we must admit is badly constructed because you have probably forgotten how it began, but is about positioning the subject and verb, is badly written.

> If the liquidator or trustee does not comply with any provision of this section (or fails as trustee duly to pay the long service leave charges for which the liquidator or trustee is liable under subsection (3)) the liquidator or trustee must to the extent of the value of the assets which have been taken into the liquidator's or trustee's possession and which are or have been available at any time for the payment of the long service leave charges be personally liable to pay the long service leave charges and is guilty of an offence.

Most sentences that are suitably succinct will not have room for much more than the subject, verb, and object, preferably in that order. That sentence has:

Subject:	Most sentences
Adjectival clause:	that are suitably succinct
Verb:	will not have
Object:	room
Adverbial clause:	for much more than subject, verb, and object,
Adverbial clause:	preferably in that order.

Subject, verb, and object are close together at the beginning of the sentence, interrupted only by a clause whose position there is essential and which is not long enough to derail the reader. The adverbial clauses at the end supplement, rather than interrupt, the sense, and are therefore easier to slot into our mental parsers as we read.

For a possible revision, see Example F on p.239.

Classically educated lawyers will be familiar with the different (and more flexible) word order which Latin permitted by inflecting words to alter meaning; the sense depended on the form of the word rather than its position in the sentence. We have lost this in most English words, and rely on the word order to distinguish

Man bites dog

from

Dog bites man

whereas

Dog man bites

could refer to the propensities of a man with some sort of dog connection. Latin usually puts the verb at the end of the sentence, with subject and object before it but either way round. Presumably this is why some lawyers write

the clauses ... in the said Agreement mentioned

instead of

the clauses ... mentioned in the agreement.

Active or passive voice

For those English lawyers educated when grammar was exiled from the curriculum, here is a brief, non-technical explanation of active and passive voice, which should show why the active usually works better.

Active and passive voice are two ways to express a verb. (A verb is the part of speech that expresses action.) Take this example, using the verb *to love*:

Adam loves Eve.
Eve is loved by Adam.

These two sentences, both correct English, both short and clear, convey the same information. The first does it in the active voice, the second in the passive.

Notice that in the passive voice, you need two extra words to give the same information. That is one reason to prefer the active voice. Another is that, as one of those words is always part of the verb *to be*, the passive can become repetitive.

Although the two sentences give the same information, there is a difference, not only of grammar but of tone and emphasis. This comes partly from the word order.

So, in the two examples just given, the focus is on:

- Adam in the active voice, focusing on who is doing the loving. The doer of the action is so important that you cannot use the active verb form without first saying who or what is doing the action. (*Loves Eve* and *Loves Adam Eve* are gibberish.)
- Eve in the passive, focusing on who or what is on the receiving end of Adam's affections. You can even leave out the doer of the action. (*Eve is loved* is a correct English sentence in the passive voice).

This difference is a good reason to prefer the passive voice when you want to avoid focusing on who or what is doing the action. For example, you can avoid criticism and soften accusations by not mentioning who made the mistake. Or you may not know or care who the doer is.

DP: The best use of the passive voice I ever saw in a legal document was at the start of a written argument by barrister Michael McParland QC, in support of a claim for exemplary damages on behalf of three men who had met a dreadful death:

In September 1998, three telecommunications engineers employed by [the Defendant] **were sent** abroad to work on the Defendant's largest ever and potentially most profitable contract.

The three men never returned.

Instead, they **were kidnapped**, **held** for ransom, **tortured**, **starved**, and after at least 64 days in captivity, they **were beheaded**. Their severed heads **were found** dumped on a roadside on 8 December 1998. Their bodies **were recovered** 3 weeks later.

The eight passive verbs highlighted in this short passage focus entirely on the three victims. We do not know who captured them or found their bodies. It makes no difference in this context.

However, omitting to say who or what is doing the action can deprive the reader of important information. For example, s.3(3) of the now defunct Inheritance (Family Provision) Act 1938 read:

> A copy of every order made under this Act shall be sent to the Principal Registry of the Family Division for entry and filing ...

This does not specify who is to send the order: is it the court or the applicant? As the reader is left to guess, they might both do it, or each leave it for the other (so neither does it), or perhaps argue about who is responsible. Similarly, passive wording doesn't work where a person's connection to an act must be explicitly stated, as when establishing a cause of action.

Another unfortunate use of the passive is in apologies. When we are to blame, an apology should admit what we did and say we are sorry. It is not the moment to edit out who did it, or even to delay the admission:

> The firm regrets that the payment **was not made** on time. (Passive)

> We are sorry that **we did not pay** on time. (Active)

But sometimes in avoiding the passive we focus on the wrong subject. For example,

> Change is needed

might become

> Change needs to happen

instead of

> We need change.

Traditional legal language uses a high proportion of passive verbs – often more than 50 per cent. This tends to make writing wordier and less direct and there is a danger that the writer will unwittingly omit the doer or focus on the object of the doer's action.

The passive voice makes text more elaborate, indirect, impersonal, and formal. In some contexts, this is polite; taken too far, it sounds pompous or evasive. The active voice makes text more direct and personal. Often this is business-like; taken too far, or in the wrong context, it could be curt or rude.

Some plain language enthusiasts (for example, Wren (2002, p.13)) have eliminated all use of the passive voice, along with some other wordy writing habits, by editing out every use of the verb to be – each *is, am, are, was, were, been, being* and *be*. But this deprives the writer of a correct and useful way to focus on the object of the action and omit the actor where that's appropriate. Indiscriminate surgery is poor medicine.

Microsoft Word, Outlook, and style-checker software can count the incidence of passive verbs and express it as a percentage, which can give a warning that you might be overusing it. We recommend that you use the passive as often as there is a good reason for it but never otherwise. Consider each case on its merits.

> **DP:** In my experience, 20 per cent is normally ample for good uses of the passive in legal writing. A score of 40 per cent or more usually indicates overuse.

To edit out passive verbs you might:

- Identify who or what is doing the action and place them before the verb. So, *The message was delivered* becomes *Mrs Smith delivered the message*.
- Change the verb to one that focuses on the object of the action, if you don't want to draw attention to the fact that you are not saying who was responsible for it. So, *The message was delivered* becomes *the message arrived*.
- Recast the sentence to omit passive verbs that you can do without. So, *The relevant factors to be considered when making this decision include* could become *Relevant factors include*.

Positive or negative thoughts   Double negatives

Using a positive phrase is generally more direct and may be shorter than the negative. So:

> A court shall not make an order under subsection (1) without first considering a report by a medical officer.

This is 19 words long and a double negative; it can be rephrased:

> The court shall only make an order under subsection (1) after considering a report by a medical officer. [*18 words*]

or better (reorganising the sentence to reflect the order of events, which helps the brain):

> The court must consider a medical officer's report before making an order. [*12 words*]

Double negatives are difficult but we can with patience pick them apart. Triple ones are harder. Look at this example from s.1 of the Protection of Badgers Act 1992:

> (3) A person is guilty of an offence if, except as permitted by or under this Act, he has in his possession or under his control any dead badger …
>
> (4) A person is not guilty of an offence under subsection (3) above if he shows that …

127

    (a)   the badger had not been killed, or had been killed otherwise than in contra-vention of the provisions of this Act or of the Badgers Act 1973; or …

It took a great deal of head-scratching to rewrite that as

(3) It is an offence for a person to have a dead badger in their possession, or under their control … unless:

    (a)   It is permitted elsewhere under this Act; or
    (b)   They show that the badger had not been killed in breach of this Act or of the Badgers Act 1973.

The multiple negatives *unless … not … in breach* survive because the essence of the exception is *unless they show*. It is tempting to cancel out the double negative in 3(b) to get:

They show that the badger had been killed as permitted under this Act or the Badgers Act 1973

but that changes the meaning to permit a conviction if you are caught with a badger that had died of natural causes. (We express no view on whether *dead* is another negative.)

Sadly, legal publishers can offer their subscribers such logic puzzles as the following, in case-summaries which ought to give the reader a quick answer to the question 'What did this case decide?':

A Nigerian national (N) appealed against a decision of the Upper Tribunal (U) allowing his appeal against a decision of the First-tier Tribunal (F) refusing his appeal against a decision of the Secretary of State for the Home Department (S) refusing his application for a residence card.

Here is a rather subtle negative, from a newspaper headline:

Scientists have created 'supermice' … which age almost half as fast as other mice.

This suggests that the supermice age not quite (= slower than) half as fast as normal ones; at, say, 40 per cent of the speed. But the story read:

The resulting mice age 40 per cent slower than those whose genes have not been modified

which must surely mean at 60 per cent of normal speed. Maybe the writer tripped over the negative.

Avoid negatives if you can, but beware changing the sense when there are more than two alternatives. The negative of

I was made welcome

could be either

I was made unwelcome

128

or the quite different

> I was not made welcome

(perhaps because no one knew I was there). So the two negatives in

> I was not made unwelcome

cannot be cancelled out to become

> I was made welcome

though you could re-write the sentence without a double negative:

> They entertained me politely but without enthusiasm.

The world isn't one-dimensional. In the words of the last *Jewish Chronicle* column written by journalist Melissa Nathan, then terminally ill:

> The opposite of ageing isn't getting younger. It's dying.

This rare quadruple negative was attributed on the radio to Boris Johnson (who had been teasing the interviewer):

> I could not fail to disagree with you less.

Such a simple sentence! But what does it mean?

And spare a thought for the defendant (temporarily) sentenced to two years' imprisonment and taken down to the cells after a juror's cough masked the first word of the verdict.[2]

Endnotes

1   Government Digital Service 'Style guide' (Sentence length) at **www.gov.uk/ guidance/style-guide/a-to-z-of-gov-uk-style**.
2   Report in *The Independent* (16 April 1999): **www.independent.co.uk/news/ untimely-cough-sends-innocent-man-to-jail-judge-jails-man-after-jurorors-innocent-cough-puts-1087503.html**.

Chapter 18

Choosing words

Words are like leaves; and where they most abound
Much fruit of sense beneath is rarely found.
Alexander Pope (1688–1744)

Trimming what isn't necessary

Traditional legal writing can be radically trimmed by applying the purpose test: Does this word (or phrase, sentence, paragraph) have a purpose? If not, leave it out. The purpose might be in what you are saying or in how you say it.

Excessive detail

Much unnecessary space is taken up with details. Some may be obvious and need not be expressed; some may be implied by law (though it may be convenient to include them); some may be redundant; others may be wrong.

Most legal documents are full of redundant details. Decorating requirements in a lease can fill a whole page when all that most landlords want is that the tenant should decorate *to their reasonable satisfaction*, or *to a standard consistent with a high-class shopping centre*. If the lease just said that, no one would be worse off. You can be sure that no tenant gives a copy of the repairing covenant to the decorator, nor even checks the lease in order to pass on the instructions to *grain varnish distemper wash stop whiten colour or suitably treat*. Nor do tenants take care to decorate in every fifth year of the term; they do it – if they are conscientious – when the premises need it. If the premises do not need it in the fifth year because they were decorated in the fourth, the tenant is unlikely to repeat the job (and why would the landlord care?). However, sometimes the right to assign, extend, or end the lease depends on whether the tenant is in breach of covenant. Then, even a trivial breach can lose a tenant a valuable right, turning the detailed requirements into a trap for the unwary. For example, in *Bairstow Eves* v. *Ripley* (1993) an estate agent lost the right to renew its lease because it had decorated the premises just before the last year of the lease rather than during the last year as the lease required. The judge found that this technical breach made no material difference but the Court of Appeal held that the wording of the lease allowed no flexibility – a point to be borne in mind by tenants' solicitors when amending an unreasonable draft. Life would be better if we didn't lay these arbitrary traps for each other.

In *Norwich Union* v. *British Railways Board* (1987) Mr Justice (later Lord) Hoffmann said, about a repairing covenant in a lease:

> According to normal rules of construction the additional words should be given some additional meaning. But [counsel for the landlord] says, with some justification, that this rule frequently cannot be applied in its full force to documents such as leases, where a torrential style of drafting has been traditional for many years …
>
> Now I accept that in the construction of covenants such as this one one cannot … insist upon giving each word in a series a distinct meaning. Draftsmen frequently use many words either because it is traditional to do so or out of a sense of caution so that nothing which could conceivably fall within the general concept which they have in mind should be left out. I also accept that *if the language is not entirely clear* the covenant should not readily be assumed to impose unusual obligations [our italics].

The torrential style is self-defeating. Because judges know that lawyers pour in unnecessary words with little thought about their meaning, they generally (though with occasional unpredictable exceptions) treat a repairing covenant in much the same way however it is phrased, and the exact wording chosen by the drafter is largely irrelevant. This point was analysed in detail in Adler (1996), which also looked at a typical repairing covenant and asked whether the torrential style is justified by the case law, as its proponents imagine. It isn't.

It has also been customary to impose covenants to *do or cause to be done*, although the last five of those six words will rarely be necessary. If a party gets someone else to perform its duty, there is often no breach and usually no loss. In those few cases where it matters who performs a contractual duty, it is sensible to say so expressly.

Another class of examples comes from management clauses. One schedule several pages long will list all the things the landlord or managing agents must do, or may do at their discretion. Another schedule will list the items whose cost the landlord can include in the service charge. The second list will usually duplicate the first (though often inconsistently); it might include a reference to the other schedule, and it might be used as a back door through which items may be implicitly added to the list of things the landlord can do. Such lists can be replaced, much more tidily, by a general obligation – and discretion – to manage, with a right to recover the cost.

Detailed lists are not just a waste of space and time but a threat to the drafting solicitor and the client. Forget one item, or fail to anticipate one circumstance, and you let your opponent slip through the net. And some impressive-looking lists turn out on closer inspection to be incoherent and incomplete.

Drafters try to patch that problem by including a catch-all generalisation intended to cover all possible circumstances, linking it to the detailed list by such phrases as *Without prejudice to the generality of the foregoing* … or *or any other* … But this can be pointless and dangerous:

- If the general rule is stated, what is the point in adding details?
- No matter how long and detailed the list, it is still vulnerable to restrictive interpretation using the principles outlined in Chapter 30. (Examples of the many cases in which this has happened are *Kudos Catering* v. *Manchester* (2013) and *Scottish Power* v. *BP* (2015).)

A better approach, we suggest, is to state the general rule first, and then consider whether any particular borderline cases should be explicitly included or excluded (although the impossibility of anticipating every-thing is discussed in Chapter 23).

Buried verbs

Buried verbs are those converted into nouns with a different, vaguer, verb added to tack the noun into the sentence. They are sometimes called 'nominalisations'. Here are some examples, with the simpler equivalent on the right:

be on a learning curve	**learn**
come to the conclusion	**conclude**
for the simplification of	**to simplify**
give (be of) some assistance	**assist, help**
I am in receipt of	**I have (received), thank you for**
I am of the opinion that	**I think**
impose an obligation	**oblige**
make an application asking for	**apply for**
reach an agreement, decision	**agree, decide**
take into consideration	**consider**

Another way to bury a verb and increase wordiness is to substitute an adverb. For example:

it is possible that	**may, might**
it is necessary to	**needs to, must**
it is apparent that	**appears, seems**

A clue to detecting nominalisations and other wordy writing is the word *of*. Another is the verb *to be*. Try hunting down *of, is, am, are, was, were, be, been,* and *being*; they might indicate where one word could replace three.

Other redundant words

Often one or two words can replace other types of phrase with no loss of meaning:

ahead of [an event]	**before**
a majority of	**most**
as a matter of urgency	**urgently**
as at (of) [date or time]	**on, at**
a sum equal to £x	**£x** (requiring payment in sterling)
at a later date	**later** (if 'date' is obvious or unnecessary)
at a rapid rate	**rapidly**
at this (point in) time	**now**
during the course of	**during**
for and on behalf of	**for**
for free	**free**
for the purpose of [doing]	**to [do]**
at your early convenience	**soon**
I authorise and request you to …	**please** …
I'm not in the business of …	**I don't** …
I'm not someone who does …	**I don't** …
impact upon	**affect**
in and of itself	**in itself**
in excess of	**more than**
in order to	**to**
in the event that	**if**
it is maybe	**it may be**
it's not part of my job description	**it's not my job**
legal services industry professional	**lawyer**
live your life	**live**
on a regular basis	**regularly**
on a weekly basis	**weekly**
on the occasion of	**on**
place of safety	**safe place**
plus the fact that	**and**
provided always that	**if, but, however,** (sometimes) **and**
subsequent to	**after**
that particular (thing)	**that (thing)**
there are people out there who …	**there are people who** …
the reason why	**the reason**
this [that] particular point in time	**now [then]**
two years down the road (track, line)	**in two years, two years later, after two years**
until such time as	**until**

upskill the level of	**improve**
[say] whether or not	**[say] whether**
within that time frame	**within that time**

Duly is generally unnecessary. It means *properly and punctually* but that is usually implied, and the word is often used when no time element is involved.

The next two examples, although alternatives are given, can be avoided altogether by restructuring the sentence:

so far as X is concerned	**concerning X**
with regard to X	**regarding (about) X**

For instance,

So far as contact is concerned, Mr White prefers the weekend arrangement

can become

Mr White prefers weekend contact.

Some phrases reveal the need to ramble while the speaker wonders what to say:

We have been proceeding with the business of developing our plans for the future of the economy (= 'We have been planning the economy')

Give some clarification as to what is going on

It depends on what happens in terms of addressing these issues

I would argue that

Some phrases can be omitted entirely without loss of meaning:

I write to inform you that

Please note that.

Lawyers (and others) often use pairs of words of identical meaning, where one, or perhaps either, can be used instead of both:

Each and every

Fixtures and fittings

Full and final

Null and void

Rules and regulations

Suffer or permit

Terms and conditions

Then and in any such case

Tried and tested.

Occasionally we expand these doublets to triplets, as in:

Give devise and bequeath.

The pre-Woolf-reform

Reply to Request for Further and Better Particulars of the Particulars of Claim

which was rather unwieldy as the name of a document, was reducible to

Better [or More detailed] particulars of claim

but some years after Woolf an enterprisingly loquacious barrister named a document

RESPONSE TO REQUEST FOR FURTHER INFORMATION IN RELATION TO THE PAR-
TICULARS OF CLAIM.

On the other hand, not all candidates for deletion really are redundant. *That*, *who*, and *which* are common victims of editors trying to squeeze text into a limited space. These words can often be omitted without loss of meaning (although it might affect the rhythm, and in this example slightly affects the formal register):

The Court of Appeal, upholding the arrangement, said [that] the obligation is equita-
ble.

But if the omission creates an ambiguity or risks a miscue, *that* should be retained.

Stating the obvious

Lawyers particularly like describing the obvious:

Now this deed witnesseth as follows:

The sum of one hundred pounds

The 29th day of September.

What else is £100, if not a sum, and what is 29 September if not a day?

In an agreement, it is not necessary to say

> It is expressly agreed that

since that will be apparent from the inclusion of the terms set out. And

> It is hereby further expressly agreed and declared that

is worse, especially when haphazardly included in only some paragraphs. Nor does

> I certify that

seem any more necessary than

> I say that

as long as it is clear that this is a formal declaration of truth. No particular form of words is needed. In *Roberts* v. *Watkins* (1863) an oral expression of approval by an architect was accepted as a certificate of satisfaction. In *R* v. *St Mary, Islington* (1890) it was held that a letter asking for payment of an amount spent was a certificate that that had been the cost. In the *Minster Trust* (1954) case, in which a document was held not to be a certificate for other reasons, the court treated the absence of the 'certifying' expression as irrelevant. More recently, in *Beyers* v. *DETR* (2000) the Administrative Court considered the meaning of 'certify' in the context of a statutory requirement for a local authority to certify its satisfaction when granting or refusing consent under a tree preservation order. The deputy judge, Mr Robin Purchas QC, said:

> In my judgment it requires a formal and communicated act of attesting or declaring the authority's satisfaction in accordance with the Article. Thus one officer giving instructions to another officer to issue a certificate would generally not constitute certification for the purpose of Article 5. There must be at least a public or communicated act of certification.

This leaves open what constitutes *a formal act*. But a letter, on headed paper from the official responsible to the person awaiting certification, saying *I am satisfied* must be sufficient.

Often, having introduced some elaboration, for instance by the words *as follows*, we add quite pointlessly (as though reluctant to move on) *that is to say* or even *in manner following, that is to say*.

In witness whereof the Authors hereof have hereunto set their hands the day and year first above written.

Archaic words

A useful test for words best avoided, other than terms of art, is whether lay people use them. A word without technical meaning used only by lawyers must have an alternative preferable to everyone else.

Here are some common examples, with alternatives on the right:

bequeath	**give**
devise	**give**
dispatch	**send**
user (as a noun to mean 'use')	**use**
vendor	**seller**

The first two words are special to wills. We were taught that *devise* is appropriate for real property and *bequeath* for everything else but Mellinkoff (1963, p.164) says that

> Not until the nineteenth century did it become a lawyerly custom to *devise* realty and *bequeath* personalty, a subtlety contrary to the linguistic and legal history of the words and never uniform in practice.

The distinction may be quaint but it is not useful. Here is a typical example of its use:

> I give devise and bequeath all my real and personal property whatsoever and wheresoever situate unto my said wife Janis Andrea Mitchell for her use and benefit absolutely.

This means

> I give all my property to my wife

so why not say so? Then the family and the executors can understand the will without what might be an unnecessary and expensive visit to their solicitor. (A little more detail will be needed if the testator is in the habit of calling someone else his wife, but the principle is sound. The famous case of *Thorn* v. *Dickens* (1906), the shortest known UK will (*All for mother*), was litigated because the testator called his wife *mother*. The will was valid and the wife took.)

Another archaic word is *moiety*. Although this strictly means *half* it is sometimes used to mean some other, unspecified, proportion. Better to say what you mean.

Hereby

Hereby is one of the profession's favourite useless words. If A must give B notice of X, the obligation is satisfied by the act. *I give you notice that …* is as superfluous as *I am telling you that …* And *I hereby give you notice that …* adds the obvious to the obvious.

One beautifully succinct piece of legislation is s.2(1) of the Torts (Interference with Goods) Act 1977, which says *Detinue is abolished.* Perhaps this is the only Act whose main clause is shorter than its short title. However, s.15(1) reads: *The Disposal of Uncollected Goods Act 1952 is hereby repealed.*

Donald Revell, formerly chief legislative counsel for Ontario and a long-standing supporter of plain language, has argued that *hereby* can be useful in this special (legislative) case (which will rarely apply to most lawyers). His example is *The XYZ Corporation is hereby established.* Leave out the *hereby*, he says, and you are left with a statement of fact rather than an act of creation. The corporation might have been established by something else. This is a seductive argument, and Phil Knight, a legislative drafter also based in Canada, replied:

> I have long avoided its [*hereby*'s] use because it sounds to my ears like a rank bit of legalese. But on reflection, I think the problem may be that, like so much strictly 'legal' vocabulary, people use it because they imagine it makes them 'sound legal' instead of using it to do its job. The resulting overuse and unnecessary use, combined with the unfamiliarity of the word in most other contexts, may be what has led to the near universal condemnation of the word. But neither personal opinion, nor misguided overuse, justify abandoning a word, if it indeed performs a useful function, and adds to certainty of a legal text.

But he goes on to explain why he thinks 'hereby' *can* be omitted in this context. Knight is a thoughtful and original writer, and his note is worth reading in full. Both these issues of *Clarity* (49 and 50) are freely available from www.clarity-international.net.

Our own preferred revision of Revell's example would be *This Act establishes the XYZ Corporation.*

Hereinafter

Many other useless 'here …' words pad out a sentence to no purpose and help the reader forget what it's about:

Herein

Hereinafter

Hereinbefore

Hereunto

Herewith

and (yes, really[1])

Hereinunto.

138

Similarly, we have

Above

Above-mentioned

Above-named

Aforementioned

Aforesaid

Beforementioned

and, legal resourcefulness being what it is,

Hereinbefore mentioned

though not yet as one word.

It would be more useful to give page and clause references.

Then there is the 'soever' group:

Whatsoever

Whosoever

Whosesoever

Whomsoever

Wheresoever

but not, so far as we know

Whysoever

though Dr Michael Arnheim has recorded

Whensoever.

The said

The is one of the most concise and informative words in the language, and much under-valued by lawyers.

Bertrand Russell wrote a classic article about it in the 1905 issue of *Mind*. He took the example

The King of France is bald

and argued that it was a combination of three statements in one:

There is a King of France;

There is only one King of France; and

He is bald.

Only if all three statements are true is it true that the King of France is bald. Adding *said* – The said King of France is bald – adds nothing but a clumsy word.

More often we use *the* to mean not that there is only one such thing in the world, but that there is only one which is the subject of our conversation. If I refer you back to the Russell article you know exactly which one I mean – his 1905 *Mind* article; I am not implying that he only wrote one article in his life. And there is no need to refer to *the said article* or *the article hereinbefore mentioned*; anything conveyed by the extra words is already covered by *the* alone.

The phoney plural

If we can say *all the money in the world* how much extra is implied by the plural, *monies*?

Advices grates even more.

Complex words

Lawyers, and others, often use a complex word (by which we mean *long and unfamiliar*) where a simple one would do. It sounds more important. But if it does nothing but pad out the text, what is the point? Here are some common examples, with alternatives on the right:

cease	**stop, end**
commence	**begin, start**
donate	**give**
endeavour	**try**
expeditious	**quick**
initiate	**begin, start**
purchase	**buy**
terminate	**end**

We are sometimes advised to prefer words of Anglo-Saxon origin to those of foreign descent (though of course that involves knowing which is which). But the many people whose first language is one of the Romance group (Spanish, Portuguese, French, Italian, and others) might more easily recognise a word of Latin origin, from which their language – but not English – evolved.

Although Latin itself is no longer widely understood, some expressions have been incorporated into English (e.g. *e.g., i.e., a.m., p.m.* and *vice versa*) and are familiar to some but not to everybody. Others are familiar only to (some) lawyers.

> **DP:** I have found in my workshops that even lawyers who regularly use phrases like *mutatis mutandis* are unable to agree with colleagues on their meaning.

Mistakes often creep in (or are introduced by spell checkers), annoying the few who still remember the correct expression.

The noun *burglar* apparently pre-dated the word for their activity. When selecting a verb the British opted for the economical *burgle*. In America, where there is more space and everything is bigger, their polysyllabic exuberance produced *burglarize*, and perhaps *burglarizers* will follow. On the other hand, sometimes new verbs formed in this way can have a usefully different meaning, as does *servicing*.

Many leases impose a covenant to repair *the main structural parts of the building*, leaving open the responsibility for the other structural parts and the problem of distinguishing between them. One landlord's legal department was unable to say what it meant by the distinction, yet refused to amend – even to clarify – the point because the lease was standard.

As we try to show in Chapters 23 ('Vagueness') and 24 ('Ambiguity'), even familiar, everyday words are open to hostile interpretation. But they do have a better chance of being understood.

Shall

Lawyers like to use *shall* because it is traditional. They imagine it to be an unambiguous word of command.

At least until recently, *I shall* and *you will* both meant one kind of thing, whereas *I will* and *you shall* meant another. Few people now remember or care about the distinction, and the *Oxford English Dictionary* says that *The interchangeable use of shall and will is now part of standard British and US English*.

For those still interested, *The Oxford Guide to English Usage* neatly summarises the use in the second and third persons:

> *You, he, she, it*, or *they shall* express intention or determination on the part of the speaker or someone other than the actual subject of the verb, especially a promise made by the speaker to or about the subject, e.g.
> 'In future you shall have as many taxis as you want' (G.B. Shaw).

The long entry on *shall* in *Garner's Dictionary of Legal Usage* (Garner, 2011) begins (on p.952):

> This word runs afoul of several basic principles of good drafting. The first is that a word used repeatedly in a given context is presumed to bear the same meaning throughout … The second principle is strongly allied with the first: when a word takes on too many senses and cannot be confined to one sense in a given document, it becomes useless to the drafter. (Depending on how finely you slice

the semantic nuances, *shall* can bear five to eight senses even in a single document. *Black's Law Dictionary* [9th edn, 2009] lists five main senses.) The third principle [is] …: good drafting generally ought to be in the present tense, not the future.

The legal *shall* has even been held to refer to the past, though the cases go both ways. For example, a reference in one will to a child who *shall die in my lifetime* included a child who had already died when the will was made. For a review of the two conflicting lines of cases see Butt (2013, p.265).

Here are some of our own examples of *shall*, with *shall* highlighted:

> 1 The Lessor **shall** be entitled at its absolute discretion to vary the proportion of the Service Costs payable by the Lessee as defined in clause 1(n) in the event of rights being granted pursuant to the terms of paragraph 5 of the Fifth Schedule hereto Provided that such variation **shall** not result in the said Service Charge proportion being increased

The first *shall* here is obviously not commanding the landlord to be entitled; *shall be entitled at its absolute discretion to* means *may*. Nor is the second use commanding the variation not to result in an increase in the service charge; it means that the discretion accorded by the first *shall* does not apply if the charge would be increased. (The whole absurd and redundant paragraph really means *The landlord may reduce the service charge – but only if certain conditions are fulfilled*. Is the tenant likely to object to an unauthorised reduction?)

> 2 If the deposit actually paid on exchange of contracts **shall** be less than 10% then notwithstanding payment of a lesser amount by way of deposit the balance of the 10% **shall** at all times remain due to the Vendor and in the event of rescission or failure to complete through no fault of the Vendor payment of the balance of the 10% deposit **shall** be a legal liability of the Purchasers to the Vendor as a condition of this contract.

The first *shall be* means *is* (especially as the deposit is paid when the clause comes into force); the second and third *shalls*, while seeking to impose an obligation, do so indirectly using words other than *shall*, which is used here to indicate the future tense of the verbs *to remain* and *to be*.

> 3 Not to erect on the Vendor's land … any buildings which would overlook the property provided always that the walls and/or fences and/or hedges to be erected by the Purchaser on the boundaries of the property **shall** be at least six feet in height

Is this ordering the purchaser to make any boundary structures at least six feet high, or (bearing in mind the repeated *ors*) only some of them? (It would be difficult to plant a hedge that is already six feet high, even if you could get it back from the garden centre.) Or is the drafter saying that the vendor must not erect buildings that would still overlook the property even if all the boundaries were at least six feet high?

> 4 The Agreement **shall** be governed by English law.

Again, this clause imposes no obligation. The best replacement for *shall be* is *is*, unless you prefer to say that *English law governs this agreement*.

Shall offers no precision; it merely sounds archaic and portentous.

Current normal use among non-lawyers and plain-language lawyers is to replace *shall* by:

- *will* to express the future;
- *must* to command;
- *may* to express permission;
- *may not* or *must not* to forbid;
- another verb in the present tense in other cases.

But even *must* can be unclear, as in

> The chair must be a member of the committee.

Does this limit the candidates for the chair or appoint the chair to the committee? The sentence should read either

> The chair must be appointed from the committee

or

> The chair is ex officio a member of the committee

or, if the expected audience might have trouble with the Latin

> The chair is by reason of office a member of the committee.

But the distinction between the imperative and the future tense can be blurred, in that a contractual term that someone *will* do something will normally be broken if they do not do it. The Law Society's *Standard Conditions of Sale* use *is to* to express contractual obligation. Richard Castle, who was on the original drafting team, has said (in conversation) that this was intended to sound less harsh than *must* and was thought more suitable for an uncontentious transaction.

In the Australian case of *Sillery* (1981) the trial judge and the Court of Criminal Appeal interpreted

> The punishment for an offence against this section is imprisonment for life

as imposing a mandatory life sentence. The High Court (in Australia the equivalent of Britain's Supreme Court) contrasted similar provisions using *shall* and disagreed (largely because the mandatory life sentence would have been draconian in many circumstances). But this does not justify the reintroduction of *shall*: the dispute would not have arisen if the Act had read *The maximum punishment … is …* or *The prescribed punishment … is …* or *An offence against this section must be punished by imprisonment for life*.

143

Both *shall* and *must* are sometimes used loosely in the form

A must do X within two weeks

to mean

If A does X it must be within two weeks

which is quite different. The mistake is to attach the auxiliary *must* to the wrong verb.

The policy of the Office of the Parliamentary Counsel in the UK is to avoid using the legislative *shall*, with exceptions (for example, where the text is being inserted into an Act that already uses *shall*).[2] Other OPCs around the Commonwealth have similar policies.

Here are just two examples of *shall*-free UK parliamentary drafting:

From s.12 of the Human Rights Act 1998

Freedom of expression

(1) This section applies if a court is considering whether to grant any relief which, if granted, might affect the exercise of the Convention right to freedom of expression.

(2) If the person against whom the application for relief is made ('the respondent') is neither present nor represented, no such relief is to be granted unless the court is satisfied – ...

(4) The court must have particular regard to the importance of the Convention right to freedom of expression and ...

From s.40D(3) of the Finance (No.2) Act 1992, added by s.81 of the Capital Allowances Act 2001:

(3) An election under this section –

    (a)   must relate to all expenditure incurred (or to be incurred) on the production or acquisition of the master version in question,

    (b)   must be made by giving notice to the Inland Revenue, in such form as the Board of Inland Revenue may determine, and

    (c)   is irrevocable.

These final comments are taken from Mr Justice Reid's judgment in the Canadian case *UAW* v. *Massey-Ferguson* (1979):

The question of the interpretation of the word 'must' in a collective agreement has come before the courts on only two occasions known to counsel. In both of those cases, it was held that 'must' was mandatory.

No case has been cited to us in which 'must' has ever been otherwise interpreted.

The word 'must' is a common imperative. It is hard to think of a commoner. There is no dictionary of stature of which I am aware that accords to the word any other connotation. In its present or future tense, it expresses command, obligation, duty, necessity and inevitability. This is so according to the Oxford dictionaries, from the Pocket through the Concise & Shorter to the O.E.D. itself.

I can find nothing but confirmation for this in Roget's Thesaurus.

In contrast, the word 'shall' is an equivocal word that can express either command or simple futurity.

Since 'must' bears only one meaning, an imperative one, it is inappropriate and unnecessary to search in the context for something that strengthens it.

However, for those who cannot bear (or are not allowed) to draft with *must*, we offer a shortcut to avoid some of the confusion. Write the first draft using *must*, not *shall*. Then, when the document is ready, change every *must* to *shall*. You will find you have used it only for obligations.

Abstract words

Abstract words refer to concepts. Concrete words refer to things you can point to, so are easier to grasp.

Another unfortunate tendency of traditional legal writing and modern jargon is to replace concrete and specific words with abstract generalities. As much as possible is standardised to save thought. So we have *mortgage products, insurance products,* and *this product* instead of *mortgages, insurance policies,* and *these peas,* losing all shades of meaning in the interests of uninformative uniformity. In the same way, these goods and services are *delivered* by ubiquitous *providers,* rather than supplied by *lenders, insurers,* and *greengrocers* (so the language will be ready when we order them all online from the same superstore).

Delivery is no longer by a van coming to the door. We even *deliver on* our promises instead of *keeping* them, and we are expected to *deliver a quality product* (using three pretentious, inappropriate, polysyllabic words) rather than *give a good service* (the plain, appropriate alternative). *Quality* is useful in its traditional role as an abstract noun but we don't need a three-syllable synonym for the adjective *good*.

> **MA:** A minicab with the slogan *We deliver destinations* tempted me to ask the driver to bring me Gatwick Airport.

Solutions has been used by all sorts of suppliers who sometimes mystify the public by failing to indicate their trade, which can't be good for business. Now the word is incorporated into law firms' names and mission statements with such verbose and clumsy titles as *ABC Claim Solutions Solicitors.* What do they solve that other firms do not?

Issues have been vaguely extended from their useful role as the contested points in dispute, and must be *addressed,* even if we don't really know what we're talking about. For instance, did *until the issue of IRA criminality is addressed* mean *until the IRA stops committing crimes, until someone stops them committing crimes,* or just *until someone starts thinking about it*? Are the now-ubiquitous *issues* problems, points in dispute, doubts, questions, or something else? What relationship do *issues around X* have to X?

This lack of precision is the enemy of thought.

Clichés

What's wrong with clichés

Spike Milligan called clichés *the handrail of the crippled mind*. We think of them as stepping-stones – words forming a pre-ordained route which the writer must follow even if led off-course.

With modern communications, expressions like John Major's nebulous *back to basics* become almost instant clichés when they go viral and are used to signal group membership rather than to convey meaning. *Going viral*, in contrast, is a useful neologism and was – until the effect wore off – a vivid metaphor.

Clichés give readers the message that you have nothing new to say, and that you are not bothering to think. Would you want a lawyer like that?

Types of cliché

Some clichés add a useless word to one with meaning:

brand new	**new**
full right	**right**
learn lessons	**learn**
mutually agreed	**agreed**
potentially dangerous	**dangerous**

Others add by habit a word that has come to be associated with the useful word, even when it is inappropriate in the circumstances. So we routinely hear of a:

Health warning, for a warning that has nothing to do with health;

Laundry (or *shopping*) *list*, when a different sort of list is meant;

Marketplace, when *market* is meant, rather than the place at which it is held;

Price tag, when the price is meant, rather than the label on which it is written;

Question mark for question;

Road map, when another sort of map is meant;

Success story, when it's the event on which we are focused, rather than a narrative about it. (In the same way that we used to say *It's a success* we still say *It's a failure*, and never *It's a failure story*.)

Track record, when a different sort of record is intended.

Other vague and inelegant clichés call for re-writing rather than just omission, notably

in terms of

a *Blank* v. *Waffle* situation

Some clichés show an ignorance of the meaning of words (an inadvisable failing in an expensive professional writer). For example:

A window of opportunity (in which *window* is intended to indicate that the opportunity is for a limited time although that is already implicit in the meaning of *opportunity*)

and

He literally got the government out of a hole it dug itself into

In the worst examples, the lack of thought is given away by careless metaphors, whose literal meaning distracts the reader:

A falling marketplace

Back me, or the grass roots will rise up (populist politician warns about triffids)

Cutting edge (but non-surgical) treatment for myeloma

Government 'tried to bury' report on Temple Mount excavations

The Teflon Don finally comes unstuck

When your back's against the wall, turn round and fight

Last year we were on the edge of an abyss. This year we have taken a giant leap forward.

Metaphor should be used to elucidate a difficult point, or to provide a memorable image, but it should not distract or mislead:

The ball is in Cuban hands and the door is ajar

The prime minister is in the driving seat in terms of delivering a UN resolution

Hold the fort in terms of moving the business forward (= 'Making progress in a stationary sort of way'?)

As George Orwell said in his essay 'Politics and the English language':

> This invasion of one's mind by ready-made phrases … can only be prevented if one is constantly on guard against them, and every such phrase anaesthetises a portion of one's brain.

Many solicitors have adopted the vacuous *mission statements* whose mere existence, let alone the content, is a cliché, though the inaccurate platitudes of advertising puff contrast unfavourably with the rigour and integrity of professionalism. To give a typical (though at least concise) example (distorted to protect the perpetrators) a firm that seemed unusually *un*caring proudly boasted *We care*, as though the rest of the profession do not. Another firm, now defunct, adopted the catchphrase *Your satisfaction is our reputation*, a poorly expressed banality that did nothing to distinguish them from their competitors.

Two hundred years after William Wilberforce, what were once people with their own lives and humanity have been downgraded to their employers' *human resources* (instead of the plainer and more dignified *staff*). This is so even in solicitors' offices, where the employers ought to know better.

Pronouns

Traditional drafters are reluctant to use the usual short, useful, familiar pronouns which help avoid repetition.

They will repeat nouns, despite the clumsiness, or replace them with lawyers' own artificial pronouns, 'the same' and 'such'. The example on p.105 had a good instance:

> … utilise the rest of the monies for the good cause for which she bequeathed the same.

Dispensing with the other jargon in that line, a translation into English would read

> … use the rest of the money for the good cause for which she left it.

Even more gauche is:

> We shall let you have the Request for Further and Better Particulars as soon as such has been settled by Counsel.

Of course, you must watch out for ambiguity before using a pronoun, but that is a danger only if there is more than one noun to which it might refer. Where there is risk of confusion, neither 'such' nor 'the same' will avoid it.

While on the subject of pronouns, may we make a plea for *I*? Writers go to inordinate lengths to avoid it by referring to themselves indirectly as *the writer* or *the present writer*. Since you can only mean *I*, you might as well bite the bullet and use the word.

A similar habit, coupled with deference to the supposedly senior profession, still affects instructions to barristers, in which *I* is replaced by *Instructing Solicitor* and *you* by *Counsel*, so that

Instructing Solicitor represents the Claimant and Counsel is asked to advise

is longhand for

I represent the claimant. Please advise

which could be reduced to

Please advise the claimant.

> **MA:** This word-processor input facilitator, then a sole practitioner, was reprimanded by a young solicitor for writing *I* in correspondence. He thought I should say *we* to show that I was not identifying too closely with my client. I said that I wrote *I* because there was only one of me and I was not the Queen, but some time later he complained again. He overlooked the possibility that if I had been plural, we could all have identified with our client.

There is some logic to using *we* when writing in the name of a firm, and of course it is the natural pronoun when there is more than one author. But however many partners you have, it sounds pompous to write as though they have all collaborated in your email or letter, and this inappropriate *we* creates an impersonal tone. We prefer *I* (which is neither immodest nor ungrammatical) for emails and letters, with the writer's name given on the letterhead or at the end. It is pleasanter to deal with Mrs Brown than with reference KB.4/F/02938, and it saves time when you telephone.

But a word of caution when replacing names with pronouns.

Bill said that John had been there and that John had seen Bill.

In casual speech we would use pronouns rather than repeat names in this context. But if we rewrite this as

Bill said that John had been there and that he had seen him

we cannot tell who saw whom. On the other hand, there would be no problem (would there?) with

Leslie said that Lesley had been there and that she had seen him.

Prepositions

Prepositions are the (usually short and familiar) words like *in*, *at*, *by*, *for*, and *of*, explaining the relationship between two things. They are useful when properly used but otherwise indicate wordy writing. Many of the redundancies on pp.132–6 include prepositions. Here are some more examples:

> Prior *to* the signing *of* the agreement (= 'before signing the agreement' (*or* 'before the agreement was signed'))
>
> *By* reason *of* the matters aforesaid (= 'consequently')
>
> *under* or *by* virtue *of* the provisions *of* this Act (= '*under* this Act')

or, to borrow (and Anglicise) an example given by Garner (whose insight this point was):

> The defendant is contending that delays *on* the part *of* Penney have resulted *in* delays *by* the defendant (= 'The defendant claims that Penney's delays have caused the defendant's delays')

Over-prepositioning can be caused by the unnecessary use of passive verbs (p.124) or by nominalisation (p.132).

Some redundant prepositions can be omitted without rewording what is left:

> ~~as~~ from
>
> off ~~of~~
>
> stop X ~~from~~ doing
>
> weigh ~~in at~~

Some prepositions are more vague and wordy than others. *With regard to* and *in relation to* have long left the precise relationship unclear. *About* and *around* are now commonly used to express vaguely a relationship between two things so that neither writer nor reader need consider what that relationship is nor who is to do what:

> Economic recovery is as much about confidence as it is about deficit financing.

A clumsy though accurate construction is

> … a memorandum of the order shall be endorsed or permanently annexed on or to the probate …

Sometimes, if a third verb governs yet another preposition, the result is even more pedantic, to give something like this fictitious example:

… a memorandum of the order shall be endorsed, permanently annexed or otherwise linked on, to or with the probate …

The grammar is faultless but the style is pompous and wordy. It is difficult to unravel because there is too much distraction between each verb and its preposition. And sometimes this form is absurd. One house-buyer was asked to covenant *not to erect or grow any wall fence hedge or other division*; and a landlord unintentionally committed himself by a similar barbarism to *decorate the foundations* and was lucky that his subsequently disgruntled tenant didn't hold him to it. The easiest way around this problem is to put each word with its pair, keeping auxiliary words with their principal. But it might be neater to rewrite the sentence, if you can find a way. One possibility is to combine the sense of the different verbs into the single verb; in this case the best we can think of is *add*:

… a memorandum of the order must be added to the probate.

But we do not think that is good enough, and prefer

… a memorandum of the order must be filed with the probate or endorsed on it.

Emphasis

Avoid extremes: they may erode your credibility and can provoke disagreement:

Our clients are totally unhappy.

Your version is completely inaccurate.

Total unhappiness is a Platonic ideal to which few can have aspired (though Job and Eeyore deserve honourable mention). And a solicitor was accused of writing a *totally inaccurate* letter which began uncontroversially *I have received your 10 September letter* and continued by putting his client's case.

Even if it doesn't undermine the complainer's credibility or provoke disagreement, emphasis is best avoided. For example, suppose you read that an argument is *very strong*. How much stronger is the argument than if the writer had said only that it was *strong*? The extra word gives no new information. Delete it, or be specific (the argument has a better than 70 per cent chance of success). The following advice is sometimes attributed to Mark Twain:

Substitute 'damn' every time you're inclined to write 'very'; your editor will delete it and the writing will be just as it should be.

The same is true of *really, particularly, significantly* and many other adverbs; and of *obvious, shocking, terrible* and many other adjectives.

Writers are sometimes advised to improve their writing by deleting all adverbs or adjectives. This is absurd: both have a useful role. But the advice followed selectively offers a shortcut to detecting over-emphasis and redundancy.

We'll return to the drawbacks of overstating your case and to the value of being specific in the next chapter.

Hedging

Traditionally reluctant to say what they mean, the British tend to veer from one extreme to the other, replacing over-emphasis with the mealy-mouthed euphemism of those too genteel to condemn, as in *perhaps not quite so good* when they mean *awful*. *Perhaps*? *Not quite*? We call this *the wimp's doubt*. Sometimes things *are* bad, and accuracy and integrity require us to say so. Zoologists who expect to be taken seriously would not say *Elephants weigh about five tons; mice are perhaps not quite so heavy*, however anxious they *may or may not be* not to offend rodents.

Careful lawyers rightly question the accuracy of their assertions. And among the points that should be checked is the degree of authority with which the statement can be made. Can I say that? How do I know it? What evidence have I got? Is it always true? How long will it take me to check? Does it matter if there are exceptions? No? Then I'll qualify it with *usually* or *sometimes* (as appropriate) and move on.

The trouble starts when, through habit or example, a lawyer qualifies statements without thought, introducing vagueness and avoiding responsibility. The passive voice contributes to this style, with *it is said that* or, more tentatively, *it has been suggested that* or *it may be considered to be.* With every *perhaps* and *possibly* the text and writer lose authority, certainty, and credibility. Moreover, it is meaningless, but common, to compare X with *perhaps* Y, as in

John has as many as perhaps Bill does

instead of

Perhaps John has as many as Bill does,

since *perhaps* always implies *perhaps not*.

Endnotes

1   Electronic Governance – Page 187 – Google Books Result (17 August 1999); Patent US4315244 – Vehicle alarms – Google Patents (17 August 1979).
2   **www.gov.uk/government/uploads/system/uploads/attachment_data/file/ 622457/drafting_guidance_june_2017.pdf.**

Chapter 19

Persuasion

Much of lawyers' writing – not just speech – is (or should be) intended to persuade. For example:

- Letters to clients should persuade them to accept your advice.
- Letters to opponents should persuade them and their clients to accept your point of view (or, if it is a dispute which goes to trial, should persuade the judge that you had been reasonable).
- Pleadings and written evidence should similarly persuade the other side or (failing that) the trial judge (although this takes second place to their main functions of defining the dispute and presenting the facts).
- In non-contentious work, draft documents should persuade the other party to accept them unamended.
- A judgment should persuade the parties (and, if necessary, appeal courts) that the judge has listened attentively and correctly applied the law to the evidence.

Any document should persuade its readers that it would be a waste of their time to try to challenge its effect.

Following the guidelines in this and similar books should by itself make your writing more persuasive. It will help you produce:

- an attractively presented document;
- step-by-step arguments;
- text in manageable chunks;
- transparent vocabulary; and
- a suitable tone.

So, your arguments are more likely to be read than those in a traditional document, and more likely to be understood. This gives you an advantage over a writer whose arguments are either not read, or if read merely bewilder.

But there is more. We believe that a fresh, unpompous style will incline readers to like (or at least respect) you; and that either liking or respect will incline them to accept what you say. Legalese alienates readers and can provoke resistance.

Here is a letter written by solicitors newly instructed by a landlord to manage its property. Until then the landlord (a one-person company) had dealt directly with the tenant. The rent had always been paid on time; there was no dispute between them; and they were on reasonably friendly terms, having been neighbours for years. The plan was to ask the tenant to pay the rent by standing order (though the lease did not require that) and to pay the tenant's share of the insurance premium (which was not payable until the following quarter day).

> Dear Sirs
>
> We are instructed to act on behalf of your Landlord, K ... Properties Ltd.
>
> We should be obliged if you would arrange for all future rental payments to be made by Standing Order to K ... Properties Ltd, Account ...
>
> We would advise you that you are also liable for a rateable proportion of the cost of insuring the above premises. There is a further insurance rental due therefore in the sum of £200. We should be pleased to receive a cheque in respect thereof, forthwith.
>
> Yours faithfully

The tenant was so irritated by the peremptory tone that he checked his lease, and was delighted to find that the landlord was not entitled to a standing order or (until the next quarter day) to the £200. He therefore refused both.

It seems from the use of this example in seminars that this was not the isolated reaction of a difficult tenant; the question 'What would your reaction be to this letter?' routinely produced the answer (to the landlord, not the speaker) 'Get stuffed!'

The solicitor, like many in the profession who habitually write hostile letters, was perfectly amiable on the telephone; he had not realised that the tone of his letter was alienating.

On p.17 we quoted the disparaging reactions to a typical letter from a solicitor (reported in Adler (1991)). The letter ended:

> If you are in agreement with this, we should be grateful if you would let us know as soon as possible so that the appropriate Deed can be drawn up for your respective signatures

and a selection of lay people were asked:

> If you received a letter like this from your spouse's solicitor, and it reflected the terms you had agreed informally, would you do as they ask?

Only 25 said 'Yes'; 48 said 'No'.

What more can you do to make your writing persuasive? We offer a few suggestions in no particular order.

Be (and be seen to be) honest and accurate

Being caught in a lie or exaggeration will undermine the credibility of everything else you say. This increases the burden of proving any contested fact, decreases the likelihood that you will be given the benefit of any doubt, and weakens any argument based on your word.

It is also likely to lose you the sympathy of any tribunal, reducing the likelihood that it will find for you in this or any other doubtful case.

Frank admission of valid points against you has the opposite effect, as shown in a study comparing the effect of damaging information when used against a litigant, and when revealed by that litigant first. The authors concluded that revealing the damaging information improved the litigant's credibility, leading to better outcomes (Williams & Croyle, 1993).

Minimise the differences between you

The smaller the gap between opposing positions, the easier it is to bridge it. So, minimise the differences between you. Most important, ensure that you start from shared premises.

If your arguments are based on the assumption that your client's interests are paramount, or that your client's account of disputed facts is correct, nothing you say can persuade your opponent to accept your conclusions.

If, on the other hand, you base your arguments on the assumption that both clients will benefit from a fair outcome, you have the makings of a settlement. Then you have a chance to help your client by persuading the other side that your proposals *are* fair (or, perhaps more persuasively, better than the opponent would do at trial).

Meet all counter-arguments

To convince your opponents that your client is right, or that your opponents would do well to accept your proposal, you must evaluate the evidence objectively, refuting or giving credit for any counter-argument. Failure to do this will lead to the conclusion that you have overlooked the weakness in your case; your opponents will then either point it out triumphantly or soldier confidently on, convinced (with some justification) that you are an idiot and that your client will lose at trial.

If you lack integrity you might gamble on the hope that your opponent will not spot the weakness, but it is a dangerous game. Even if the opposing litigant and solicitor have missed it, counsel might not; nor is it likely that the judge will; and by that time you will be in trouble over costs. If *you* can see the difficulty, why should they not, helped by their lesser predisposition to your client's welfare? It is safer and more ethical to state the facts and reasons that counter the objection, although you may not need to do your opponents the favour of spelling out the objection for them.

Surprisingly often, opponents reply to an argument by saying they disagree, or that they *refute* the argument. But if it is to convince anyone the refutation must explain the error. Both your opponent and the judge will automatically dismiss an assertion unless it is supported by objective reasons and evidence.

Help the persuadee

Most parties want to avoid the stress of litigation and its cost in money and time. They want to feel that their grievances have been heard and given due weight. In both contentious and non-contentious negotiations the parties want to get out of the hands of lawyers and on with their lives as soon as possible. They want to feel that the outcome is fair. They don't want to lose face. So craft proposals that will come as close as possible to satisfying everyone. Aim to convince your opponents that you are offering the best outcome they are likely to get. Look at the dispute or disagreement from the point of view of the person you're trying to persuade. Forget why *you* want what it is you're arguing for, and try to show what's in it for them.

Judges generally want to do justice, apply the law, and avoid being reversed on appeal. To help them, quote legislation or binding authority; show them the moral merit of your case; base your arguments on unappeal-able facts.

Questions can be powerful. Readers tend to prefer their own ideas to anyone else's. While suggesting a conclusion makes your argument clear, getting the reader to form that conclusion can be better. For example, if you believe a conclusion is unjustified, you might say *There is no evidence to support that conclusion*, but it would be better to ask *What is your evidence for that conclusion?* (Sometimes, the reader may surprise you by producing an answer. In that case, you will not have gained the point you expected but you will have gained useful information.)

What should you do if, despite your best efforts, you cannot make a persuasive case for your clients? Advise them to settle. They will probably do so anyway, at the door of the court if not sooner, and the less the wasted costs the better.

Don't overstate your case

There is nothing to be gained from asserting that your case is stronger than you can establish by argument. It will not fool anyone, and you will lose credibility.

Minimising the difference between you and your opponents means setting the bar no higher than it needs to be. If all you need to prove is that an error was made, what do you gain from suggesting it was inexcusable or deliberate? The extra accusation is likely to provoke resistance.

Over-emphasis can undermine the argument it is intended to reinforce, making it harder for your opponents to agree with you. If they have got something wrong, what do you gain from suggesting it was *clearly* wrong? You are asking them to admit not only that they made a mistake, but that it was an obvious mistake; not only that they are wrong, but also that they are stupid. If it really is clear, they can see that for themselves. But it probably isn't, or you wouldn't be having the argument.

MA: My father (to whom I was articled) once said that he could always tell when I didn't know what I was talking about because I became dogmatic. His anecdotal insight has since been supported by experiment: Kuhn & others (1994) played the recording of a murder trial to mock jurors, questioned them in detail about the reasons for their subsequent 'verdicts', and found that *more competent reasoning was associated with lower certainty*. Which brings us to the next point …

Be specific

Facts convince; assertions don't. In Garner's (1999, p.333) words, expanding on the advice *Show, don't tell*:

> Don't say that something is unfair; show why it is, and let the reader conclude that it is …
> If you follow this advice, you'll find yourself being more concrete, more careful in marshalling facts, more adept at arousing the very emotions you feel.

For example, suppose a claimant has got judgment and wants a freezing order to help enforce it. The judge needs evidence to decide whether there is really a risk that the defendant's assets will disappear if not frozen. The evidence supporting the application might say:

> The claimant is extremely concerned that, unless the court grants a freezing order, the defendant will dispose of its assets to defeat the judgment. This fear is based on the defendant's reponse to the claim, the location and movability of his assets, and the history of insolvent liquidations defeating the claims of creditors of his wholly-owned companies.

Being more specific, the applicant might have said:

> In the last six years, the defendant has owned four companies in the financial services business, three of which have entered insolvent liquidation, leaving unpaid debts exceeding $15 million. His present business is based in Ukraine. It has few fixed assets and its main income of commissions from high net worth clients could easily be

157

diverted. When the present claim was first raised, the defendant said 'You can sue if you like – don't think you will ever see a penny of it' (see the transcript at page x of exhibit XX1).

If you were the judge, which version would you find more convincing?

Help readers understand an abstract argument by applying it to familiar facts. Use names rather than generic expressions like *the first defendant*. Garner (1999) offers this example:

> At 7:30 one morning last spring, Father Michael Prynne, a Roman Catholic priest, was on his way to buy food for himself at the grocery store when his car collided with Ed Grimley's pickup truck. The Catholic Church neither owned Father Prynne's car nor required its priests to buy groceries as part of their priestly functions. Was Father Prynne acting as an agent for the Church at the time of the accident?

Develop your arguments in logical steps

It is not enough to put all your arguments in; you must do so coherently. Build your case in an orderly manner, step by step, moving from what is familiar to the reader to what is not. An argument is less persuasive when it takes for granted facts or connections that are obvious to the writer but not to the reader. Spelling them out makes it easier for your readers to follow the argument and harder for them to dissent from it. It will also help you notice any weakness in your position (in which case go back to *Meet all counter-arguments*). The extract from Lord Scarman's judgment on p.67 is a skilful example of this process.

Although this approach works well when the reader is hostile to your conclusions, other methods may be just as logical and more suitable in other contexts. Armstrong and Terrell (2015) suggest various other possibilities, including:

- Stating a conclusion, and then backing it up (for a reader who is inclined to accept your conclusions, as when you are advising a client).
- Setting up a debate or choice (to encourage the reader to make an informed decision).

Use visual aids

A picture is said to be worth a thousand words. In fact, any type of image might be better than any number of words: sight-bites can be more persuasive than sound-bites.

This weapon, like any other, can be misused. For example, just as statistics can be manipulated in their numerical form they can sway readers unfairly in pictorial format. The impact of a graph can be adjusted, as illustrated by those at Figure 19.1, by:

- Changing the scale of one axis to alter the gradient from dramatically steep to reassuringly gentle, or vice versa;
- Changing the range of an axis (from, say, 0–100 to 90–100) to make differences look more significant; or
- Changing the frequency of the sampling (for example, whether the figures are daily, weekly, monthly, quarterly, or annual) to emphasise or hide a short-term dip.

Figure 19.1

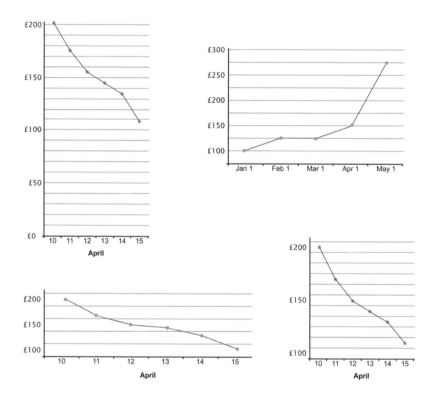

Consider your reader's needs

Many readers are short of time; most have pleasanter things to do than read your prose. Give them the key messages straight away: *What does this writer want? Why should I do it? What will happen if I don't?* Relegate the details and other material to later sections, well-signposted with headings. English judges, in particular, have for years been pleading with the writers of litigation documents to respect their time and give them only the information they need to do their job. Why irritate them by ignoring this? And

159

why increase the risk that they'll miss the golden needle buried under the dross? Do everything you can to reduce length and help the reader.

Judges and other decision-makers also need respect for their authority. Their job is to decide the questions the parties bring to them. They get annoyed if one party or another tells them what to do (and most people are annoyed if you tell them what to think). Statements of fact, suggestions, and questions are more acceptable. Garner (1999) recommends that in a written argument for the court you:

> Write fair but persuasive issues that have only one answer. Cast each one as a syllogism. And when you have multiple issues ... preface each one with a concise, neutral heading.

Written evidence

Evidence should be, as far as possible, accurate, complete, relevant, coherent (therefore well organised), easily understandable, and concise. Errors should be corrected and apparent inconsistencies explained. Lawyers have an additional duty to their clients to ensure that the evidence is as persuasive as possible. On the other hand, in civil litigation in England and Wales, Practice Directions 32.4.1 and 32.18.1 tell us that written evidence *must, if practicable, be in the [witness's] own words.* This means, as Toulson J emphasised in *Aquarius* v. *Lloyds* (2001) para.46:

> the words which the witness wants to use and not the words which the person taking the statements would like him to use.

Lawyers routinely draft witness statements in language that only a lawyer would use. If they would draft evidence as we recommend the statements would be more useful, and perhaps more compliant with the practice direction.

Two examples

Here (slightly changed) is a letter which, with the carefully prepared defence and counter-claim, persuaded a formerly robust litigant to abandon his claim without payment:

Dear Mr Gunner
Thank you for your letter of the 23rd.
When you telephoned, apparently in response to my 26 October fax, you said that the Wilsons' offer was unacceptable but that we were 'not far apart' and you invited them to increase it. I made it absolutely clear in my 16 August letter that I was not going to negotiate that way. Instead I invited you to make a counter-offer. You said you were not able to do that without considering the file but that you would write to me. You did not do so until 23 November. So the complaint in your letter that we have

let matters slip is wrong. It is clear from your letter that you do not have a note of that conversation but are relying on your memory, and that that is unreliable. This encourages the Wilsons to be optimistic about the outcome of any trial.

Your conduct of these negotiations has also been erratic: on 3 August you offered to accept £14,000; when on 16 August I counter-offered £7,000 you asked for £17,000, denying that it was more than you had sought before. This reinforces the Wilsons' confidence that you would make a poor witness.

Since you rejected their £7,000 offer they have prepared a careful counter-claim and have spent a substantial amount on legal fees in doing so. They now feel that they have a strong case and are increasingly disinclined to make concessions – especially while it seems that you are having difficulty supplying the information in my 21 October request. However, they will agree that both sides now drop their respective claims if you pay their costs (to be assessed by the court if not agreed). But this offer will remain open only until 4 pm on 2 December.

Yours sincerely

The letter is not as terse as it might have been but the detail was helpful. It covered the tactical dispute while the defence and counter-claim had dealt with the merits.

DP: I can offer another example from my first year of practice at the Bar. I was asked to help produce a deliberately aggressive letter about some proposals for organising the copy documents for trial. I was proud of my draft, which I remember mentioned *these pointless collections of photocopies*. The client was pleased with the tone. However, we did not get co-operation over our proposals for trial and I personally regretted my draft when I finally saw the point of the copy documents.

Chapter 20

Editing

I saw the angel in the marble and carved until I set it free.
Michelangelo (1475–1564)

Before you send out any document, however brief, you should read it with the ear of the recipient, and re-read it after any alterations. Our minds tend to run along rails, especially during familiar activities. When editing, we need to get off the train and look at what we're saying from different perspectives.

You need to check that:

- There are no clerical errors.
- You have made all the points you want to.
- They are in a sensible order.
- There is nothing superfluous.
- No part of the document is (or sounds as though it might be) inconsistent with another part, or with the available evidence.
- All numbers, dates, names, and facts are correct.
- No change has spoilt other parts of the text (for instance, by using a word which already appears nearby, or unnecessarily repeating an idea expressed elsewhere in the document).
- The formatting is consistent.
- It sounds and looks right for your purposes, both stylistically and in its tone.

The need to read with the ear of your reader is particularly important when considering the tone. Will your readers react as you want them to?

However often you check the document on screen, always read the hard copy. It is surprising how often errors appear at this stage when they have been lurking, despite previous checks, in the blind spot under your nose. Beware in particular changes imposed automatically and without your knowledge by your computer's settings, especially if you edit your stylesheets. The *replace all* command is dangerous.

A sensible precaution for a complicated or sensitive document is to ask someone else to check it. If you must check your own work and time allows, leave it at least overnight and if possible a lot longer, so that you come back to it as a new reader. Here is the advice of two outstanding writers who specialise in making difficult text comprehensible:

> When I finish a business letter (these days I type my own), I'll hand it to two or three colleagues – perhaps to the two lawyers who work at Lawprose ... and to an intern ... – and ask them to proofread it for me. But I don't stop there. I insist that each reader find two suggested improvements before giving it back to me. No one is allowed to say, 'It looks alright to me; I didn't find anything'.[1]
>
> Whenever I write I have a particular imaginary reader in mind (different imaginary readers oversee and 'filter' the same passage in numerous successive revisions).[2]

This idea is not new. Michael Foot[3] wrote that:

> In accordance with his custom, [Jonathan] Swift read large chunks [of *Gulliver's Travels*] aloud to his servants, to make sure that every sentence attained his rigorous standard of simplicity.

One (expensive) possibility is to employ a plain language organisation to edit and accredit a much-used document. This takes some of the burden from you, while you can learn from an expert with a view to editing for yourself when you have the skills. Another benefit is a mark of approval on the document, advertising your commitment to clarity – although this will have to be renewed if the document is updated. But choose carefully: not all these organisations have high standards.

Look on suggestions and criticism not as a personal attack on your writing skills but as a constructive contribution to a team effort. If someone tells you that something isn't clear, then it probably isn't – at least to them and so perhaps to some of your final audience. And if they say text is vague or ambiguous then it almost certainly is, even if you can't see it. Keep looking, and if necessary ask them to explain, and don't give up until you can see the problem. Then fix it.

Endnotes

1   Bryan Garner (2009).
2   Richard Dawkins (1989).
3   Michael Foot, in his introduction to the 1967 edition of *Gulliver's Travels* (first published in 1726).

Chapter 21

Computer aids

Why use style-checker software?

Even the best writers are fallible. However carefully they've edited, they can be tormented by mistakes they notice only after publication. Software applies to your text some of the guidelines we have recommended and points out what it thinks are your failings. Sometimes it will be right, and you may want to accept its suggested alternative.

A longer-term advantage, however, especially for firms, is in improving not just a particular piece of text but the overall skill of lawyers who already pride themselves on their writing and think they don't need help. It allows discreet, self-administered, ongoing correction, without the need for superiors or colleagues to criticise; and it provides independent support if inter-personal criticism is needed.

DP: Even able and influential partners usually fail to pass on their own clear writing style to more than a few colleagues. Where they have been successful, in my experience, management has been the vital ingredient, with style-checking software an important tool. Motivation, training, and the revision of templates play a part but I have not seen any organisation succeed in changing its writers' habits without using software. If whoever decides on pay and promotion sets specific achievable writing goals, and then monitors and insists on performance, the team will comply. For the experience of one organisation that did so using StyleWriter software, see plain2015.ie/wp-content/uploads/2015/11/18-Sept-Perry.pdf. (I must declare an interest here. I recommend whatever software I think will work for a user. When a client buys StyleWriter on my recommendation, its makers pay me a commission (which doesn't affect the price to the user). If I thought another program would work better, I would recommend it.)

What software does

By counting words, characters, full stops, and paragraph breaks, software can measure, and offer the writer targeted advice, on:

- **Sentence length.** The software counts the number of whole words between full stops and paragraph breaks. There are differences of detail but most count average sentence length quite fairly. Microsoft Word and other software can also display the word count for selected text. A good style-checker will identify long sentences for the writer to edit, and make the average sentence length visible while editing. It cannot suggest a rewritten sentence.
- **Readability scores.** Most readability scores are based on word and sentence length. On this basis, the software may report a (US) grade level, a recognised readability score, or its own measure of readability. This tells the writer if the document needs editing for length and complexity, and may suggest where to edit, without identifying the changes needed. For more on this, see *What is the use of readability scores?* on the next page.

By recognising word patterns (like a spell-checker), software can highlight and sometimes offer alternatives for:

- **Passive voice.** The software recognises and highlights typical word patterns for passive verb forms, such as *is [verb]ed*. Sometimes it misses an unusual one, or picks up what only looks like a passive verb form, but on the whole this is useful for writers not familiar with passive verbs.
- **Wordy expressions.** For example, the software may offer to replace *in order to* with *to*, or *in respect of* with *about, for, of*, and so on. WordRake inserts these suggestions into a Word document in 'track changes' and does something similar in Outlook. Unfortunately, it does nothing else.
- **Hard words.** Software can highlight whatever long and unfamiliar words are in its vocabulary, and may offer an alternative. Most vocabularies are designed for general use and do not identify or offer alternatives to legal terms, or for words that only lawyers misuse, such as *said, such,* and *shall*.
- **Hidden verbs.** The software may identify nominalisations, with or without suggesting a verb to replace the abstract noun.
- **Empty words.** Some words, perhaps useful in their place, more often add only length without meaning (see Chapter 18 ('Choosing words')). Some software can recognise and highlight these, with or without prompting the writer to delete them.
- **Jargon.** Some software will identify abbreviations, acronyms, and unusual words. Some will detect business jargon such as *granularity* or *in the xxxx piece*. Most have not been programmed to detect legal jargon.
- **Writing patterns added by the user.** Some software allows the user to specify unwanted word patterns and alternatives. It takes skill to use wildcards to catch all the unwanted patterns and nothing else, and to suggest advice and alternatives that will work wherever the patterns appear.

- **Consistency.** Some software will check and compare text for compliance with a style sheet or for internal consistency. This makes only a small difference to clarity, but it might engage support for using the software for other reasons.

Some software allows the user to switch off unwanted advice. For example, one style-checker kept prompting its user, Felicity, to change her name to Joy, until it was taught to ignore the word when written with a capital F. In theory, this feature could be abused, as reluctant users could switch off all the advice. In practice, only a few patterns are usually switched off, and this small amount of control may reconcile a new user to targets set by an employer.

As we write, we know of one style-checker, Acrolinx, that goes beyond recognising word patterns. It can distinguish between the same word used as a noun and a verb, and tailor its advice accordingly.

Most style-checker software is meant for the individual writer to use on one document at a time. But Acrolinx is designed to analyse large numbers of documents.

In future, no doubt style-checkers will appear that can learn from the user's reaction to their suggestions, as predictive text programs do now.

What is the use of readability scores?

The best-known readability statistic is the Flesch test, a summary of which is given at the end of this chapter.[1] As can be seen, it is a function only of the average number of syllables per word and the number of words per sentence. By that over-simplified test

DOG CHUM CAT

is a model of readability, though inarticulate and dangerously ambiguous (at least to those of us who have seen a dog and a cat separated only by a bowl of Chum). Moreover, the test's mathematical complexity is so absurd that we wonder if Flesch was pulling our legs, since the procedure is clearly not precise enough to justify three (or any) places of decimals. You get the same score (or, at worst, rounded to the next whole number) if you multiply the average word length by 85, add the average word length, and deduct both from 207. And a little more tampering could reduce even that misleadingly false precision, so that the penultimate number could be deducted from 200.

Nevertheless, the Flesch test can be a useful rough guide.

> **MA:** My request to clarify one ambiguous clause was brushed aside by my opposite number with the emphatic assertion that his text was 'perfectly clear'. 'How can it be perfectly clear,' I asked, 'when on a scale from 0 (very difficult) to 100 (very easy) it scores minus 263?'

We do not suggest that writing is necessarily good or clear if it meets these tests, nor that a good writer should never make exceptions. You cannot write by numbers. But these scores are fairly reliable, particularly if they are consistent, and if poor they serve as a useful and discreet alert. We suggest that the most useful of the widely-available computer-generated scores, with guideline targets for readability in legal writing, are:

- Average sentence length: target 20 words maximum.
- Flesch score: target 60 minimum.
- Passive verbs: A score over 20 per cent (or more than 20 passive verbs in 100 sentences) may indicate over-use. But regardless of numbers a good writer will check that each one is appropriate and convert any that are not to active voice.

StyleWriter and other software also offer their own measures of readability. You could test these on samples of text from *The Economist* (or a magazine on a serious subject aimed at your main target reader) to see if the software's scores and suggested targets match your needs.

What software doesn't do

Style-checkers are automatons, with limited intelligence and no imagination. They cannot always offer suggestions and their suggestions are not always useful. They cannot detect reasons for the writer's word choice. They make mistakes and lack creative style, so are no substitute for careful editing by a human with an ear for the language. But they are an invaluable second pair of eyes to field our own lapses, to challenge traditional writing styles, and help to train the user in new writing habits.

Software cannot yet analyse the structure and organisation of text. It cannot prompt the writer to add more headings, suggest what those headings should be, or identify misplaced text. Nor can it help with format and layout, beyond allowing list format to reduce average sentence length.[2]

Some software claims to correct its users' grammar. The problem is that it is impossible to reduce the rules of English grammar to a set of coherent mathematical principles based on recognisable word patterns. Software that recognised parts of speech might have more chance. We have not investigated grammar checkers in as much detail as we have style-checkers but those we have seen missed too many mistakes and questioned too much good text to be reliable. One program passed

> The fat. Sat on the mat

(without a closing full stop) as correctly spelt and grammatical with a perfect Flesch score.

Finally, software alone will not change an organisation any more than training or templates alone. It is only as a tool for the committed user, or as required by management, that it can help.

What software should I use?

So far as we can tell, most lawyers in 2017 write in Microsoft Word and Outlook. Anyone writing in Word should make full use of its heading styles and navigation pane. In both Word and Outlook, consider switching on the facility to identify passive verbs, ultra-long sentences and wordiness as you type. (In Word 2016, switch on all the clarity and conciseness categories.)

The help available in Word and Outlook is better than nothing, but it is limited and inconvenient. Its readability settings are buried deep in the menus for checking grammar and style, and its readability scores are available only at the end of a complete spellcheck. Sadly, it ignores many difficult word patterns, such as sentences up to 60 words long; some other suggestions are unhelpful, for example discouraging writers from beginning a sentence with *And*.

For more help, given in a more user-friendly way, try a style-checker. The range and detail of the software is constantly changing so, rather than recommending or reviewing current products, we suggest some questions to help you compare those available.

- **Security and confidentiality.** Does the software upload my text to computer servers outside my control? How is work-in-progress saved?
- **Compatibility.** Does it work with my computer and my other software?
- **What text does it check?** Can it check my emails or only word-processed documents? Does it ignore quoted text? Does it check text in tables?
- **What does it look for?** Does it check sentence length and passive voice? What words or phrases does it identify?
- **What help does it give?** Does it tell me what's wrong with highlighted text? Does it offer alternatives? Can I focus on one writing habit by hiding advice on other points? Is it easy to measure performance against specific writing targets?
- **How can I edit?** Can I view scores and comments while I edit? Can I edit using my usual software, or must I cut and paste text between that and the style-checker?

- **Tailoring.** Can I add word patterns? Can I teach it to stop offering unwanted advice? Is it suitable for my local language?
- **Networking.** Can I run it on a computer network? What are the most common problems for a network? How will it interact with my document management system? How can the firm or individual users tailor networked software?
- **Support.** What IT support does the supplier give?
- **Price.** What does it cost? Is that an annual charge or one-off? Per user? Per computer? How often is it updated? Must I pay for updates?

Armed with these questions, we suggest you shortlist two or three products. If it's a big investment, most software publishers will give you a free trial.

Using the Flesch test[3]

To work out the readability score of a passage of writing using the Flesch test, follow the method set out below.

1 **Count the words**

   Contractions, hyphenated words, abbreviations, figures, and symbols (for example: wouldn't, full-length, TV, 17, &, $15, 7%) all count as single words.

2 **Count the syllables**

   Count the syllables in words as they are spoken, except that abbreviations, figures, symbols and figures count as one-syllable words.

3 **Count the sentences**

   Count as a sentence each full unit of speech ending with a full stop, colon, semicolon, dash, question mark or exclamation mark. Do not count paragraph breaks, colons, semicolons, dashes or initial capitals within a sentence.

4 **Calculate the average number of syllables per word**

   Divide the number of syllables by the number of words.

5 **Calculate the average number of words per sentence**

   Divide the number of words by the number of sentences.

6 **Find your readability score**

   There are two ways to find your readability score:

   - *The formula*
     Multiply the average number of words per sentence by 1.015. Multiply the average number of syllables per word by 84.6. Add

the two numbers. Subtract this sum from 206.835. The balance is your readability score.

(This can be done online.)

- *The Flesch Readability Chart*
  On the chart, draw a straight line from your calculated 'Words per Sentence' to your calculated 'Syllables per Word.' The intersection of this line with the centre column shows your readability score. Flesch considers that 60 is the minimum score for text to qualify as plain.

  (The chart can be found online or in *How To Write Plain English* by Rudolf Flesch (Harper & Row, 1979).)

Endnotes

1   For a detailed study of the origin, testing, and use of this and other readability measures, see *The Principles of Readability* by William DuBay (2004).
2   Law firms can edit contracts in Word, without creating formatting problems or changing the unique appearance of each firm's documents, by using the UK Document Excellence Group's suggested list of Standard Styles for Legal Agreements. This small contribution to clarity of contracts is available at **www.ukdeg.co.uk**.
3   © Rudolf Flesch 1979.

Chapter 22

Testing documents[1]

Why should lawyers test their documents?

Readability formulas and computer software are a quick, easy, routine first test but suffer the inadequacies described in Chapter 21.

The next step is to pay attention to readers' responses. What do they question; what do they miss; what do they misunderstand? How could you edit a much-used document to improve these results? And how could you improve your writing habits to reduce these problems in future?

Formal testing is time-consuming and expensive and is therefore rarely possible for legal documents. But it should be considered when the cost of misunderstanding would be high.

How can lawyers test their documents?

Informal testing is simple. You show someone the document (anonymised if necessary) to check that it achieves its purpose. For example, does the document convey the message you want? Does it say anything that confuses or counters that message?

The simplest way to test a document is to ask a colleague to review the draft. For example, suppose you have drafted a written argument for use in court tomorrow. You might ask a colleague to read it from the judge's point of view and mark up what sounds convincing and what provokes their scepticism.

It is best to ask someone as much like the intended reader as possible. For example, suppose you've written a marketing piece. Email the draft to a few client contacts, asking for their advice. Their comments will improve the text and the process of seeking and accepting their views will help build the client relationship. If the document is aimed at lawyers, ask a lawyer friend or colleague to read it. If the intended reader is a non-lawyer, ask someone unused to legal documents: a friend, perhaps, if your client's confidentiality is protected, or one of your support staff.

It is helpful to the reviewer, and gives better results, if you spell out what you need to know. Depending on the document and the reviewer, this might vary widely, though you are always looking for the impact on the reader. You might ask them to point out anything you've said that looks odd. Or you might ask more specific questions: Does it leave any of the reader's questions unanswered, or raise new questions? Are the suggestions workable in practice?

At a Clarity meeting in 2016, Caroline Jarrett demonstrated the 'pens of power': one technique used by the Government Digital Service to test gov.uk webpages.[2] It's easy and quick. You give the reader two pens, and ask them to highlight in different colours the things that promote the document's purpose, and those that don't. Mrs Jarrett suggests these examples of useful questions, according to the purpose of the document. If it is:

- **To give an answer:** one pen for text that helps with the answer and another for text that doesn't.
- **To explain a duty:** one pen for text that helps to explain, another for text that confuses.
- **To create confidence:** one pen for text that increases confidence and another for text that creates doubt.

Or, if you are more concerned to check whether text is understandable, she suggests you could ask the reader to highlight familiar and unfamiliar words. Once the reader has marked up the text, it can be illuminating to ask them to explain why they marked it as they did. That can often suggest what changes to make.

Ask questions that can only be answered correctly if the reader has understood. This can reveal a surprising level of hidden incomprehension as to the significance of the information as well as the literal meaning of the words, even with intelligent and well-educated readers (Adler, 1991). It can also reveal alternative meanings arising from your own ambiguity or vagueness interpreted from the reviewer's different perspective.

You can also assess the intended readers' emotional reaction to the document and to you.

Don't assume that your consequent changes have fixed the document. You might need to test again.

Running a timed test

Organisations rewriting important documents are often reluctant to test the results. The time already spent in writing and editing might rule out further delay or expense, especially if it is only to confirm the value of the work already done. But the confirmation could encourage work on other documents.

Testing can support a decision to start rewriting an organisation's most used documents. We suggest rewriting just 200 words of text using all the techniques in this book. Then carry out a timed test on typical readers who are not already familiar with either version. It's easy to include as part of a workshop on effective writing. It takes about 10 or 15 minutes and is an excellent teaching exercise if you follow it up with discussion about the different effect of the two versions and what writing techniques made the difference.

For the simplest version of this test, set up an exercise similar to the 'Reader's needs' exercise on p.228. Set readers a simple question to test the intended effect of the document, such as *What does the writer want?* or *What should I do now?* Half have the original version, half the rewritten one. Set a stopwatch going on screen and ask each participant to note on their copy of the text their answer and the time when they knew it. You can then compare the accuracy of the answers and the time it took to reach them. Perhaps a colleague can do this analysis while you discuss the difference between the two versions. Then announce the results, which will confirm what the participants have experienced as they did the exercise. And you will have data to show that, even in less than a page of text, you can make it noticeably quicker and easier for the reader to get the key message.

To demonstrate the value of plain writing techniques, but without reference to your own documents, you could use the original and rewritten text on pp.232–3.

Larger studies and academic research

The tests we have described so far are quick and easy enough for any good writer or trainer to do, and demand little from the reader. The test described on p.17 (Adler, 1991) was more demanding in time and effort. More extensive studies and academic research have also been carried out. A legal writer may hope to find in these studies evidence to support or disprove the value of specific writing techniques, or for plain language generally. We mention just a few studies that have collected and presented research evidence for use in this way.

From 1978 to 1981 the Document Design Project in the USA gathered evidence of what would improve communications and did new studies to fill gaps in the research. One result was *Guidelines for document designers*, a compilation of guidelines with citations to the relevant research (Felker and others, 1981).

In *Writing for Dollars, Writing to Please*, Professor Joseph Kimble has summarised 73 projects and studies, as evidence of the value of plain language in law and business.

In 2012, the Office of the Parliamentary Counsel and the National Archives conducted extensive user testing on legislation. They were looking for evidence of the user's experience of UK legislation published online and whether particular drafting techniques could help improve comprehension. So far as the drafters could draw useful conclusions from this research, they have changed their guidance and practice. However, the report also shows how difficult it is to isolate and test the effect of a single drafting technique (Bertlin, 2014).

Which documents should we test?

We can't test every email. But lawyers know which are their high-stakes documents, worth extra investment in writing and editing.

Endnotes

1   For a more detailed review of the options, see Mowat (2015, Chapter 5).
2   For more information, see **userresearch.blog.gov.uk/2014/09/02/a-simple-technique-for-evaluating-content**.

Part D

How misunderstandings arise

Chapter 23

Vagueness

We have been concentrating on the imprecision of legalese but many expressions that would be considered plain English are equally vague.

For instance, how precise is *precise*? Euclidean geometry and Newton's mechanics were thought to describe the world with absolute precision until increasingly sophisticated instruments showed that they were slightly inaccurate.

In the familiar, everyday world of precise legal texts, a parcel of land *100 metres long* might measure 100.1 metres; and a parcel more precisely described as 100.0001 metres might in reality be 100.0000009 metres long.

In *OFT* v. *Foxtons* (2009), Mann J held that the terms *associated* and *connected* were too vague in their context – the letting agent's standard terms of contract – to be *plain and intelligible* to their client landlords:

> When similar words are used in statutes they are closely defined (see for example the Insolvency Act 1986) … Without some form of definition they are vague words. That is not to say that a court could not give them a meaning or apply them if it had to. The point is not that they are void for legal uncertainty. The point is that they are too vague to be classed as plain and intelligible. How far do they go? A spouse almost certainly; but a spouse's relative? How far up, down or sideways in a family chain does the expression take one? A company of which the tenant is the sole shareholder may well be connected or associated, but what about a lesser shareholding? What of a company by whom he has long been employed? On one reading of the clause the link is capable of being forged by more removed connections – it would cover the situation where X is connected with company C which is connected to tenant T.

Can a landlord object to a tenant's advertisement when the lease permits only a *small* sign showing the name and nature of the business? 'That's small,' says the tenant. 'No, it isn't,' says the landlord. Unless the sign is so disproportionate to the size of the building that the outcome could not be (much) in doubt, few landlords would consider the problem worth the expense and risk of litigation, so the clause is unenforceable. A drafter with forethought would specify the maximum size in the lease.

The *Shorter Oxford English Dictionary* has over 2,600 pages; *shorter* is not the same as *short*. Nor should *older* be the same as *old*, unless we want to surrender a useful distinction to the fashionable euphemism.

There are no categories in nature. We impose them on the world to help us make sense of it, and words help us do it. *Young* shades gradually into *old*, *blue* into *green*, *good* into *bad*, *rich* into *poor*, *fast* into *slow*, *often* into *rarely*, *some* into *many*, *jog* into *run*, *cottage* into *house*, *house* into *mansion*, and *careful* into *negligent*. This lack of clarity doesn't matter in nature, though it sometimes matters greatly in law. A careful drafter must decide the appropriate degree of precision, balancing flexibility against complexity.

But the fuzzy edge around the meaning of a word is not the only reason that absolutely precise legislation is impossible.

As words only approximate the reality they seek to describe, so also they only approximate the thoughts in people's heads, as accurately as they need to for the uses to which they are normally put. Greater accuracy would be tiresome and uneconomic. So the details of a concept can vary from one person to another, even when they use the same word and think they are talking about the same thing. Heffer (2013, p.215) compares Lord Goddard LCJ's dictum in *R v. Summers* (1952) …

> I have never yet heard a court give a real definition of what is a 'reasonable doubt', and it would be very much better if that expression was not used. Whenever a court attempts to explain what is meant by it, the explanation tends to result in confusion rather than clarity … The jury should be told that it is … for the prosecution to prove [the defendant's] guilt, and that it is their duty to regard the evidence and see if it satisfies them so that they can feel sure, when they give their verdict, that it is a right one

… with that of his Australian counterpart, Dixon CJ in *Dawson v. R* (1961):

> In my view it is a mistake to depart from the time-honoured formula. It is, I think, used by ordinary people and is understood well enough by the average man in the community. The attempts to substitute other expressions, of which there have been many examples not only here but in England, have never prospered. It is wise as well as proper to avoid such expressions.

How small a doubt can be without becoming unreasonable will vary with each juror's (or judge's) view of Blackstone's (1765) principle that

> It is better that ten guilty persons escape than that one innocent suffer.

Sir Matthew Hale, published posthumously in 1736 but writing a century before Blackstone, had put it at five guilty escapers. A politician 'tough on crime' may opt for a lower figure, as did the Roman Emperor Trajan and the Criminal Law Revision Committee (1972), neither of whom were prepared to let slip more than one wrongdoer for each innocent spared. The more liberal 12th century Talmudist Maimonides preferred a thousand mistaken acquittals to one wrongful conviction. In a detailed but witty historical review Alexander Volokh (1998) lists many other ratios that have been proposed. The modern alternatives to *reasonable doubt* – *satisfied so that you are sure* or just *sure* – don't help, as no juror can be absolutely sure of anything except his or her own existence. No form of words can solve the problem because the concept behind them is incurably vague, even though it is – as one perspective of the presumption of innocence – an essential part of our liberty and of the rule of law (Wolchover & Heaton-Armstrong, August 2010).

There is a third problem. A rule should be worded in sufficiently general terms to apply, in the way the legislators want, in all the circumstances that might arise. But those circumstances are infinitely variable and often unpredictable, so judges will always be needed to fine-tune the boundaries in borderline cases, and also in 'hard' cases – those where the strict application of a clear rule would produce an unwanted result.

Let's consider H.L.A. Hart's much discussed (1958) example of what he calls the *open texture* of language:

> No vehicles are allowed in the park.

It would be an ingenious litigator who challenged the meaning of *No, are, allowed,* or *the*. But is a helicopter hovering over the grass a vehicle? Probably yes (although in *McBoyle* v. *United States* (1931) the Supreme Court held that for the purposes of the relevant legislation an aeroplane wasn't a vehicle). And is it in the park? At the time of Hart's article, the *Shorter Oxford English Dictionary* defined *vehicle* (in more or less the sense intended here) as:

> A means of conveyance provided with wheels or runners and used for the carriage of persons or goods; a carriage, cart, wagon, sledge, etc. … A receptacle in which anything is placed in order to be moved.

But its other definitions of *vehicle* included

> A means or medium by which ideas or impressions are communicated or made known

and

> A material means, channel, or instrument by which a substance or some property of matter (as sound or heat) is conveyed or transmitted from one point to another.

So does the bye-law ban children's pedal cars, wheelchairs, baby carriages, skateboards, skis, shopping trolleys, books, and any wires and conduits needed for the park's facilities? A purpose clause would help answer the more difficult questions, and drafters and legislators will want to provide some exceptions, and exceptions to exceptions, to give effect fairly and reasonably to the spirit of the law. Do they want to stop children playing, or to create a safe area in which they *can* play? Do they want to stop tired shoppers from taking a short cut? Easily foreseeable exceptions include emergency vehicles and park maintenance vehicles. Against that it is easy to imagine circumstances in which such vehicles *should* be excluded from the park, for instance if they are not on official business.

Bayless Manning, a former dean of Stanford Law School, took the counter-intuitive view (1982) that blocking the loopholes in legislation was pointless, as it inevitably created just as many new loopholes. Taking as his example the US Treasury's proposed 110 single-spaced pages of s.385 regulations (devoted to distinguishing for tax purposes between *equity* investments and *debt* investments), he

> predict[ed] that the regulations will not reduce the aggregate of ambiguity that attends the problem of distinguishing between debt and equity. New ambiguities will substitute for old; the seeds of new litigation will be sown; and new pressures for still further elaboration will ensue. These things will happen, not because the regulations are poorly drafted (though the … proposed regulations are), but because that is the nature of the process.
>
> Consider the United States Constitution. The Constitution is open-ended, generalised and telescopic in character. What has it spawned? Pervasive ambiguity and unending litigation.
>
> Consider the extreme counter-model of law, the Internal Revenue Code and its festooned vines of regulations. The Code and regulations are particularised, elaborated and microscopic in character. What have they spawned? Pervasive ambiguity and unending litigation.

Andrew Stumpff (2012) helpfully illustrates what Manning called 'The Law of Conservation of Ambiguity' (though *vagueness* might have been a better term than *ambiguity*) with the analogy of fractals – shapes that are identical regardless of scale. Increase the scale of the map to clarify the boundary between *lawful* and *unlawful* and see on which side a case falls, and the new line will be just as vague, though the details will be different. A large-scale coastline viewed from the clifftop is as jagged as the longer stretch of that coast visible from space.

This depressing doctrine seems to us as under-argued and implausible as other forms of fatalism. We accept that one can never rule out the possibility of uncertain cases, for the reasons already given. But nothing Manning says disproves the intuitive view that blocking loopholes will *reduce* the number of uncertainties, continuously approaching precision even if it never arrives there. It should reduce to an even greater extent the economic viability – and so the likelihood – of tax avoidance and of litigation in general, as the uncertainties become more fanciful and less worth the risk or costs of the argument. A sensible drafter will recognise that you cannot legislate for everything and must agree with the client a sensible cut-off point. For instance, in drafting a will with a gift to A it is sensible to ask who is to take it if A predeceases the testator. It might be worth including a second reserve in case both A and the first reserve have died. But you have to draw the line somewhere, and the sensible place to do so depends on a balance involving the amount at stake, the cost and convenience of adding further precautions, and the likelihood of mass extinction.

We see three flaws in Manning's reasoning:

- Taking Manning backwards in time, removing the accumulated complexities of the tax code and back through the various drafts of the Constitution, we arrive not at the same amount of ambiguity and legislation as when we began the journey but at a blank sheet of paper, with no power to tax and nothing to litigate. Or is he saying that the doubts only arise when the first word is written, whatever that is, and then can never be reduced or increased?
- The Constitution and the regulations have different functions: respectively to enable and to do. The relevant clause of the Constitution (the opening paragraph of Article 1, §8) reads:

  > The Congress shall have power to lay and collect taxes, duties, imposts and excises, to pay the debts and provide for the common defense and general welfare of the United States; but all duties, imposts and excises shall be uniform throughout the United States;

  and §385, the section under which the regulations were made, reads:

  > The Secretary is authorised to prescribe such regulations as may be necessary or appropriate to determine whether an interest in a corporation is to be treated for purposes of this title as stock or indebtedness (or as in part stock and in part indebtedness).

  No one would suggest that these clauses specify the taxpayers' liability with as much precision as the Code – or at all.
- Manning offers no systematic comparison between the litigation generated by the Constitution and that generated at different stages of legislative development; nor between that generated by laws drafted with different degrees of skill.

If, on the other hand, Manning was writing a polemic and didn't mean to be taken literally, he had a point. Over-legislation is counter-productive.

Some vagueness is desirable, being often essential for flexibility: how could we legislate without *reasonable*? (Note the vague words *some* and *often* here; it would be neither possible nor desirable to be precise.) Necessary vagueness also makes use of words like *immediately*, *sufficient*, *believe*, and of course *necessary*, *vague*, and *precise*.

But we must contrast this useful vagueness with the lazy vagueness that reveals woolly thinking, although there is of course – as with so many things – no clear boundary between them.

MA: In seminars I used to ask students how they would interpret a rule entitling patients to see their medical records unless it was *likely* that the disclosure would compromise a confidential source. If no possibility of compromise was described as a 0 per cent chance, and certain compromise was described as a 100 per cent chance, what figure would they give as the threshold of 'likely'? They were asked

---

> to think about it for a moment but to keep their answer to themselves until everyone had decided. Then each answered in turn. Although many students suggested 51 per cent, the responses were surprisingly diverse, sometimes ranging in a well-attended seminar from one per cent to 99 per cent. The lower figures seemed to me more thoughtful.

So lawyers must live with vagueness, but they should be aware of and minimise the risks.

And/or

We single out this expression for discussion because of its exceptional contrast between vagueness and apparent simplicity and because of its malign grip on the legal mind. Everyone thinks they know what it means: *either A or B or both*. If that were always so, *and/or* might be an (inelegant) shorthand. But it is not always so.

Its meaning must depend on the meaning of the '/' alone. That too is vague but seems to be the same as the meaning of the whole 'and/or' expression, creating an infinite regress: *and and/or or*. Only lawyers could have added a third level with longer words:

Further and/or in the alternative ...

Too often the expression is a lazy alternative for the drafter who has not considered which option is appropriate: (*A and B*) or (*A or B or both*) or (*A or B but not both*). Is a bequest to *A and/or B* to be shared between them (as in *In re Lewis* (1942))? If so, in what proportions, and what is the function of /*or*? Or is it a gift to one or the other? If so, who chooses, and what is the function of *and/*? The confusion is compounded in *A or B and/or C*.

In *Situ Ventures* (2013) para.26, where a drafter meant *or* but wrote *and/or*, Lord Justice Mummery said:

That this document is not the product of skilful drafting is also evidenced by the presence of the expression 'and/or.' Its use in this clause is unnecessary and confusing. ... I would add that the use of the expression 'and/or' in any legal document is in any case open to numerous more fundamental objections of inaccuracy, obscurity, uncertainty or even as being just plain meaningless, as explained by Sir Robert Megarry in his erudite philological discussion of 'and/or' in 'Andorandororand' from *Law at the Centre* (1999) at pp.71 to 78.

For a history of the extensive case law, see Mellinkoff (1963, especially pp.147–152). Since then, one 'respected law firm' has been reported (Henderson, 1989, p.185) as being so concerned about the expression's vagueness that it insisted on putting this definition in a partnership agreement:

'*and/or*' means that the thereto precedent and subsequent words grammatically associated therewith are connected thereby in the conjunctive sense (whether cumulative as to the whole thereof, or in any combination of more than one thereof) and also, as an equal alternative, in the disjunctive sense, and (except where specially restricted to the conjunctive sense, for example by use of the phrase and (but not or)) ordinarily means that the conjunctive sense should be applied thereto unless by reason of the context, subject matter and circumstances then concerned substitution of the disjunctive sense would reasonably be necessary to give meaning to the words used therewith, and or (except where specially restricted to the disjunctive sense, for example by use of the phrase or (but not and)) means the converse (both ordinarily and substitutionally) of the foregoing meaning and implication of and.

So now you know.

Chapter 24

Ambiguity

Whereas vagueness is an absence of any clear meaning, ambiguity is a choice between alternative meanings. But it's in the nature of vagueness and ambiguity that there is no clear boundary between the categories.

Barbara Child (1992) writes of

> an experiment I perform in my classroom every semester when we talk about ambiguity. I have the students look at [Figure 24.1 opposite]. Many of them have seen it before, but not all. And so far, without exception, semester after semester, there are always some who see only one face and some who see only the other. In fact, *you* may be looking at this picture and wondering what I'm talking about. You may be seeing only the young woman with the necklace, the fine features, and the downcast eye looking away. Or you may be seeing only the crone with the babushka over her hair, facing more forward. If you see only one or the other, it may help you free yourself from your set vision if I tell you that the young woman's chin is the old woman's nose, and the young woman's necklace is the old woman's mouth. It may help you, and it may not. Semester after semester, try as they might, some students take nearly an hour, even with help and the best of intentions, to see the other face.
>
> It is [she says] the most powerful lesson I know about ambiguity.

This tunnel vision applies to words as well as to pictures. It blinds us to ambiguities that might be obvious to a fresh mind and makes it difficult for us to understand another's *misunderstanding*. *Time flies like an arrow* is a good example, which changes its meaning depending on whether you read *Time* as a noun or a verb, a phenomenon we'll discuss more fully in the next chapter (on miscuing).

Ambiguity can be as surprisingly difficult to spot in words as it is in pictures. In 1926 H.W. Fowler used

Our object is to further cement trade relations

in his now-classic *A Dictionary of Modern English Usage* to recommend splitting an infinitive in some circumstances. He pointed out that moving *further* outside the infinitive to read

Our object is further to cement trade relations

suggests that this might be a further object rather than another way to improve relations; similarly,

Our object is to cement further trade relations ?

suggests that we might want to cement a new trade relationship. Sir Ernest Gowers left this unchanged in his 1965 second edition and we are not aware of it being challenged until Richard Oerton (1993) pointed out that, unlike most adverbs, *further* can be read as a verb, in which case the object could be to improve relations with (or – another ambiguity – within) the cement trade. This example has disappeared from later editions but (rightly) not the principle it illustrated.

Figure 24.1   Hill, W.E. 'My Wife and My Mother-in-Law', originally printed in *Puck* (November 1915)

Easier to spot is this common and less complex construction, unnecessarily ambiguous and clumsy to some ears. It avoids the unnecessarily split infinitive in

He decided to quickly run

by substituting

> He decided quickly to run

(which makes it unclear whether it was the decision or the pace that was quick) when

> He decided to run quickly

would be natural and clear.[1]

Lawrence Solan (2004, p.878, citations omitted) defines pernicious ambiguity as that which occurs when the various actors involved in a dispute all believe a text to be clear, for instance when

> a court determines that reasonable doubt is a concept well enough understood by the community so that a definition is neither needed nor appropriate. The United States Court of Appeals for the Seventh Circuit, among others, has taken this position. When this happens, there is absolutely no way of knowing how different from each other the jurors' concepts of reasonable doubt really are.
>
> In fact, experimental evidence suggests that they are likely to be quite different.

But even definition by the court might not resolve the problem. Solan (p.879) quotes Smith's (1991) research as

> suggest[ing] that jurors' everyday understanding of the definitions of crimes more than likely plays a role in their deliberations, pushing aside the legal definitions that are read to them in instructions ... The results were that it is very difficult to convince people that the legal definitions should trump their [own] notions of the crime.

So, when someone tells you that text can be read in a way you don't see, it's rash to insist, as one solicitor did, that *It's perfectly clear*. Keep an open mind, get them to explain if necessary, and (unless you can refute their interpretation) keep looking until you see it.

Types of ambiguity

There are traditionally three types of ambiguity:

- **Semantic**: when a word carries more than one possible meaning;
- **Syntactic**: when the sentence is constructed in such a way as to give more than one possible meaning; and
- **Contextual**: when a document says two inconsistent things.

Semantic ambiguity

Words are used differently:

- From place to place: *pavement* means in Britain what *sidewalk* means in America, but it means in America what *roadway* means in Britain. And *no* (short for *ano*) means *yes* in informal spoken Czech.
- From group to group: *launder* has a special meaning in law enforcement; and in England the slang *job* varies radically between police and criminals.
- From century to century: in the 16th century a *machine* was a structure of any kind (according to the *Oxford Dictionary of Word Histories*).
- From moment to moment (and from one area of legal practice to another): when two lawyers discussed the Jones *estate*, one meant a housing development owned by the Jones family while the other meant the property left when Mr Jones died.

Everyone knows that many words have more than one meaning but it takes a dictionary to remind us just how many different meanings a word can have. For instance, the *Shorter Oxford English Dictionary* has a column-and-a-half on *house*, including (among other uses):

as a noun:

- a building for human habitation,
- the part of a building occupied by one tenant or family,
- a place of worship,
- a religious community,
- a school or college subdivision (referring either to the building or the members),

and as a verb:

- to receive or put in a house, and
- to place in a secure or unexposed position.

So even apparently simple, common words can be surprisingly slippery. William DuBay has suggested (informally) that *the older a word is, the more meanings and uses it has*. The problem often arises when drafting time limits, as in these examples:

- *By* a date can mean *any time before* that date or *not after* the date. Similar confusion arises with *until, from,* and *to*. We reluctantly suggest using *on or before* and *on or after* instead. Nick Wright of Editor Software rightly points out that *before* and *after* are shorter and unambiguous. However, we are afraid of misdirecting the reader; in an instruction to complete an action *before 1 January*, the one date mentioned is already too late. A good alternative is 'no later than 31 December'.
- *Midnight on 26 January* could be just after the 25th or just before the 27th. Any other time of day is safe from this problem, at least if you use the 24-hour clock.
- The period *within three months of 1 January* lasts from October to March but *within … of* is sometimes interpreted as *within … after*. Use *within …*

before or *within … after*, if that's what you mean. Or specify the start and end of the period (if necessary *including both dates*).

- *Month* (and *calendar month*) can mean the period from the first to the last day of a month, or the period from any date to the same date in the next month (or its last day, if earlier).[2] Defining *month* as a calendar month doesn't help: it just confirms that it's not a lunar month. Days and weeks are free from this problem, but require more counting.
- Dates expressed in numerals can be ambiguous in international contexts. So 9/11 is 11 September in the USA, but 9 November in the UK. We suggest spelling out the month if there is any risk of confusion (or as a safe habit).

Subject to, without prejudice to, and *notwithstanding* cause much confusion among lawyers, and at least as much among their clients. The solution is to spell out the relation between the related propositions. For example, *Notwithstanding clause 6* could become *This clause has priority over clause 6.* Counsel once advised that:

Subject to

(a)   any increase due to psychiatric injury;
(b)   successful extension of the limitation period to include [damage]

I am of the opinion that … a global award for damages of £20,000 should be considered a starting point.

Condition (a) is fairly clear: £20,000 is the minimum, but that threshold would be raised if psychiatric injury can be proved. But couldn't (b) be read either way, so that the damages might be less than £20,000 unless the limitation period was extended?

Even such short words as *and* and *or* are open to interpretation:

- *And* can mean *or*: In *Associated Artists Ltd* v. *Inland Revenue Commissioners* (1956) the court held that a power *to present classical, artistic, cultural and educational dramatic works* meant that any production had to be classical, artistic, cultural, *or* educational, rather than a combination of all four. This is the commonsense answer, so you may wonder why the drafter didn't use *or*. But a power *to present classical, artistic, cultural or educational dramatic works* might be read as a once-and-for-all choice between them, as *or* can be either exclusive or inclusive.
- *Or* can mean *and*. In s.2 of the Human Rights Act 1998:

  A court … must take into account any–

  (a)   judgment …
  (b)   opinion …
  (c)   decision … in connection with Article 26 … *or*
  (d)   decision … taken under Article 46.

The fashionable verb *face* can be particularly vague. When journalists report that someone *faces* a life sentence, are we to understand that the sentence has been passed, or that it will be passed, or that it might be?

Using short, familiar, 'Jack-and-Jill' words is not always sufficient for clear expression.

And this is before the lawyers adapt words, giving unusual meanings to the words listed on p.207 and many others.

The 1971 *Stroud's Judicial Dictionary* had 48 entries for *house* filling six pages, and cross-references to other entries. (The much briefer – but still extensive – entries in later editions say that much of the old case law has been rendered 'largely' obsolete by the modern conveyancing practice of relying on title numbers or plans.)

Often the context identifies the intended meaning and saves us from ambiguity. But often it does not, which is how *Stroud's* came to be. Sometimes the meaning will be clear enough for informal use, while the need to guard against a perverse interpretation requires what seems like pedantry. Perverse arguments are sometimes raised in litigation and might win at trial. An example concerned a covenant against constructing *any building on the Property which shall be greater in height than the buildings now existing on the Property.* A solicitor advised – and the trial judge held – that this allowed buildings higher than the existing roofline, though not higher than its chimneypots. The Court of Appeal called the judge's finding *a little unexpected* and held the solicitor was negligent to give that advice without warning that a court might disagree (*Queen Elizabeth's School* v. *Banks Wilson* (2001)).

Humans have a surprising capacity to get things wrong, and the drafter must balance the risk of misunderstanding and the seriousness of the consequences against the advantages of brevity and of not labouring the obvious. Of course, the risk is much greater when the reader will be looking for a loophole.

Syntactic ambiguity

The Daily Telegraph once asked: *Is not ironing your baby's clothes a sign of neglect?* The answer depends on whether it meant *Is the failure to iron ...* or *Isn't it true that ...*

Noun strings are a common form of ambiguity. For example,

the landlord's solicitor's costs and expenses

could be

the landlord's solicitor's costs and the landlord's expenses

or

> the landlord's solicitor's costs and the landlord's solicitor's expenses

or perhaps even

> the landlord's solicitor's costs and the expenses of every party to the arrangement.

List format can help here, with all information common to all items in the introductory line. Another way is to replace lists of examples with a general description. For example, assuming *costs* and *expenses* are two categories of charge:

> You must pay the landlord's solicitor's charges.

What risks were covered by a *Voluntary Accidental Death and Dismemberment Plan*? Hyphens can be a useful though sometimes clumsy remedy: this was presumably a *Voluntary Accidental-Death-and-Dismemberment Plan*, it being the plan rather than the death or dismemberment that was voluntary, but our hyphenation doesn't help decide whether deliberate or disease-related dismemberment are insured.

As with semantic ambiguity, apparently simple language can cause problems:

> It's too easy to resist

could mean either *You can resist* or *You can't resist*. And

> It was nearly the end of their marriage

could mean either

> The marriage was drawing to a close

or

> The incident just recounted nearly brought the marriage to an end.

Traditional legal writers create much syntactic ambiguity by pouring words and phrases into a sentence without making clear what relates to what. Here are two typical examples:

1

> 'The Building' means the building forming part of the Development comprising several flats and all structural parts thereof including the roofs gutters rainwater pipes foundations floors all walls bounding individual flats therein and all external parts of the Building and all Service Installations except those used solely for the purpose of an individual flat

Is it the building or the development that comprises? And does *thereof* – a word shunned by non-lawyers – refer to the building, the development, or the flats? *Therein* cannot refer to flats but it could refer to the building or the development. And *except those used solely for the purpose of an individual flat* could relate to every item in the list or only to the last.

Redrafting this example as a list (cutting out the superfluities, clarifying the vagueness, and using small caps to flag defined terms) gives, depending on the meaning required, either:

THE BUILDING is that edged red on the plan, but excludes:

(a) (which?) internal walls; and

(b) CONDUITS used only by an individual flat.

or

THE BUILDING is that edged red on the plan, but excludes those of the following items which are used only by an individual flat:

(a) (Which?) internal walls.

(b) CONDUITS.

The following slightly different form of syntactic ambiguity comes from an opinion by counsel:

2

Only normally domesticated animals may be kept (in the flat)

might restrict pets to

animals which have been domesticated in the usual way

or

animals of a domesticated species

or perhaps (at a stretch)

animals which usually behave themselves.

Ambiguity can also result from omitting words commonly omitted informally:

Do you trust Brown more than Green?

could be asking:

Do you trust Brown more than Green does?

> or
> Do you trust Brown more than you trust Green?

Similarly,

> The judge wants the statement drafted by counsel

could be disambiguated by inserting either *that was* or *to be* after *statement*.
Before leaving syntactic ambiguity we can't resist two more examples:

- A dictator's election promise (which we cannot trace so, sadly, suspect is apocryphal):

  > You will live badly, but not for long.

- A newspaper cutting quoted on BBC radio's *News Quiz*:

  > Too many police can't shoot straight or take bribes.

Contextual ambiguity

This is the ambiguity arising when a document says conflicting things.

It might be obvious to the alert reader but is a trap for anyone too bored to read critically. Two common legal examples are:

> 'The contract' means and includes

(*means* means that the definition excludes anything which is not mentioned and *includes* means that it doesn't) and

> From time to time and at all times

(which means *both intermittently and continuously*).

It is easier to miss the inconsistency when a provision in one part of a document contradicts something in another part, perhaps because the solicitor adapted a precedent without reading the unchanged bits. An example of this problem is the contract that gives a right to end the contract on grounds of breach (in a clause headed *Termination*) and a different right to end it on grounds of delay (which is also a breach), in a clause headed *Time of the Essence*.

A borderline case

A borderline case between contextual ambiguity and no ambiguity arises when a reader suspects that the writer meant something different from the natural meaning of the words used.

In casual speech we sometimes say things that should not be taken literally, but it can cause confusion and should be avoided in a formal context.

Nelson Mandela may have had a twinkle in his eye when he made this discreetly tautologous comment:

It was one of my only failures.

A more common example is the use of expressions like *the second after X*, as in:

The house mouse has become the second most intensively studied mammal species after our own.

Strictly, this means it is the third most intensively studied, though a comma after *species* or parentheses around *after our own* would promote it one place.

A general recently said that a particular military campaign would need *5,000 boots on the ground*. Did he mean 2,500 soldiers?

Legally qualified readers might guess that

... (we) HEREBY GIVE YOU NOTICE of her desire to sever the joint tenancy in equity of and in 19 Holt Lane Norwich Norfolk now held by you and John Thomas Chatterbox both at law and in equity by virtue of a Conveyance dated ...

was intended to convert the joint tenancy into a tenancy in common (so that each owner would now have separate half-shares they could leave by will to other people). But they might at the same time doubt its effect; there is, after all, a difference between wanting to do something and doing it. Lord Denning MR held in *Burgess* v. *Rawnsley* (1975) that the wording of s.36(2) of the Law of Property Act 1925 vindicates the notice; nevertheless, it would be clearer to write *The joint tenancy is severed* (and clearer still with an explanation to a lay recipient).

Solicitors seem particularly attached to asking for information by requesting people to *confirm* that something is the case when they have no reason to believe that it is. They should be asking *Is [it so]?* An even worse variant is *Please confirm whether ...*, which invites the mischievous reply *Confirmed*.

The uses of ambiguity

Lawyers sometimes create ambiguity deliberately to avoid trouble (at least in the short term).

This might be to camouflage guilt or avoid ill-feeling. Or it might ease negotiations, either openly or slyly, when the acceptance of an unclear document by disagreeing parties is better than a failure to agree. Perhaps the blurred details can be clarified later, when the general principles have been agreed or the parties' commitment to the deal is stronger. Or perhaps the clause need never be interpreted, and the dirt can remain under the carpet until the building is redeveloped. Or perhaps (if you like to gamble) it will be construed in favour of your own client.

Overt ambiguity is also the basis of puns and can be used to create a catchy title.

Endnotes

1   Good (1989). There are two versions of this guide to clear writing: one general, the other aimed specifically at lawyers. This example is taken from p.30 of the lawyers' edition.
2   See, for example, *Webber* v. *NHS Direct* (2012, unreported, Appeal No UKEAT/0627/11/DM), where both meanings were arguable. The Employment Tribunal chose the first but the Employment Appeal Tribunal preferred the second.

Chapter 25

Miscuing

What was *hot oyster mushroom salad* doing in a vegetarian cookbook? It turned out to be referring to *hot oyster-mushroom salad* rather than to a *hot-oyster and mushroom salad*. A more experienced cook would probably have read it correctly first time but this was a book for beginners.

As we read our brains unconsciously parse the text. Ambiguity and vagueness can derail this process.

Your mind's ear should just have registered 'As we *reed* our brains ...'. But if the context allowed you to 'hear' 'As we *red* ...' you were miscuing, and it would have been our fault; it is the writer's job to notice and avoid ambiguities.

Steven Pinker (1994) analyses a way in which ambiguity can make us miscue. He explains that some linguists programmed a computer to high-light ambiguities and were astonished to find five alternative meanings for *Time flies like an arrow*:

- Time proceeds as quickly as an arrow proceeds.
- Measure the speed of flies in the same way that you measure the speed of an arrow.
- Measure the speed of flies in the same way that an arrow measures the speed of flies.
- Measure the speed of flies that resemble an arrow.
- Flies of a particular kind, time-flies, are fond of an arrow.

You may have interpreted *Time* correctly as a noun; this would have prompted you to expect a verb to follow, and to understand *flies* accord-ingly; this would have led you to assume that *like an arrow* modified *flies*. But if, unfamiliar with the expression, you happened to read *Time* as an impera-tive verb, you would expect *flies* to be a noun; and you would probably have assumed that *like an arrow* modified *Time.* All this happens quickly and unconsciously, so we usually only notice the problem when the sentence does not make sense when we follow our initial interpretation. The reader is pulled up short, goes back to the beginning, and starts again. There is less harm done than if the ambiguity passes unnoticed, but it makes the readers' task more difficult, slows them down, and drains another coin from the writer's credit.

Pinker goes on to contrast the two readings in the aphorism *Time flies like an arrow; fruit flies like a banana,* where the mixture of similarity and sudden contrast is absurd enough to make us laugh.

Of course, a reader might unconsciously 'choose' the right interpretation first time, in which case there is no problem. That is how writers overlook the flaw when editing: they know what they mean, and (synapses being creatures of habit) attention is funnelled by inertia along the route it used before, as across points on a railway line.

Miscuing (when we notice it) draws our attention to ambiguities, as we realise that the writer could not have intended our initial interpretation.

Here is one from a Court of Appeal judgment showing the need to exercise care when using pronouns:

> The judge said that the other three principal witnesses were independent. However, he found Mr X to be highly partisan. He had high praise for Mrs X whom he described as honest and truthful, and, in a later paragraph, as an impressive witness who gave her evidence clearly and without hesitation and who impressed the judge as a person knowing her own mind.

Who had high praise for Mrs X? At first, it appears to be Mr X (the last male mentioned before *he had high praise*). But the reference to *an impressive witness* stops the reader: *he* must after all be the trial judge. The initial interpretation can be primed by the reader's prejudices: a divorce lawyer might assume that husband-and-wife witnesses were on opposite sides, while a less cynical reader might assume that spouses supported each other.

And what of this one?:

> The Senate passed the measure, a day after it passed the House of Representatives.

Chapter 26

The loss of nontextual clues

In speech, our words are disambiguated by sound – pronunciation, intonation, pauses, loudness, speed – and by body language – gestures, facial expressions, posture. This process is routine, automatic, and fast, so we are often unaware of it. Consequently, when writing we tend to forget that all these clues are lost, leaving ambiguity in text we think is plain.

The wider context can also play an important role. Although this can be represented as well in writing as in speech, the need for it to be spelled out increases as writer and reader become more separated by time or distance than speaker and listener usually are. In an interesting history of technology, from cuneiform to texting, Peter Tiersma (2010) traces the development of this distinction between speech and writing and its effect on the legal interpretation of language, notably in the continuing tension between the literal and liberal approaches championed by Justice Scalia and Lord Denning respectively.

This inadequacy in our writing should not surprise us. Humans have had sophisticated speech organs for at least 100,000 years and language might have been evolving for a lot longer (Ostler, 2005, p.9). Communication by sound, gestures, and other signals are of course much older still. By contrast, writing is only 5,000 years old, and it is still rudimentary by comparison, representing sound inexactly and gestures hardly at all. The alphabetic system was introduced by the Phoenicians around 1,300 BCE and most of our punctuation, which helps us disambiguate, is so recent that lawyers are only now being persuaded to use it. But however sophisticated writing becomes, a finite range of symbols could not represent the infinite ranges of sound and gestures.

Intonation

Simple sentences can have multiple possible meanings depending on which word is stressed. For instance,

- THIS is your kitchen now (= *this room (rather than that one) is now your kitchen*)
- This IS your kitchen now (= *confirms what the listener already thought*)
- This is YOUR kitchen now (= *notes the transfer of proprietorship from the previous chef*)

- This is your KITCHEN now (= *changes the use of the room*)
- This is your kitchen NOW (= *makes the change immediate*).

Compare also two possible inflections of

You should try sleeping upstairs

in response to the complaint 'My room is too hot to sleep in at night' to mean either:

- 'It's better upstairs. Why don't you try it?'; or
- 'It's worse upstairs, where I sleep, so stop moaning'.

You might experiment with these:

- John could only see his wife from the doorway.
- I'm going to let him ask you.
- Why couldn't her sister know someone more focused?
- I was sick. Mother wanted me at home.

Some languages use diacritical marks to indicate which syllable within a word is stressed, but in English we make do without them and hope that the context will give us the correct reading. CONduct (the noun), for example, is stressed differently from conDUCT (the verb).

Speakers and their listeners avoid misunderstanding by the many clues that, automatically and often unconsciously, they give and interpret. Writers and readers have no such luxury. Each will 'hear' the words in their mind's ear, the writer according to the intended meaning but readers at random, strongly influenced by their expectations. So a lawyer writing to a client

I filed the claim I was preparing yesterday

might 'hear' in her mind's ear

I filed (the-claim-I-was-preparing) YESterday (= *Yesterday I filed the claim that I was preparing at some unspecified time*)

while the client might read it as

I filed (the-claim-I-was-preparing-yesterday) (= *Either yesterday or today I filed the claim I was preparing yesterday*).

An ideal editor will experiment with different possibilities when reading a draft, and mark words whose stress should be drawn to the readers' attention. An easier and safer approach is to recast the sentence:

I was preparing the claim yesterday and have now filed it

or

Yesterday I filed the claim I had been preparing.

Context

The contributors to Heffer, Rock, and Conley (2013) show how meaning can be distorted as text moves through the legal system from one context to another.

So, for example, a series of questions and answers in a police interview, or a series of interviews, are subsequently edited and paraphrased by a police officer into a more condensed first-person narrative which the witness is expected to sign. That narrative is eventually presented in court as though it were the witness's own words, all uttered on the same occasion. It might then be further contracted during counsel's closing speeches and the judge's summing-up. Those summaries are likely to be themselves summarised in press reports of the trial.

We all make judgments about people based on the way they speak. But in this process the subtle clues arising from word choice, intonation, gesture, and facial expression are replaced by clues applicable not to the defendant but to the officer or one or more of the later editors. Was a remark serious or flippant, literal or ironic, sarcastic or a joke? Was it arrogant and hostile, or polite and helpful? What *did* Derek Bentley mean when he called out *Let him have it, Chris*?

Chapter 27

Misleading expectations

We learn from experience, our own and that of others. We rely on unquestioned assumptions and other habits of thought in all aspects of our lives: in our use of language, in our thinking, and in our perceptions.

This has the obvious advantage of sparing us the need to work out everything afresh for ourselves each time a decision is needed (while we die of predators, starvation, old age, or boredom). It also allows us to pool our knowledge and it gives us the benefit of others' skills that we don't have.

But it makes us less flexible, and open to error and abuse. Our thoughts and perceptions travel too often like railway carriages, trapped in a single perspective, instead of whirling and pirouetting like birds.

Why we are misled

Our ability to make connections between brain cells is innate. But few of the connections are themselves innate; most are created by experience, and are strengthened by repeated use while unused connections are dropped.

Our brains have to learn how to translate the code of internal electro-chemical events into coherent and accurate messages from the outside world. Recent medical advances that have given sight to adults blind from birth have shown patients confused by visual chaos until they learn to make sense of the light show; some, lacking a baby's adaptability, prefer to be restored to blindness. Neuroscientist David Eagleman (2015) gives this gentler example:

> (T)he language that you're exposed to in infancy (say, English versus Japanese) refines your ability to hear the particular sounds of your language, and worsens your capacity to hear the sounds of other languages. That is, a baby born in Japan and a baby born in America can hear and respond to all the sounds in both languages. Through time, the baby raised in Japan will lose the ability to distinguish, say, the sounds of R and L, two sounds that aren't separated in Japanese.

A familiar piece of boilerplate – particularly one too familiar to read carefully – might match our expectations in 99 ways yet be different in a crucial 100th. While the text runs rapidly, easily, and unconsciously along well-established neural pathways we are likely to overlook the difference. One firm used this clause in its standard conveyancing contract for some time before anyone read it thoughtfully enough to notice that it did not have the intended (or any) effect:

> A person who is not a third party to this Agreement has no right under the Contracts (Rights of Third Parties) Act 1999 to enforce any term of this Agreement …

In all our perceptions and thoughts we can easily jump to the wrong conclusion, unaware that we have jumped anywhere. We see and hear what isn't there, and miss or misinterpret what is, baffling and sometimes infuriating those affected by the misunderstanding. Sometimes the tone, context, or implausibility of a misperception alerts us to its inaccuracy (as with dreams). Often it will not. Those who think of their consciousness as a private cinema, with objective reality projected on to the screen, should remember that the camera *does* lie, especially if its electronics are scrambled.

Memory can be similarly corrupted, as becomes increasingly apparent as we age. False memories being indistinguishable to their owners from accurate ones, an honest witness will convincingly insist on their truth unless the memories can be discredited by compelling external evidence.

How context misleads us

Figure 27.1 Bruner, J.S. and Minturn, A.L. image from 'Perceptual identification and perceptual organisation' originally printed in *Journal of General Psychology* (1955, 53: 21–8).

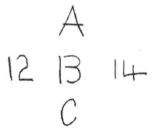

Figure 27.1, an illustration from Bruner and Minturn, shows how context primes us to see (in this case) either a letter or a number. But it's not always so straightforward. Tracking instruments show that the eye does not run uniformly along the line and then down to the next as we read; nor do we interpret a sentence a word at a time in the order in which they are presented. So, as a lawyer familiar with the statute mentioned three paragraphs above, you might have taken in the reference to the Act without

untangling the comparatively complex wording of the first line, and have jumped – as so many have jumped before you – to the wrong conclusion.

How suggestion misleads us

As has become evident from sexual abuse scandals, even dramatically false memories can be implanted, despite the absence of supporting context. Perception is similarly susceptible to suggestion.

In 1994 David Bain phoned the emergency services in New Zealand to report that he'd come home to find his parents, brother, and two sisters dead. The following year he was convicted of their murders. In 2007, during the preparations for the last of a series of appeals, a detective thought he heard a short but damning confession made under the defendant's breath in the recording of the original phone call. No one had noticed it before. The Privy Council quashed the conviction on unrelated grounds and the defendant was acquitted at a retrial. Meanwhile, several speech experts, instructed by prosecution and defence, had expressed different views as to what, if anything, had been said, but all agreed that no version was clear enough to be included in the transcript of the call. In the words of Elias CJ, when the NZ Supreme Court ruled that the disputed extract should be kept from the jury and meanwhile from the public:

> None of the experts is able to say that the sounds relied upon in the recording are words, rather than meaningless exhalation of breath. If they are words, none of the experts is able to say that they amount to the words the Crown wishes to rely upon as evidence. Some consider such words can be heard in the recording, with effort. But all experts caution as to the dangers of hearing something that may not in fact be there, because of accident in arrangements of sounds. The principal Crown expert uses the analogy of an image glimpsed in a cloud formation to illustrate the dangers ... And all express the view that, if the recording is admitted, the jury should not be told what the sounds are thought to amount to. All are agreed that such 'priming' entails a high risk of suggestibility, which would be difficult to counter.

Helen Fraser and others (2011) tested the priming risk on 190 volunteers. First, the whole tape was played to them. None heard words at the disputed point in the recording. Then 96 of them (group A) were given background information based on the Bain story, primed with his alleged confession, and told where to listen for it. The others (group B) were given a story and alternative words suggesting that the caller's father had killed the others and then himself. Listening to the tape again, 32 members of group A and 3 members of group B 'heard' the confession; none heard the alternative words. At the end, after both groups had been told the experts' view, 17 in group A still heard the confession, and were surprisingly joined by 11 in group B. We have held back the words in case you want to test your own resistance to suggestion; if so, listen to the full recording and then the extracts at forensictranscription.com.au/audio before, and then again after, reading the alleged confession. The effect might surprise you.

This case was not an isolated one, as the quality of the covert recordings routinely used in the prosecution of serious offences is often far poorer than those made in more favourable conditions by the emergency services. The homepage forensictranscription.com.au details some consequent miscarriages of justice and a presentation by Dr Fraser explaining why transcript vetting by defence lawyers and judges is inadequate: they are as prone to suggestion bias as anyone else.

How speakers mislead us

In all speech and writing we unthinkingly omit that part of the essential information that is so clearly understood by both parties that it is taken for granted. We have to do this because the amount of relevant information is infinite. But some of the context automatically relied on in conversation (where the listener can be helped by non-verbal clues and by asking questions) must be spelled out in writing, where writer and readers are separated by space and time, or if the parties have different motivations or habits of thought.

For example, *I am buying the shop* need not specify the address if that is apparent from the context. But if the address is needed, the name of the city might not be, and the country will rarely have to be stated. Moreover, the unspoken subtext – indicating the relevance of the statement and the type of response that would be appropriate – will vary. If spoken to the shop assistant the statement might mean *I am to be your new boss*; to someone coming out of a nearby house, *We are going to be neighbours*; to a solicitor, *I need someone to do the conveyancing*; to a rival buyer, *Go away!*

H.P. Grice's (1975) analysis of the techniques we automatically apply in co-operative conversation offers helpful insights. He phrased them as recommendations aimed at avoiding misunderstanding, on the assumption that that is what those conversing usually intend. He proposed four maxims:

Quantity:	Give as much information as necessary for the purpose of the exchange, but not more.
Quality:	Do not say what you believe to be false or that for which you lack adequate evidence.
Relevance:	Be relevant.
Manner:	Avoid obscurity of expression and ambiguity. Be brief and orderly.

That our expectations can be manipulated by breach of these maxims is a particular danger to lawyers because the parties may not have been co-operating and because courts tend to construe words literally. In *Bronston* v. *The United States* (1973) the president of a company seeking the American equivalent of voluntary winding up was questioned under oath about his personal assets:

Q: Do you have any bank accounts in Swiss banks, Mr Bronston?

A: No, sir.

Q: Have you ever?

A: The company had an account there for about six months, in Zurich.

Surprisingly, this fudge seems to have passed unnoticed, and it later emerged that Mr Bronston had once had an undisclosed but well-filled personal Swiss bank account. Nevertheless, the Supreme Court overturned his perjury conviction because his second answer, though intentionally misleading, was literally true.

How our views mislead us

Confirmation bias is our tendency to perceive, remember, and actively seek out evidence that supports our beliefs and to avoid, ignore, or dismiss anything that contradicts them. This censorship is sometimes conscious and deliberate (as when people choose a newspaper sympathetic to their views) but it need not be. The headline *Trump backer claims Muslim registry is the same as Japanese internment* is likely to be read as a disenchanted supporter's condemnation of the proposal or as an enthusiastic supporter's endorsement of it, depending on the view the reader thinks most reasonable – although in this case that bias might be affected by the expectation that a Trump backer would hold illiberal views. Similarly, Winston Churchill's comment that Clement Attlee had *a lot to be modest about* is likely to be interpreted by a Conservative hostile to socialism as a witty put-down; someone who knew of Churchill's regard for his former deputy prime minister might read it as a compliment.

What we can do about it

We can reduce – but never eliminate – the risk by remaining aware of these traps and taking more care than is usual to avoid them.

The techniques in Part C are designed not only for economy but also to reduce the likelihood that we or others will jump into a hole hidden by verbiage. In particular, when checking our own documents or reading those of others, we should resist the temptation to skim. That temptation will be significantly reduced if documents are clear, concise, and as enjoyable to read as their contents permit. A well-known generalisation says that the one thing we do not check will be the one that is wrong.

A pleading or witness statement (and instructions to draft them) should be checked for consistency with the witness's other statements and with whatever other evidence is available.

In the search for common ground we should also look for differences in belief and perception that might underlie the disputes we need to avoid or resolve. If the difference is irreconcilable we will at least see where the problem lies.

Humility helps – especially the willingness to learn from others regardless of their status.

We suggested some other precautions in Chapters 20 ('Editing') and 22 ('Testing documents').

Chapter 28

The boundaries of literacy and intelligence

Normal literacy and intelligence

The National Literacy Trust reports[1] that fewer than one per cent of adults in England are completely unable to read or write, but that

> Around 16 per cent, or 5.2 million adults[,] ... have literacy levels at or below those expected of an 11-year-old. They can understand short straightforward texts on familiar topics accurately and independently, and obtain information from everyday sources, but reading information from unfamiliar sources, or on unfamiliar topics, could cause problems ...
> Around 5 per cent, or 1.7 million adults in England, have literacy levels below those expected of an 11-year-old.

But a short browse in a good dictionary should convince you that nobody will know more than a modest fraction of the words and phrases in their native language, even discounting the jargon of unfamiliar disciplines and vernaculars.

Anyone less literate than most has extra difficulties. These can arise not only from their more limited vocabulary but also from lack of confidence, embarrassment, fear that others will take advantage of their ignorance, a consequent wish to keep their incomprehension secret, or just boredom. There is a great temptation to smile and nod. These readers need the writer's special care if the message is to arrive.

Some terms, whose words are familiar in one sense, might puzzle or mislead lay people – and even lawyers from different specialisms – when used in a special legal sense. For example, many contracts exclude *consequential loss*, which the Court of Appeal has defined in a way known only to scholars and litigators. As a result, many a contracting party, thinking it has excluded all but the immediate consequences of a breach of contract, finds it has not excluded much. Applying the Court of Appeal's definition, the judge in *McCain* v. *Eco-Tec* ((2011) paras.62–87) found that every item of damage claimed, totalling £1.7 million, was direct recoverable loss. And in *GB Gas* v. *Accenture* (2009) an exclusion of consequential loss had no impact on claims totalling £29 million.

Other deceptively familiar terms include:

administrator	perverse [verdict]
assent	plead
average	possession
[in] camera	prescription
charity	presents
child	privilege
consideration	profit
constructive [trust]	prove
costs	purchaser
deed	qualified [privilege]
devise	quiet enjoyment
estate	real [property]
equity	recital
execution	recorder
general [damages]	remainder
house	settlement
instrument	several
interest	special [damages]
issue	tail
land	term
light	title
liquidated	trust
malice	value
nuisance	waste
occupy	without prejudice
peppercorn	

It doesn't help that some terms have more than one technical meaning.

Even knowing the superficial meaning of the words might not be enough. Specialised knowledge, particular intelligence, or imagination might be needed to grasp their underlying significance. Even greater – or a different sort of – intelligence might be needed to translate the information conveyed into an informed decision. (Intelligence is not a single ability, far less can it be reliably quantified. Different parts of the brain process different information in different ways, and ability in any one area does not imply ability in another – which helps explain the follies of otherwise intelligent people.)

Adler (1991) (quoted on p.17) showed how a volunteer group whose literacy was above average misunderstood many aspects of a routine letter written by a solicitor proposing financial settlement terms to his client's unrepresented wife. Many in the group were well-educated and all were experienced in the use of lawyers. Although many were confident that they understood the letter, none of them understood it fully, and some of the misunderstandings were serious. Among the imaginatively misconstrued phrases were *matrimonial home, net proceeds of sale*, and *without prejudice*. Sometimes the superficial meaning was understood but not the significance (in brackets):

> Irretrievably broken down (your husband is about to divorce you).

> Transferred to joint names (will be inherited by the survivor regardless of your wills).

> All or any claims you may have now or in the future ... to be dismissed (you will be giving up all your other rights but your husband won't be giving up any of his).

> If you are in agreement with this, we should be grateful if you would let us know as soon as possible (your agreement will then be irrevocable, even though you've had no legal advice, unless you can persuade a judge to release you from it).

We doubt that this obscurity was intentional. The routine use of any expression can reduce it to such familiarity that the user forgets its unfamiliarity to others.

Peter Tiersma, a professor of law who was also an academic linguist, wrote (1999):

> Some of the best evidence that people have trouble with legal terminology comes from the fact that jurors, after they have received their instructions, all too often turn to dictionaries for their enlightenment ... A survey of American decisional law found many cases in which jurors have been accused of misconduct for looking up words, including *assault, battery, culpable, custody, entrapment, interference, insanity, legal cause, malice, malpractice, motive, murder, negligent, possession, premeditate, preponderance, proximate, prudent, rape, reasonable, undue, utter* (as in *utter a forged cheque*), and *wanton*.

We quote this in support of our general thesis that the law should be more clearly expressed, but this may be a convenient moment to consider juries in particular. Their understanding and reasoning are largely unchecked (especially in Britain, as a result of s.8 of the Contempt of Court Act 1981), yet they have the power to wreck lives. Since Tiersma wrote that passage, much work has been done to improve the standard instructions given to jurors on both sides of the Atlantic. Yet however well the instructions are drafted, jurors will still be obliged to decide cases without a clear grasp of the law they are supposed to be applying, for two reasons:

- Many jurors (sometimes, no doubt, all those deciding a particular case) are less literate than law students are expected to be, and less used to thinking like a lawyer. But no student would be expected to give a complete and accurate answer applying an unfamiliar area of the law to a set of facts after listening once to a lecture, without help from a dedicated teacher, and with no opportunity for further study. (However, the *steps to verdict* described on p.95 are helpful.)

- A large part of the problem is not that the law has not been clearly *expressed* but that it is inherently and incurably vague, as we argued in Chapter 23. It cannot help if the jurors are unaware of this.

It is not only jurors whose literacy is finite. *The Independent Online* (31 October 2007) reported these remarks of Sir Igor Judge not long before he was appointed Lord Chief Justice:

> For the Court of Appeal to decide the issue, we heard detailed submissions about the legislative provisions in no less than five statutes … The problem was so complicated that three judges had to reserve judgment because at the end of the hearing we could not work out whether or not the defendant was guilty. After reserving judgment we concluded that no offence had been committed. Yet the appellant had spent time in custody.

But the seeds of injustice can be sown long before trial. Goldstein and others (2012) say:

> Although many juvenile offenders read near the sixth-grade level, their linguistic deficits make comprehension of the [*Miranda*] warnings unlikely even when they are written at an appropriate level. Furthermore, adolescent characteristics associated with developmental immaturity seem to impact *Miranda* comprehension in ways that create unique challenges for youths attempting to comprehend their rights. These characteristics may interact with language factors, suggesting that a sufficiently low reading and comprehension level of the warnings may be necessary but not sufficient for comprehension.

One suspect (of unspecified age), when told that he was *going to be charged with the damage on the door* seemed to think that meant that he would have to pay for the door (Heydon, 2013, p.68).

How many wrongful convictions are founded on misunderstandings? And how much legal advice is inappropriate or misapplied?

Even when aware of their failure to understand, many people will often lack the time, patience, or funds – or will fear that their lawyer lacks the time or patience – to resolve all their doubts, and they will unwisely hope for the best.

Fluctuation

An additional layer of difficulty arises from the constant fluctuation of any individual's ability to understand and process information, according to their physical and mental condition. A person's usual abilities can be reduced by illness, malaise, tiredness, preoccupation, stress, lack of interest, hunger, thirst, other cravings, discomfort, pain, and external distractions. Mental abilities fluctuate even with the normal daily rhythm of our bodies and with longer-term hormonal variations.

Stress

Anxiety diverts the mental resources needed for thoughtful response. Hormones released into the prefrontal cortex as a response to stress immediately impede memory, learning, judgement, and decision-making. As failure to understand can itself generate anxiety, particularly when understanding is essential, this can create a vicious cycle.

Lawyers sometimes forget how stressful any contact with the law can be to someone threatened by it, or even to someone not threatened but out of their depth in a strange environment. Giving evidence in court is stressful even to a disinterested and honest witness, especially when they are, or soon will be, cross-examined. This must be as nothing compared to the anxiety of litigants in person, never before in court, forced to argue their own case because they cannot afford a lawyer. Even receiving a lawyer's letter in a non-contentious matter can be stressful until the reader is convinced that there is no threat.

Rock (2016) gives this example of the effect of anxiety, putting herself in the position of a newly-arrested suspect who badly needs to understand the rights to silence and counsel, the limits of those rights, and the risks involved in choosing to exercise them:

> You are in a small room which is lit rather too brightly by harsh fluorescent lighting panels. A strange smell hovers. It reminds you of something unpleasant but you are not sure quite what. The room is furnished with a metal toilet and a wide, thigh-high bench covered by a thin mattress encased in very thick, very cold, blue plastic. There is a piece of paper beside you covered in tight-set type which you cannot bring yourself to concentrate on. You have a nagging, queasy feeling, however, that you should have read that paper and that you should have read it carefully. You are particularly concerned that the words at the top of the page, the same words which you heard when you were arrested and brought to this police cell, might be some of the most important you'll ever encounter as they might affect the rest of your life. However you just cannot face reading them.

Heydon (2013, p.64) offers a transcript of a police interview showing a suspect's difficulties understanding whether she had a right to refuse to be fingerprinted. It includes this telling exchange (hesitations and transcription notes omitted but punctuation added):

O: Do you understand this information?

S: So have I got a choice whether I get fingerprinted or not?

O: Do you wish to comment on this information? Do you understand what I've said to you?

S: Not really, no.

O: Would you like me to read it to you again?

S: No. Just I'm asking you. Have I got a choice? Do I have to be fingerprinted or don't I?

Endnote

1   www.literacytrust.org.uk/adult_literacy/illiterate_adults_in_england

Chapter 29

Translating and interpreting

This chapter is not a guide to legal translation, and contains nothing that will be new to competent legal translators. It is intended to warn everyone else of the difficulties and dangers and the need for professional help.

As Peter W. Schroth (1986) said, legal translators must:

> ... understand not only what the words mean and what a sentence means, but also what legal effect it is supposed to have, and [they must] know how to achieve that legal effect in the other language.

This calls for deep knowledge of both languages and some knowledge of both legal systems. It is no place for amateurs. Sometimes, however, lawyers know as they write that their reader will be working in a second language, without access to a professional translation.

We follow the usual convention that, broadly, writing is translated and speech interpreted. The difficulties we identify for translators apply also to interpreters, but interpreters have additional problems.

Professional translators are required (by the Institute of Translation and Interpreting's Code of Professional Conduct[1]) to

> translate only into a language that is either (i) their mother tongue or language of habitual use, or (ii) one in which they have satisfied the Institute that they have equal competence

and to

> translate only from those languages in which they can demonstrate they have the requisite skills.

As we said in Chapter 2, we agree with the traditionalists that accuracy and precision are of the greatest importance in legal writing. But we have tried to show that absolute precision (sought by those imposing rights and duties) and absolute accuracy (sought by those explaining those rights and duties) are unattainable ideals. And if meaning can be lost even between those who share language and culture, how much worse must it be for those who do not? The greater the difference between languages, legal systems, and other aspects of culture, the more serious will be the problem, particularly where cultural differences change (and in some cases obliterate) the significance of what is communicated. This is particularly serious for legal translation, where fine shades of meaning can deprive people of their rights.

Let's look at the concepts *theft*, *trust*, and *equity* to illustrate the difficulties.

On p.52 we quoted the French definition of theft, which, unlike the English definition, does not specify an intention to deprive the owner permanently. So, one may be guilty of *vol* in France while innocent of *theft* in England. Moreover, *vol* doubles as the word for *robbery*, losing the distinction available in English, although lawyers in Quebec interpret it differently from those in France. And *frauduleusement* – which is part of the definition of *vol* – sometimes does and sometimes doesn't mean *fraudulently*.

The common law notion of trusts was (and to some extent still is) alien to civil law systems. The French version of the Civil Code of Quebec uses *fiducie* where the English version uses *trust*, but in both languages the law is codified and differs from common law.[2] The 1985 Hague Convention on the Law Applicable to Trusts and on their Recognition differs in substance from both common and Québecois law, though it imports the English word *trust* into its non-English versions:

Article premier

La présente Convention détermine la loi applicable au trust et régit sa reconnaissance.[3]

Garner (2011) identifies at least 13 meanings for *equity*. Most of these are unknown to non-lawyers, who are likely to think it means either *fairness* or (in England) *the value of their house less the amount owing on their mortgage*. Civil lawyers have the same difficulty as non-lawyers. They often see the word translated as *équité* (in French), *equidad* (in Spanish), or *equità* (in Italian), which they understand only as *fairness* or *reasonableness* (Sarcevic, 2015).

These conceptual differences matter to individuals (and their accountants, lawyers, and judges) who need to understand a foreign document. They also complicate the work of legislative drafters in the many plurilingual jurisdictions (for instance, Canada, Switzerland, and Hong Kong) where the same concepts must be enacted in different languages with the same effect, each version having equal status. The EU has perhaps the greatest headache, legislating in 24 official languages from several branches of the Indo-European family, and from outside this family; by comparison with that range, English and German are similar.

Translators have an easier job than interpreters. They have time to think and edit; they can consult dictionaries, thesauruses, style guides, precedents, colleagues, and the internet. If there is no sufficiently precise translation they can usually add explanatory notes.

On the other hand, we expect from interpreters instant, complete, and accurate renderings, often unscripted, even when two people are talking at once, and sometimes in stressful conditions or when the interpreter is too tired to function well. We expect them also to set aside any sympathy they have for the outsiders whose culture they share, although this will sometimes be difficult when they are interpreting 'for' – see the bias sneaking in – a migrant seeking asylum or accused of a crime. And if the interview is unrecorded there might be no way for anyone to know when there has been a serious misunderstanding.

A particular danger lies in interpretation by someone whose apparent competence in the language is misleading, or (similarly) by someone operating without an interpreter in a language not their own. A single word or fragment missed, mispronounced, misheard, misused, unrecognised, or misunderstood can distort the meaning: from positive to negative, future to past, singular to plural, male to female, or from one topic to another, derailing all that follows. In the nasal accent of a windy, wine-growing region of southern France, *vent* and *vin* sound indistinguishable, as do *cent* and *cinq*.

> **MA:** The first time I saw a sign *Boissons frais* in a shop window I absent-mindedly read it as *fresh fish (poissons frais)*, and might not have realised my mistake had the shop not been a launderette (offering in fact *cold drinks*). Later, since my wife and I have lived in this region long enough to conduct whole conversations in French with apparent understanding, we sometimes discover afterwards that her understanding and mine have been radically different.

Vulnerable interviewees – whether police suspects, victims, children, claimants, migrants or tourists struggling with the language of their hosts, or other fragile witnesses – may see the interpreter as a friend, the only person available who can understand and explain what is being said to them and what they have to say in reply. On the one hand, the interpreter is expected to remain neutral and objective, and not to step outside the role of interpreter by editing undiplomatic, unfortunate, or unwise statements or speech styles (for instance, making the witness sound more articulate). On the other hand, the interpreter's primary function is to create understanding, and for this they sometimes need to intervene to avoid *mis*understandings arising from imprecision in either language. Ideally, they should also correct misunderstandings where the meaning of verbal or non-verbal cues differs between cultures.

The misinterpretation of style can work both ways. Jieun Lee (2011, p.2) warns that:

> [C]ompared to speakers who use elaborate or formal forms and convoluted illogical structures, speakers who use simple, congruent forms and logical structures are considered more committed to what they say. Powerless speech is marked with the use of linguistic markers such as hedges, tag questions, polite forms, and other features that mark vagueness and uncertainty, whereas powerful speech is devoid of these features. Numerous social psychology-based studies, which have investigated the effect that witness testimony styles may have on courtroom participants, have consistently found that speakers with powerful speech style are perceived more favourably in terms of credibility, intelligence, and attractiveness.

The mistranslation of style may not be deliberate, or even conscious. In a detailed and useful guide to lawyers instructing translators and interpreters, Corsellis and Clement (2006, p.223) claim that:

> interpreters are rarely qualified to be a source of accurate knowledge on the beliefs, perceptions, attitudes and demeanour of the individuals with whom they share a language.

Sharing a language that has spread worldwide by empire or commerce does not imply sharing a culture.

Nor does sharing a country. Australian courts, for example, have had to learn that in some aboriginal cultures courtesy requires people to appear to assent to statements with which they disagree. This signals respect, not dishonesty. The Legal Services Commission of South Australia advises that:[4]

> gratuitous concurrence [as it is called] during a conversation is ... used to build or define the relationship between the people who are speaking.

Similarly, Dr Diana Eades states (2002, p.164):

> Silence in Aboriginal English is seen as a valuable and positive part of interaction, and is not taken as an indication that something is wrong, or that the speaker is evasive, lying or ignorant.

Corsellis and Clement also warn (2006, p.222):

> Interpreters should be advised [in their brief] of any specific techniques which will be used, e.g. for interviewing children, as these could impact upon the interpreting. The interpreter's task is to match as fully as possible the level of formality and type of language used by both parties, as well as the content of the message. They will need to know where it is vital, for instance, to use a non-leading question in particular circumstances: for example, there is no generic sign in [British Sign Language] for 'weapon' and choices would have to be made between 'gun', 'knife' and so on.

215

The risk of misinterpretation is high when bilingual police officers double as interpreters, especially while taking part in an interrogation. In England and Wales they are not allowed to interpret when questioning suspects or taking witness statements to be used in evidence, but it is permitted in the United States – with worrying consequences (Berk-Seligson, 2016).

Finally, Berk-Seligson (2016, quoting Sonia Russell's 2000 study of the English police's administration of the caution to French suspects) also expresses concern about the extra difficulties caused by police officers stating the law in their own words, and so adding a preliminary layer of (amateur) interpretation for the interpreter to work from.

Writing to reduce the dangers

In general, the easier the text is for the native speaker, the more likely it is to be translated accurately. This can be seen from the resources for translators published by the European Union.[5] In recent years, most EU legislation has been drafted in English and then translated into the other 23 languages, so their advice to writers is particularly relevant to English writers. Nearly all that advice is the same as ours.

However, a few techniques that work well for readers whose first language is English (and for first class professional translators) can create difficulties for unaided speakers of English as a second language, for whose benefit you should:

- Avoid where possible expressions that cannot be translated literally, either because of cultural differences – if you're aware of them – or because they are idioms whose meaning is not immediately apparent.
- Avoid, or if necessary explain, phrasal verbs. Who could guess the difference between *hold* and *hold up*, or *set up*, *set down*, *set in*, *set to*, *set back*, and *set off*?
- Spell out connections in full, including the words you might otherwise omit for brevity. For example, instead of *I thought you said this would work* you might write *I thought **that** you said **that** this **proposal** would work.*
- Use any knowledge you have of the target language. For example, native speakers of Romance languages like French, Spanish, and Italian are more likely to recognise words imported into English from their languages or from Latin (typically, but not reliably, those ending *ion*) than words derived from Anglo-Saxon.

The process of translation often reveals ambiguity or confusion in the original text (as usefully highlighted by the misunderstandings of automatic online translators). If you encourage the translator to contact you with queries, not only should you get a better translation but you may also discover new ways to improve your writing.

216

Endnotes

1 www.iti.org.uk/attachments/article/154/Code%20of%20professional%
   20conduct%2008%2009%202013_Final.pdf.
2 ccq.lexum.com, from s.1260, about which the Supreme Court of Canada
   confusingly said in *Caisse populaire Desjardins de Val-Brillant* v. *Blouin*
   (para.43): 'Parliament may, however, call a plan a trust even if the plan cannot
   be characterized as such under the rules of Quebec's civil law'.
3 www.hcch.net/fr/instruments/conventions/full-text/?cid=59.
4 www.lsc.sa.gov.au/dsh/ch03s04.php.
5 ec.europa.eu/info/resources-partners/translation-and-drafting-resources_en.

Part E

Common law rules of interpretation

Chapter 30

A brief look at the interpretation rules

We will say little about the rules of interpretation, as it is a mistake to rely on them when drafting. They apply only when people cannot use our documents without the expense, delay, prolonged stress, and ultimate uncertainty of asking a court to guess what we meant, with the risk that (if it guesses wrongly) it will impose a meaning we don't like. The courts will not apply them at all if they consider the meaning clear from the face of the document. Even when applied they are an unreliable remedy, being not rules so much as a jumble of mutually inconsistent maxims. In Mellinkoff's (1992) words:

> A maxim is to law as a fortune cookie is to philosophy.

But we'll consider a few of the maxims because they serve as warnings of the lurking traps and because what guidance they do give supports the use of plain language. A fuller treatment is given in Butt (2013).

The overriding principle is that *words are to be given their ordinary sense*. As the then Mr Justice Hoffmann said in *Norwich Union* v. *British Railways Board* (1987):

> After all that analysis, however, I come back to what seems to me to be the plain question: what as a matter of ordinary English do the words of the covenant mean?

He came back to the point as a law lord in *Investors Compensation Scheme* v. *West Bromwich Building Society* (1997), and his opinion was adopted by Lords Goff, Hope, and Clyde. Introducing his formulation of the current position, Lord Hoffman said:

> I do not think that the fundamental change which has overtaken this branch of the law … is always sufficiently appreciated. The result has been, subject to one important exception, to assimilate the way in which such documents are interpreted by judges to the common sense principles by which any serious utterance would be interpreted in ordinary life. Almost all the old intellectual baggage of 'legal' interpretation has been discarded.

His summary of the principles may itself be roughly summarised:

Take the meaning that the document as a whole would have to a reasonable person with the background knowledge that should have been available to the parties at the time of the contract. This background includes everything except (for policy reasons) their negotiations and statements of subjective intent. Words should be given their 'natural and ordinary meaning' unless one can conclude from the background 'that something must have gone wrong with the language'. The background can also be used to resolve ambiguities.

Lord Hoffman was speaking only about construing contractual documents, but similar principles apply to other documents.

Since then the English courts have to some extent swung back from giving effect to what the parties must as reasonable people have meant (even if it's not what they said) to giving effect to the ordinary meaning of their words (even if it's hard to believe they could be so *un*reasonable). But *Investors Compensation Scheme* v. *West Bromwich Building Society* has not been overruled or even criticised.[1] Words should still be given their *natural and ordinary meaning*, although that was at first *unless* and now *even if* that leads to a harsh result.

The old intellectual baggage

The old principles are still alive to the extent that they can help establish the ordinary meaning.

Eiusdem generis

This is the principle that if a list of things of a particular type ends with a catch-all expression like *or anything else* (or, possibly,[2] begins with general words followed by a list), then the meaning of the general words is restricted to things of the same type. *Eiusdem generis* has been called the *limited class rule* by Arden LJ, in *Davies* v. *Meadwestvaco Calmar Ltd* (2008) and elsewhere, and the *class presumption* (Torbert, 2007). This name-change must be an improvement, and timid practitioners should be encouraged by the Court of Appeal's willingness to abandon traditional expressions in favour of clearer neologisms.

In *BOC* v. *Centeon* (1999) the Court of Appeal said:

> Mr Strauss' submission that there is no such thing as an *eiusdem generis* rule ... in my view goes too far. Admittedly the Latin ought to be replaced by English words and the interests of clarity may well be served by doing so. Maybe it is wrong to regard it as a rule. Sometimes it has been called a maxim or an aid to construction. What cannot be denied, in my view, is that the considerations which underlie it are ones which a reasonable man would take into account as a matter of commonsense.

In that case a list comprised

any transfer of any of the equity interest in Delta, the transfer of any or all of Delta's assets or business, the dissolution of Delta, the termination of the business of Delta (or any part thereof), the success or failure of any research projects undertaken by Delta, the future commercialisation or otherwise of any products, Delta's future business prospects or technological or technical successes

but ended

or by any other matter whatsoever.

Mr Strauss, having failed in his attempt to bury *eiusdem generis*, had

submitted that … the lawyers knew the power of the word 'whatsoever' and that as an exclusion it effectively precludes limitation by, for example, the *eiusdem generis* rule …

But his opponent

submitted that the parties, as well-informed lawyers, likewise would know that the right of set-off had to be excluded by, as Lord Diplock put it, 'express or clear or unequivocal language', so much so that even express words might be regarded as necessary to make it clear that that was intended.

The court agreed with both of them:

It seems to me that both of those submissions are valid. But of course the question of construction remains.

And it applied *eiusdem generis* to restrict *any other matter whatsoever* to matters connected with the subsequent fate of the Delta project.

But it is not always easy to define a class to which the general words are to be restricted.

In *Heatherington v. Grant* (1960), *all kinds of merchandise* was not restricted by the listed types because no class could be identified. On the other hand, in *Cosco* (2010) the Commercial Court found a class in

the loss of time from default and/or deficiency of men including strike of Officers and/or crew or deficiency of … stores, fire, breakdown or damages to hull, machinery or equipment, grounding, detention by average accidents to ship or cargo, dry-docking for the purpose of examination or painting bottom, *or by any other cause* preventing the full working of the vessel

on the basis that these

all related to the physical condition or efficiency of the vessel (including its crew) or, in one instance, cargo and did not include truly extraneous causes.

The sleight of pen here lies in the *or*, which extends the *eiusdem generis* principle so that it applies not to a single list of related items but to a list of unrelated sublists.

223

The cause of succinct drafting was not helped by Rix J's tentative (and expressly *obiter*) view in *The Laconian Confidence* (1997) that while *any other cause* should be applied restrictively *any other cause whatsoever* was probably wide enough to reach the opposite conclusion. But, as we saw a few lines back, the Court of Appeal took the opposite view soon afterwards in *BOC* v. *Centeon* (1999).

However, context (meaning the verbal context of this and associated documents as well as the factual background) is everything. Driedger (1974) put it this way:

> General words, whether associated with two words, one word or none, may be restricted by anything comprised in 'context' in its widest sense.

In *Skinner* v. *Shew* (1893) the Court of Appeal interpreted the class of threats made *by circulars, advertisements or otherwise* to include those sent by letter. The relevant context was the Act's purpose, which was to restrain threats, and the means of transmission were neither here nor there. The Court concluded that the examples were given not to exclude other types but for the avoidance of doubt.

Expressio unius (est exclusio alterius)

This is the other side of the *eiusdem generis* coin, being the principle that mentioning one or more things implies the intentional omission of anything that has *not* been mentioned. Like *eiusdem generis*, it can be subsumed under the general principle of deducing the meaning from the context. If you want to anglicise it, it might be called *the full list rule*.

In *Hare* v. *Horton* (1833) Parke J held that the mortgage of a foundry and two dwelling-houses

> with all grates, boilers, bells, and other fixtures in and about the said two dwelling-houses

did not include the fixtures at the foundry, although of course those would normally have passed as part of the land even if not mentioned.

But again, the decision whether to apply the rule depends, in Lord Macnaghten's words in *Pasmore* v. *Oswaldtwistle* (1898),

> on the scope and language of the [document] ... and on considerations of policy and convenience.

Noscitur a sociis (qui non cognoscitur ex se)

This is the principle that a word is understood by the company it keeps: its immediate verbal context. In this it is similar to the previous two maxims but, unlike *eiusdem generis*, no identifying class is needed. Anglophones might want to call it *the associated words rule*.

The Court of Appeal applied the rule in *Tektrol* (2005). The owner of a stolen computer was unable to recover from its insurer as if this were *other erasure loss distortion or corruption of information*. Sir Martin Nourse said

> The expression 'other erasure loss distortion or corruption of information' demonstrates that the loss contemplated is loss by means of electronic interference ... It is not just the effect of the other three words, but the order in which the four appear.

But why didn't the drafter just refer to *other loss of information by electronic means*?

Contra proferentem

This is the commendable principle that ambiguity will be construed against the interest of the party responsible for it. We might call it *the careless drafting rule*.

In principle, *contra proferentem* is not available unless one party was clearly 'responsible' for the clause (*Transocean Drilling UK Ltd* v. *Providence Resources Plc* (2016)). And it may not apply to a commercial contract negotiated between parties of equal bargaining power (*Persimmon Homes Ltd* v. *Ove Arup & Partners Ltd* (2017)). In practice, it doesn't matter. The courts can interpret a clause strictly in the interests of justice, without invoking this or any maxim.

The Court of Appeal made limited use of it in *Tektrol* (2005):

> A limited version of the [*contra proferentem*] doctrine is ... of some relevance in construing exceptions in insurance policies, as the court has to do in this case. As Lindley LJ put it in *Cornish* v. *Accident Insurance Co* (1889, p.456):
>   '...in a case of real doubt, the policy ought to be construed most strongly against the insurers; they frame the policy and insert the exceptions. But this principle ought only to be applied for the purpose of removing a doubt, not for the purpose of creating a doubt, or magnifying an ambiguity, when the circumstances of the case raise no real difficulty.'
>   In the present case, as will be seen, there are some genuine difficulties in determining the factual situations to which the clauses absolving the insurers from risk, read in context, can properly be applied. It is at least a relevant factor in such an enquiry to recall that the insurers indeed could have made things much clearer in their own favour if that was indeed their intention when they drew the policy.

Falsa demonstratio non nocet

This is the principle that a document will not be invalidated by an inaccurate description. It only works if the misdescribed person or property can be identified, a point that might be used to excuse the scattergun approach of multiple descriptions. Against that is the amount of litigation that has arisen, and we offer instead our own maxim – *The more words, the more mistakes* – and suggest instead frugal precision.

Endnotes

1 Lord Sumption gave a readable account of these changes, and of his own disagreement with Lord Hoffmann's position, in 'A question of taste: The Supreme Court and the interpretation of contracts' (**www.supremecourt.uk/ docs/speech-170508.pdf** (8 May 2017)).

2 In *Ambatielos* v. *Anton Jurgens* [1923] the House of Lords refused to intepret general words *eiusdem generis* with a list of examples because (among other reasons) the general words preceded the list.

Appendix A

A legal writing workshop

Training aims

We believe that, if their lives depended on it, most lawyers could make their writing shorter and clearer without any training. What stops them is not lack of skill, but habit, conservatism, the lack of time and incentive, and what has been called *the curse of knowledge*: in this case, the difficulty lawyers have in adopting the perspective of those who are unfamiliar with law.

Our suggested aims for a plain language workshop are therefore to:

- Give participants the reader's experience, so they understand how badly their clients and managers suffer from their poor writing style.
- Convince them that they personally have at least some of the poor writing habits noted in the reader's experience.
- Show them what they personally can gain by improving their writing style.
- Identify three writing habits that will make the most difference to their writing for the least effort. Depending on their training needs, these might be taken from those suggested in Chapter 8.
- Give practice in an easy, practical way to change each of those three writing habits.
- Check that, by the end of the workshop, participants can recall each of those habits and explain how to change them.
- Invite each participant to pick one habit that they will start work on immediately after the workshop. Suggest that they write it into their current year's performance objectives.

We suggest that a half-day workshop is enough to achieve these aims. For continuing support as a participant works on changing their writing habits, we recommend style-checking software.

Here, then, is an outline for a workshop for up to 12 lawyers, focusing on word choice and three other writing habits from the five offered here. Law firms and legal departments are welcome to use and adapt these exercises and materials for inhouse training if they credit *Clarity for Lawyers* and acknowledge our copyright. (Suggested wording: '© Mark Adler and Daphne Perry, from *Clarity for Lawyers* (Law Society Publishing 2017)'.) Other professional trainers must first agree the terms of a licence with Daphne Perry.

As usual in training, the more the participants can learn by exercises and question-and-answer, the more they will learn (and the more they will enjoy the training). The main techniques taught should be revised and tested throughout the workshop.

Writing samples

Every point in the workshop should be illustrated by examples taken from the participants' own writing. An example taken from this book might make the same points but without convincing the participants of the need to change their own writing habits.

Before the workshop, the participants should therefore supply sample documents, after deleting sensitive information. Naturally, the trainer should keep these documents confidential, use them only for the workshop, and destroy any copies afterwards. From these documents, the trainer can identify the writing techniques on which to focus and extract short, anonymised examples to use in the exercises and discussion.

Participants say that the use of their own writing is one of the most valuable features of the training, as well as occasionally the most painful. It is worth reminding everyone at the start of training not to claim authorship or try to identify a writer. And we, the trainers, should treat every fault with understanding, not criticism. There is always a reason why people write as they do; often it is just their ability to learn from those around them. Every writing fault featured in this training is one that we ourselves have made, until we learned better. Some of them still trouble us today.

Introduction to the workshop

This should be kept short – 10 minutes at most to introduce the trainer, the participants (if necessary), the training format, and the topics to be covered. Warn the participants that in a few minutes they will be asked to write down three things that other writers should do, to make what they write quick and easy for the participants to read. Tell them that, at the end of the training, they will be asked to pick one writing habit to improve. Tell them what they, personally, will gain from doing so, and make sure it is realistic.

Readers' needs – a practical exercise

The main aim of this exercise is to prove that, in one page of text, the techniques we suggest can visibly reduce the time it takes for a document to achieve its purpose. A secondary aim is to show how traditional legal writing can annoy and frustrate the reader.

For this, you need a page or less of real text that, while wordy and confusing, is still recognisable as normal legal writing, and a rewritten version applying as many techniques from this book as possible to convey the same message. Then identify the most likely question the real readers would have in mind as they read the text. Often, it's *What does the writer want? What should I do now?* If it's appropriate, you could use the example on pp.232–3. Or use a message about IT or some other expertise, to give lawyers the experience of reading someone else's jargon.

Having briefed the participants on their task, give half the group the original version, and half the rewritten version. They should all start reading at the same time, and give a clear and permanent signal when they think they have an answer to the question.

Normally, most of those given the rewritten document signal that they have an answer before the others although, in a group of lawyers, the most confident decision-makers usually come out first, no matter which version they get. (Long experience of working with documents like the original also produces a faster response. On the other hand, a non-lawyer reading the rewritten version can beat a partner with an unfamiliar original.)

You could then ask participants what feelings they experienced as they looked for the answer. Normally those reading the original experience some frustration. Asking what features of the rewritten text made it quicker to read is good preparation for the next exercise.

Three chosen techniques – a practical exercise

The next part of the workshop takes only a few minutes, but it sets the scene for everything that follows. You invite the participants to write down three things everyone else should do, to make their writing quicker and easier to read.

You then present your own three chosen techniques in detail.

Teaching the three techniques

For the next three topics you present, begin by asking who in the room included the suggested technique in their three. Follow this by asking them (and others) what makes this technique so valuable. In this way, you acknowledge the writing expertise already in the room and avoid telling participants what they already know. Continue by asking questions, discussing examples, and working on exercises until participants can explain the benefit of the writing technique and how to apply it.

After teaching each technique, you will suggest how the participants should practise it once or twice in every document they touch – and in every email – to develop a new writing habit.

After you have presented all three techniques, take a few minutes to find out what others the participants included in their three. Someone is sure to identify simple language or avoiding jargon, leading to the next topic ('Word choice' on p.231).

Here we offer suggestions for teaching some writing techniques that often feature among those chosen.

Headings

Question participants about the value of headings. Using extracts from the writing samples, help them to see how headings can save reading time and supply context for the detail that follows.

Next, ask what makes a good heading. You are looking for the answers *short*, *informative*, and *accurate*.

A good clue to the first two is a heading that is too long but tells the whole story. Ask what is good and bad about it. Show examples of headings from the participants' documents and invite participants to suggest how some could be shortened and others could be made more informative. Consider the organisation of headings within a document (or cover it under *Putting the main message first*).

To explain what is meant by *accurate*, try to tease out the metaphor of a signpost, and ask where you should arrive if you follow it. Ask how accurate a good heading should be and wait for the answer *totally*. What other kind of accuracy is there? Explain that this means a heading should describe everything that follows until the next heading or the end of the document and nothing else. Show examples of headings from a sample document alongside misplaced text and invite participants to suggest where it appeared. Discuss how this happens and how, if writers have the luxury of time to edit, moving the text will improve structure and organisation.

Putting the main message first

Ask the participants where they would look for the main message when they are reading a document.

Illustrate the value of putting the main message first, comparing examples of poor beginnings with ones that get straight to the point.

Establish the test for identifying the main message – whatever the main target reader needs to know, or what the writer most needs them to know. Suggest a useful shortcut – to take the last paragraph and move it to the beginning. Question the value of beginning a contract, or any document, with a list of defined terms. Remind participants that, if ever they have a reader's attention, it will be at the start of a document.

Short sentences

When you ask the value of a short sentence, you might offer as a clue a long and involved sentence from the writing samples, preferably one with a mistake in it. Everyone makes mistakes, and not just in the long sentences, but they are harder to spot in a long and involved construction. And, for anyone who was not taught grammar and punctuation (most writers educated in the last 30 years), short sentences are easier to get right.

Discuss how short a sentence should be. Many lawyers agree that short sentences are good, but most believe their own sentences are already short enough. Length limits may seem arbitrary, but they're a useful guide. Therefore, suggest a target sentence length for those working to shorten their sentences. The most practical is two lines maximum. For those with style-checking software, suggest keeping the average sentence length to no more than 20 words.

Show examples of long sentences, taken from the writing samples. Get the participants to edit them using the techniques of splitting, pruning, and listing. A good illustration of the value of the list format is a bulleted list written in an alphabet no one can read. Show how much information the format conveys before the participants have read a word of the text.

Paragraphing for meaning

To show the value of paragraphs, a good exercise is to take the same text and format it in several ways: as a wall of text; divided arbitrarily; divided sensibly; and with subparagraphs or bulleted lists. Discuss which version is most readable and why.

You can also take a long and convoluted paragraph and work with the group to break it into short paragraphs with in-line headings. Then review the order of the points made. The idea is to demonstrate the editing technique rather than to come up with the perfect version. There are usually several good ways to edit the text. Explain how this technique can be used to improve the structure and signposting of the document.

Active voice

This topic normally has to start with a short explanation of active and passive voice (for which see p.124). Using examples from the participants' writing samples, let them identify passive verbs in sentences showing good uses (to focus on the object of the action, or to soften a demand or criticism) and bad (omitting useful information, avoiding responsibility). Let them practise editing passive to active, using the techniques suggested on p.127.

Word choice

This rarely features in the trainer's choice of habits offering the most change for the least effort, because it is harder to change. The curse of knowledge is most powerful here: lawyers regularly fail to identify legalese as anything out of the ordinary.

Here you could display some non-legal text and ask participants to identify jargon and other difficult words, noting any ordinary words used in an unusual way. Discuss the effect of these words on the reader, and the value of writing in the reader's language for building rapport and for showing understanding of the client's needs. Ask the group if they can think of any other sort of specialist who writes to its clients in unfamiliar language, and wait for the laughs and sheepish looks.

Then take some legal text and get the group to identify unavoidable legal terms, other language that only a lawyer would use, and language that anyone would use. Discuss how their readers would express the same ideas and what the writer should do about unavoidable legal terms (explain the term if it's not one the reader would use).

If some writing samples contain Latin words, you can demonstrate how little agreement there is over their meaning, even within the group. It is easy then to suggest that using Latin is not good communication.

This might be an opportunity to mention the legal habit of interrupting text to define terms, often in bold text, brackets, and quotation marks. Like jargon, this format hinders understanding and can alienate the reader. Show alternative formats to convey the same definitions (in-line headings or a glossary).

Rewriting – a practical exercise

If time allows, you can invite the participants to rewrite about 120 words of text from the writing samples, applying the principles taught in the workshop. A workshop of 12 lawyers, working in groups of four, could look at three extracts. The main aims of this exercise are:

- To show three writers (silently and anonymously) how hard their colleagues find it to understand their most confusing bit of sample text.
- To convince everyone to focus on one writing habit at a time, rather than try to apply everything they've learned at once and lose productivity. Fifteen minutes is barely enough to edit 120 words.
- To give the participants a bit of extra interaction and relaxation at the end of the workshop.

Review

Invite each participant to identify the first writing habit they will work on. Suggest they write that habit into their year's performance objectives. Wish them luck.

> **DP:** I have attended and given many workshops. Each time I have learned more about what works (and what doesn't) when training lawyers to improve their writing. One thing I have learned is that, if the only incentive for using plain language is what the trainer can provide, training alone has little effect. The essential ingredient is that the lawyer's manager demands and praises plain language.

231

Sample practical exercise

OMNICORP *(Version X)*

Omnicorp Plc ask for your advice. They say:

- We are working on a project for a client.
- Our client has shared confidential information with us for the purpose of the project.
- Our contract with the client includes the confidentiality clause below.
- We now want to engage a contractor to help with the project.
- Can we share the confidential information with the contractor, or must we ask the client's permission first?

2. Obligations of the Parties

2.1 The party who receives the Confidential Information ('receiving party') from the other party ('disclosing party') agrees as follows:

2.1.1 to maintain the same in confidence and to use it only for the Purpose;

2.1.2 not to make any commercial use of the Confidential Information nor to use the same for the benefit of itself or any third party except for the Purpose;

2.1.3 not to copy or reproduce (whether in writing or otherwise) any part of the Confidential Information except as strictly necessary for the Purpose or as expressly otherwise allowed under the terms of this Agreement;

2.1.4 to only disclose the Confidential Information to its employees, professional advisers, auditors and consultants (and in the case of Omnicorp, any employees, advisers, auditors and consultants of the Omnicorp Group) who need to know the same for the Purpose and to ensure that all such persons are obliged by their contracts of employment or contracts of service not to disclose the Confidential Information; and

2.1.5 to apply thereto no lesser security measures and degree of care than those which the disclosing party applies to its own confidential or proprietary information but in no event less than reasonable care.

Time taken:

Answer:

Sample practical exercise

OMNICORP

Omnicorp Plc ask for your advice. They say:

- We are working on a project for a client.
- Our client has shared confidential information with us for the purpose of the project.
- Our contract with the client includes the confidentiality clause below.
- We now want to engage a contractor to help with the project.
- Can we share the confidential information with the contractor, or must we ask the client's permission first?

2. **Duties of the Parties**

   Each party agrees to treat the other's Confidential Information as follows:

   2.1 **Use**: to use it only for the Purpose.

   2.2 **Copying**: not to copy any part of it except as:

   a   necessary for the Purpose or
   b   expressly allowed by this Agreement;

   2.3 **Disclosure**: to keep it confidential; but a party may disclose Confidential Information to anyone who:

   a   needs to know it for the Purpose,
   b   has contracted not to disclose it, and
   c   is one of the following:

   - the party's employee, professional adviser, or consultant.
   - an employee, adviser, or consultant of any company in the Omnicorp Group.

   2.4 **Security**: to take reasonable care of it, and to match any greater care and security measures applied by the disclosing party to its own confidential information.

Time taken:

Answer:

Appendix B

Analysis of examples

Example A

(See p.64.)

Original

We have been consulted by your Husband regarding matrimonial difficulties which you have been experiencing during your marriage . . .

We understand that there were arguments culminating in Easter this year when there were considerable difficulties presented when your Parents were invited to stay at the matrimonial home. Our client had already intimated to you that he intended to redecorate the house, and that our client would be unable to accommodate your Parents.

Since Easter we understand that you have not spoken, and that prior to this occasion there were periods of up to 7 days when you did not speak to each other. This was mainly caused by the difficulties that our client has experienced with his Parents-In-Law, and in particular with your Father whom he finds a difficult man to get on with.

Our client has given us other grounds which have led us to advise him that he has sufficient grounds for a Divorce based on your unreasonable behaviour, and we are writing to enquire whether you would agree to allow such a Petition to proceed undefended . . .

Despite the small financial contribution that you have made towards the house, and the fact that our client has paid most, if not all, of the bills on the house during the period of your marriage, and that the house is in our client's name, we have advised our client that you may have a small claim for a share in the property, 15 Green Lane. Our client would be prepared to consider making a payment to you to discharge any interest that you may have in the property, on the basis that this would be in full and final settlement in respect of all claims that you may have against him.

In any event any payment that is to be made will have to be made out of the proceeds of sale of the house, so that any payment would be dependent on obtaining a purchaser at a suitable price.

You are of course aware that Frances is continuing her further education and there is the question of her Grant for the final year of her studies at University. Our client has confirmed to us that he will be prepared to contribute the greater part of her Grant, but that you will be required to pay the sum of £250 towards her final year's expenses. Please confirm that you are willing to do this . . .

Revision

Dear Mrs S

We are sorry to say that your husband has consulted us about your marriage difficulties. He asks if you would agree to a divorce.

As you have not been living apart for two years, you cannot divorce by consent. As a result, it seems that Mr S could only ask for a divorce by arguing that your conduct justified it. If he did, it would not be in a spirit of animosity and we would try to raise no more complaints than are necessary to convince the court that the marriage had broken down beyond repair.

Alternatively, Mr S would not resist such a petition if you preferred to bring it against him.

We also hope that we can reach agreement on a financial settlement but perhaps this is a matter which should wait until you have seen your own solicitors, if you wish to do so.

Perhaps you, or they, would contact us?

Yours sincerely

Notes

At the time, most undergraduates were eligible for a local authority grant, although reasonably well-off parents were expected to contribute. The details in the letter indicate that the husband could have afforded a more generous package than his solicitor's letter suggests.

The revision ends with the 'raised eyebrow' question mark, to denote a polite request. A full stop is a shade peremptory, and the writer has no right to demand a reply.

Example B

(See p.83.)

Original

The Guarantor in consideration of the Vendor making the foregoing assignment at the request of the Guarantor hereby covenants with the Vendor that the Purchaser will at all times hereafter duly pay the rent reserved by the Lease the service charges (if any) and all other payments and costs thereby provided for and will duly observe and perform all the covenants on the part of the Lessee and conditions therein contained and that the Guarantor will at all times hereafter duly observe and perform all covenants on the part of the Guarantor with the Landlord of the property and will at all times hereafter pay and make good to the Vendor on demand all losses costs damages and expenses occasioned to the Vendor by the non-payment of the said rents service charges or other payments or the breach non-observance or non-performance of any of the said covenants and conditions or any breach of the Purchaser's covenants as to payments observance and performance and for indemnity expressed in this assignment and notwithstanding any termination of the obligations of the Purchaser or any successors in title of the Purchaser by reason of disclaimer by any Trustee in bankruptcy or liquidator or the winding-up of the Purchaser or any successor in title of the Purchaser being a Corporation IT IS HEREBY AGREED AND DECLARED that any neglect forbearance or indulgence of the Vendor in enforcing or giving time to the Purchaser (or any Trustee in bankruptcy receiver or liquidator of the Purchaser) for any payments or observance or performance of any obligation shall not in any way release the Guarantor in respect of the Guarantor's liability under this present clause

Revision

1   In consideration for this assignment by the seller, the guarantor must:

    a   Fulfil any positive covenant the tenant has broken.

    b   Indemnify the landlord and the seller against the consequences of the tenant's breach of any covenant.

2   The guarantor's liability continues despite:

    a   Lenience by the landlord to the tenant.

    b   Disclaimer in the bankruptcy or liquidation of the tenant.

Notes

It is not necessary to say that a party covenants if this is a deed. A covenant is an agreement by deed.

Fry J said in *Evans* v. *Davis* (1878) that *observe* refers to negative covenants and *perform* to positive ones. On the other hand, *Harman* v. *Ainslie* (1904) and *Ayling* v. *Wade* (1961) applied *perform* to negative covenants. Where, as here, no distinction is needed between positive and negative, it is useful to have a single expression to cover both; if *observe* is still in doubt, *comply with* will do (and sounds more appropriate to modern ears: *observation* suggests watching rather than doing). But we have used *fulfil* in clause 1a and have expressly restricted it to positive covenants: there is no sense in asking the guarantor (for example) *not to make a noise at night* as a remedy for the tenant's disruption.

We have used a full stop at the end of each subclause (a) instead of a semi-colon followed by *and* or *or*. This avoids any argument, especially in clause 2, over whether *and* means that both limbs must be satisfied or that *or* suggests a choice; each subclause is independent of the other so neither conjunction is appropriate.

Example C

(See p.105.)

Original

$50,000 is the most that a person or persons may be required to spend by an order or orders under subsection (1) (whether made on one or more occasions) for all contraventions of any one provision of Part II which are of the same or a substantially similar nature and which occurred at or about the same time.

Revision

$50,000 is the most that any one or more persons may be compelled under subsection (1) (whether on one or more occasions) to spend for all substantially similar breaches of any one provision of Part II occurring at about the same time.

But Professor Adams' version is better (at least, if *no-one* includes corporations):

No-one can be obliged to pay more than $50,000 by an order or series of orders under subsection (1) for breaches of any one provision of Part II occurring at or about the same time. The same limit applies if the order or orders affect more than one person.

Notes

A person or persons is inelegant. We prefer *any one or more people*, though slightly longer, but unfortunately this loses the benefit of the Law of Property Act, s.61 definition of *person* to include *corporation*.

May be required:

- We dislike *required* because of its common use as a pompous alternative to *need*; but *needed* would not do here.
- *Ordered* would not be right because we are speaking of the cost of complying with an order rather than an outright fine. In any case, we are using *order* a few words on.
- We prefer *compelled*. *Required* or *needed* point us to the person with the need; *compelled* focuses on the person compelled, and by whom is less important. For the same reason, the passive is appropriate.

An order or orders: Again, this is a clumsy repetition. We think it can be omitted altogether, leaving . . . *compelled under subsection (1) (whether on one or more occasions) to spend* . . .

Contraventions: breaches sounds better.

Which are of the same or a substantially similar nature: Substantially similar nature includes *same*, so the first alternative need not be spelled out.

At or about can be smoothed to *at about*.

Example D

(See p.119.)

Original

(1) Subject to the following provisions of this section, where an order (in this section referred to as 'the original order') has been made under the last foregoing section, the court, on an application under this section, shall have power by order to discharge or vary the original order or to suspend any provision of it temporarily and to revive the operation of any provision so suspended.

Revision

Orders made under section 26 may on application to the court be:

(1) Discharged or varied.

(2) Suspended and (if suspended) revived.

It should be clear from the following provisions that subsection (1) is subject to them.

Original order does not have to be defined, since the words are used in their ordinary sense.

Suspend implies *temporarily*.

Example E

(See p.122.)

Original

1. Save that by clause 6 of the said Agreement, the Claimant was allowed by the Defendant into possession and occupation of 'the storage area' in order to carry out in a good and workmanlike manner and to the reasonable satisfaction of the Landlord's Surveyor, the works set out in a Section 146 Notice, a copy of which was annexed to the said Agreement and save that by Clause 10 of the said Agreement the Claimant was to comply with the said Section 146 Notice and save that by Clause 11 of the said Agreement the Claimant was to so comply within three months from the date of the said Agreement, that is, by 3rd September 1987 and that provided the said Notice was complied with within that time the Defendant agreed to grant the Claimant a supplementary Lease of the 'storage area', Paragraph 1 of the Particulars of Claim is admitted.

Revision

Paragraph 1 of the particulars of claim is admitted, except that the agreement provided that:

a The defendant comply with the section 146 notice (which was attached to the agreement) within three months – that is, by 3rd September 1987 [clauses 10 and 11].

b The defendant have possession of the storage area for this purpose [clause 6].

c The work was to be 'carried out in a good and workmanlike manner' to the reasonable satisfaction of the Landlord's surveyor [clause 6].

d If the work was completed in the time allowed the claimant would grant the defendant a supplementary lease of the storage area [clause 11].

Notes

• The main part of the paragraph has been moved from the end to the beginning, so the reader knows immediately what it is about.
• *Except* is shorter and more common than, but otherwise exactly the same as, *save that*.
• It is not necessary to keep repeating *the Claimant* and *the Defendant*, nor to capitalise them.

- Broadly, possession is the right to occupy, and occupation (as Lush J said in *R* v. *St Pancras* (1877))

  > includes possession as its primary element but it also includes something more. Legal possession does not of itself constitute an occupation. The owner of a vacant house is in possession . . . but as long as he leaves it vacant he is not rateable for it as an occupier.

  But the judge added that actual possession, even as a trespasser, implies occupation. The duplication looks scholarly and thorough but in this context is unnecessary.
- The inverted commas around *the storage area* are inappropriate, and look odd. The words are used in their normal meaning. We would not write *The claimant let 'the premises' to the defendant.*
- Later the area is referred to, inconsistently, as *the storage area.*
- *Good and workmanlike* is another cliché masquerading as a term of art. If the job is workmanlike, what does *good* add? And what does either word add to the effect of *to the reasonable satisfaction of the Landlord's Surveyor*? The answer may be that counsel was following the rules of pleading by quoting the original document warts and all, but then where are the quotation marks?
- A section 146 notice is not so grand that it justifies initial capitals. It is surprising – but this is not a criticism – that counsel did not name the Act.
- *A copy of which was annexed to the said Agreement* is in parentheses and must have a closing comma as well as an opening one. In the revision we have used round brackets rather than commas to indicate more clearly that it is an aside and that the important point is that the defendant had three months to comply with the notice. We have repeated *the agreement* rather than replacing it with *it* to avoid the possibility that the notice was attached to the particulars of claim.
- *The said Agreement* is repeated ad nauseam (a phrase we are too delicate to translate).
- *The said Notice was complied with* is a particularly clumsy passive.

Example F

(See p.123.)

Original

If the liquidator or trustee does not comply with any provision of this section (or fails as trustee duly to pay the long service leave charges for which the liquidator or trustee is liable under subsection (3)) the liquidator or trustee must to the extent of the value of the assets which have been taken into the liquidator's or trustee's possession and which are or have been available at any time for the payment of the long service leave charges be personally liable to pay the long service leave charges and is guilty of an offence.

Revision

a A liquidator, or trustee, who does not comply with any requirement of this section is guilty of an offence.

b A trustee who commits an offence by failing to pay the long service leave charges as required by subsection (3) will be personally liable for those charges to the

239

extent of the value of the assets which have at any time been in the offender's possession and available for their payment.

Note

The commas around *or trustee* are inelegant but are needed to establish that *who does not comply with* . . . refers to both liquidators and trustees.

Appendix C

Precedents

C1   THE LEASE OF A FLAT IN A BLOCK OWNED BY A MANAGEMENT COMPANY OF WHICH THE TENANTS ARE THE SHAREHOLDERS

Lease of flat [number], Orchard Court, Fruitree Road, Appledore, Kent, TN1 1NT

LR1	Date of lease			
LR2	Title number(s)	LR2.1	Landlord's title number	K 628496
		LR2.2	Other title numbers	
LR3	Parties to this lease		Landlord	Orchard Court Management Company Limited (registered number 812833)
			Tenant	
LR4	Property		In the case of a conflict between this clause and the remainder of this lease then, for the purposes of registration, this clause shall prevail	Flat on the ground floor of Orchard Court, edged red on the plan
LR5	Prescribed statements, etc.			None

LR6	Term for which property is released	From and including	1 January 1990
		To and including	31 December 2889
LR7	Premium		£
LR8	Prohibitions or restrictions on disposing of this lease	*This lease restricts dispositions*	*in clause 6H*
LR9	Rights of acquisition, etc.	LR9.1 Tenant's contractual rights to renew this lease, to acquire the reversion of another lease of the property, or to acquire an interest in other land	None
		LR9.2 Tenant's covenant to (or to offer to) surrender this lease	None
		LR9.3 Landlord's contractual rights to acquire this lease	None
LR10	Restrictive covenants given in this lease by the landlord in respect of land other than the property		None
LR11	Easements	LR11.1 Easements granted by this lease for the benefit of the property are in clause	4
		LR11.2 Easements granted or reserved by this lease over the property for the benefit of other property are in clause	5
LR12	Estate rentcharge burdening the property		None
LR13	Application for standard form of restriction		

LR14 Declaration of trust where there is more than one person comprising the tenant	The tenant is more than one person. They are to hold the property on trust for themselves as beneficial	[joint tenants] [tenants in common]

Definitions

Orchard Court
The freehold land registered at the land registry under title number XXX 1234, known as Orchard Court, Fruitree Road, Appledore, Kent, and edged blue on the plan attached.

The retained parts
All parts of Orchard Court not shown on the plan as a flat (defined as in clauses 2 and 3).

The service charge
The cost to the landlord of complying with its covenants under clause 7.

Share(d)
Share(d) with the landlord or with any tenant or occupier of other flats in Orchard Court.

Conduits
Conduits, wires, cisterns, and chutes carrying water, electricity, gas, communications, and domestic waste.

---

1 In consideration of the premium, which has been paid to the landlord, and the tenant's covenants, the landlord lets the flat to the tenant for the term.

2 The boundaries of the flat are:

A Between the plaster and the walls and ceilings.
B Immediately above the concrete floors.

3 The flat includes:

A Its doors, door fittings, windows, and window fittings, but not the window frames.
B Conduits within its boundaries.

4 The tenant has the right to:

A Park private cars, motorcycles, and cycles:

1 On the private parking space marked on the plan with the same number as the flat.
2 On any available marked space in the communal parking area as permitted by the rules referred to in clause 6K.

B Use the taps and hose in the communal parking area to wash private vehicles.
C Place a namecard in the space by the front-door bell at the main entrance.
D Use the cupboards next to the front door of the flat for service meters.
E Share the use of:

1 The retained parts to get to and from the flat and parking spaces.
2 The gardens.
3 The conduits in the retained parts which serve the flat.
4 The television aerial, amplifier unit and entryphone system.

5   The landlord retains the right, for itself and the owners and occupiers of other flats at Orchard Court, to share the use of any conduits passing through the flat for the benefit of other parts of Orchard Court.

6   The tenant must (and if there is more than one tenant they agree jointly and individually that they will):

A   Pay:

1   The service charge calculated in accordance with clause 8.

2   The expenses attributable to the occupation of the flat, except those for which the landlord is responsible under clause 7.

3   Any expenses (including legal and other professional fees) incurred by the landlord under subclause D3 or as a result of any breach of the tenant's obligations.

B   1   Keep the flat to the reasonable satisfaction of the landlord in good condition, clean, and well-decorated.

2   Comply within a reasonable time with a notice from the landlord to remedy breaches of paragraph 1.

C   Not damage the flat or allow others to do so.

D   Allow the landlord and its agents to enter at all reasonable times (on reasonable notice except in an emergency) to:

1   Inspect the flat.

2   Carry out emergency repairs.

3   Do any work which the tenant should have done under subclause B2.

4   Comply with its other obligations under this lease.

E   Comply as if the freeholder with the legitimate requirements of any authority relating to the flat, unless it is the landlord's obligation under clause 7.

F   Use the flat only as a home for not more than one household, without over-crowding.

G   Not do or allow in Orchard Court anything which:

1   Might annoy others.

2   Is dangerous.

3   Might prejudice the landlord's insurance cover or increase the premium.

H   Not dispose of nor part with possession of:

1   Part only of the flat.

2   The whole flat, except:

a   By transfer, assent, mortgage, charge, or operation of law.

b   By a sublease:

- in which the subtenant agrees with the landlord to abide by the terms of this lease (except subclauses 6A and J); and

- of whose terms the landlord is given at least two weeks' previous written notice.

I   Give the secretary of the landlord company written notice within one month after any such transaction, supplying a copy of the instrument and paying a reasonable registration fee on demand.

J 1   Be a member of the landlord company and, on request by it (unless circumstances make it impracticable) serve as any one of more of the following:
- a member of its board;
- company secretary;
- chair.

   2   Resign from office when no longer the tenant and pass membership of the company to the new tenant, giving as much notice of the resignation as is practicable.

K Obey (and ensure any occupiers of and visitors to the flat obey) the following rules (as reasonably varied at any time by the landlord for the benefit of the tenants as a whole):

Tenants may not:

1   Make a sound audible inside other flats (except between 9am and 6pm to an extent inevitable for normal housework, normal repairs, or normal decoration).
2   Use unsuppressed electrical equipment.
3   Dry, clean, or air anything outside the flat (except as allowed by clause 4B).
4   Leave anything on the retained parts, except for:

   a   Parking in accordance with clause 4A.
   b   Leaving wheelchairs, and prams, in each case while occupied, on grassed or paved parts of the gardens (but without obstructing the paths).

5   Leave any vehicle in a communal parking space for more than 18 hours in any 24 without the landlord's permission.
6   Leave the basement garage door open.
7   Fix an aerial or satellite dish outside the flat.
8   Put up any sign visible outside the flat.
9   Allow water to soak through the floors.
10 Interfere with the retained parts or shared facilities without the landlord's permission.
11 Use the shared facilities in a way which might damage them or inconvenience other occupiers.
12 Play ball games.
13 Allow a dog on the retained parts except on a lead.
14 Make the retained parts dirty or untidy.

7 The landlord must:

A Keep the retained parts clean, tidy, and in such condition as is reasonable having regard to the class and age of the building.
B Manage Orchard Court as a high-class residential estate, maintaining the facilities to a reasonable standard, employing a caretaker and, at its discretion, other agents.

C 1   Insure with a reputable company:
   a   The landlord against public liability.
   b   Orchard Court against the perils required of borrowers by the Council of Mortgage Lenders and to a level sufficient to reconstruct it without cost to the landlord or tenants.

   2   Provide on demand copies of the current policy and premium

       receipt (but not more than once in each period except on payment of a reasonable fee).

3   Use the proceeds of any insurance claim to reinstate Orchard Court, making significant changes only as required by law or approved by the tenants of at least 75% of the flats materially affected by them.

4   Arrange for the interests of the tenant and the tenant's mortgagees to be protected by the policy.

D   Comply with any law relating to the retained parts, paying all charges assessed on them.

E   Make good any damage done when exercising its rights, except to the extent that the damage resulted from the tenant's breach of duty.

F   1   Use its best efforts to keep the other flats in Orchard Court let on similar terms (except insofar as may be needed for a caretaker).

2   Enforce against the other tenants, so far as is reasonable, the obligations in their leases.

G   Register the current tenant as a member of the landlord company.

8   A   As soon as practicable after 31 December each year, the landlord must produce accounts for the year then ending, and will meanwhile estimate the service charge for the next year.

B   The tenant must pay by banker's order one-fortieth of that estimate (adjusted by bringing forward any balance from the previous year) by equal instalments on the 1st of each month.

9   Any management decision made on behalf of the landlord is binding on the tenant unless it is shown that no reasonable landlord could have made it.

10   The landlord may enter the flat, so ending this lease, although without affecting any rights which have accrued under it, if:

A   Any money due to the landlord is unpaid for more than 21 days after it has become due (whether formally demanded or not); or

B   The tenant has broken any other covenant.

Signed as a deed on behalf of the landlord by

Director

Secretary

Notes

This precedent was taken from a form used in 1990 for a block of 40 flats whose management company, owned by the tenants under the usual one-share-per-flat arrangement, had bought the freehold. The brief was to replace the traditionally written leases whose terms were approaching their end with plain language leases for a term long enough to outlive the structure. We have made a few changes since, most significantly adding the clauses prescribed by the Land Registration (Amendment) (No 2) Rules 2005. Those are not always as we would have chosen but we may not omit words which appear in unitalicised bold text in Schedule 1 to the rules. For instance, as this was a lease of a flat the premises were originally called 'the flat' rather than (as we now must) 'the Property'. However:

- The rules do not forbid changes in formatting, and we have used a lower-case

'p', preferring the grammatical convention applicable to common nouns to the legal habit of capitalising anything the Drafter considers Grand.
- We have also sidestepped the land registry's predilection for emboldening practically everything in sight, a custom which drowns essentials which might otherwise have been usefully highlighted.
- We have replaced some full stops after the numbers with a tab space (an omission which is presumably permitted as full stops are not words).
- We have culled the superfluous words from LR8 (*This lease contains a provision that prohibits or restricts dispositions*), replacing it with the more informative *This lease restricts dispositions (in clause 6H)*. This change also seems to be permitted, because the words are not emboldened in the regulations, and it is only bold text which must be retained.
- We have corrected the grammatical error in LR9.2 by changing it from *Tenant's covenant to (or offer to) surrender this lease* to *Tenant's covenant to (or **to** offer to) surrender this lease*. It is forbidden to omit words from that rubric but not to add them.

> **MA:** I normally inserted the plan on the back of the front page, or on the back page if that was otherwise unused.

Definitions We welcomed the land registry's abandonment of its former prefix *Her Majesty's*, which since it is a public institution seemed as unnecessary and inaccurate as the irritating communist equivalent *People's*. However, this redundancy is now being reinstated. We have rebelled against this bossiness by referring to it as *the land registry*, using the words in their natural sense rather than as a name.

Cl 1 The tenants between them own the freehold so there is no rent. There is no point in providing for a peppercorn.

Cl 2 The entire structure of the building is owned by the landlord company.

Cl 4 There are no explicit rights of support and protection because the points are covered more effectively by clause 7.

Cl 6 We are reluctant to mix up the positive and negative covenants. One group of *musts* and another of *must nots* would be neater. But we have opted to keep groups of related covenants together whether they are positive or negative; so, for example, *not damage* follows *keep in good condition*.

Cl 6 K Some of the rules are unnecessary because they are implied by law (for instance, that against putting up an aerial outside the flat, which would be a trespass). But it is worth expressing prohibitions which might otherwise be overlooked or ignored.

Cl 6 K 12 Opinion was divided about adding *at Orchard Court*. We have used the shorter form rather than state the obvious. No management company could enforce the rule in its wide sense, nor would it try unless the entire board was insane and beyond the control of its members.

Cl 7   The landlord's covenant for quiet enjoyment is implied by
        common law if not mentioned, so the only purposes for a
        landlord to mention it explicitly are to cut down or increase
        the implied right, or to reassure tenants who didn't know that
        they had it. But in practice it is unlikely to reassure them,
        because they don't know what it means (and it would be
        disproportionate to explain it clearly).

Cl 7 A The standard of repairs is not set impractically high; the
        tenants, voting through the company, can allow the building to
        age gracefully and may eventually sell for redevelopment.

MA: When struggling with Clause 7A for the original version of this lease I asked a much older and more experienced solicitor how he would avoid the conflict between the usual repairing covenant and the fact that the lease was intended to outlive the building. *Who cares?* he said. *You'll be dead by then.*

C2   LICENCE TO ASSIGN AND AUTHORISED GUARANTEE AGREEMENT

Details	
Date of this licence	02 April 2016
Premises	6 Aerobics Street, London SW1P 4PP
Lease	The 20-year lease from 15 June 2011 between the landlord and the outgoing tenant
Landlord	Johnson Estates Ltd
Outgoing tenant	Mrs Ayse Tremaine of 8 Grosvenor Road, London W1X 9GG
Incoming tenants	Mr Jeffsinka Geronimo and Ms Audrey Shepherd, both of 15 High Street, London SW6 4GT

1   The landlord permits the assignment of the lease to the incoming tenants.
2   The incoming tenants agree jointly and individually:

   A   To comply with the terms of the lease.
   B   To register the assignment at the land registry as soon as practicable.
3   The outgoing tenant:

   A   Guarantees that the incoming tenants will comply with the terms of the lease.
   B   Indemnifies (as principal debtor) the landlord against any breach of those terms.
   C   Will remain liable under paragraphs 3A and 3B (but only to the extent allowed by law):

      1   Despite any concession or failure to enforce terms.

2   Even if the terms of the lease are changed, except that her liability will not become more onerous.
3   Even if the landlord reasonably refuses to accept payment from the tenant with the intention of preserving a claim to end the lease early because of the tenant's breach of duty.

Signed as a deed for Johnson Estates Ltd by Diana Benaron and Wendy Gallant as directors authorised to sign for it	
Signed as a deed by Ayse Tremaine in the presence of:	
Witness's signature	
printed name	
and address	
Signed as a deed by Jeffsinka Geronimo and Audrey Shepherd, each in the presence of:	
Witness's signature	
printed name	
and address	

Notes

Some practitioners like to see a covenant to take a new lease if the original one is disclaimed. We have omitted it as redundant (see *Hindcastle* v. *Attenborough* (1997)).

C3   RENT REVIEW MEMORANDUM

The premises		**Unit 7, Potts Industrial Estate, London N1 6WG**
Landlord		Johnson Estates Ltd of 6 Engel Grove, London NW3 6BY
Tenant		William Daniel Marks
Lease	Date	6 March 1986
	[Original landlord	Myrtle Williams plc]
	[Original tenant	Sonia Lewis]
New rent		**£9,100** a year
Date from which it takes effect		**6 March 2017**

Signed by Myles
Sullivan
for the landlord: . . . .

Signed by the tenant: . . . .

C4   MEMORANDUM OF TRUST

Specimen memorandum of trust

between
David Cassel
and
Anne Mira
concerning
[Address]
and any replacement
house

Our holdings

1. This agreement is **[not]** to survive our marriage, if we do marry.
2. The house is bought as our home **[state contributions]** **[with the help of interest-free loans of £10,000 from David's mother and Anne's father, and these are to be repaid (if they have not already been) from the proceeds of sale]**.
3. We will hold the house as **[joint tenants (see explanatory note)]** **[or specify shares]** [regardless of our respective contributions to the purchase or to any improvements].
4. We will be **[jointly]** responsible for the mortgage and any expenses **[or specify shares]**.

Arrangements for a sale

5. If one of us (A) serves written notice on the other (B) asking for a sale of the property:
   (1) B can opt in writing within one month to buy out A.
   (2) If B does not exercise this right, the property will be put on the open market and will be sold as soon as can be arranged but not less than three months from the original notice.
   (3) If we cannot agree on a price or on a means of fixing it, then it will be decided by a surveyor.
   (4) After receiving the surveyor's notice of the price, B has two weeks to cancel the option to buy.
   (5) The sale from A to B will be completed one month after the price is fixed, or three months from A's original notice, whichever is the later.
   (6) There will be no exchange of contracts on the open market at a price less than provided by paragraph (3) until the land has been on the market for three months, and then only with a surveyor's approval.

(7) The death of one of us before completion of the sale to B or exchange of contracts with a third party will not annul the original notice.

(8) If B dies before completing the purchase from A then the option will be annulled and the property sold on the open market as above with B's personal representatives taking over B's role.

(9) If we cannot agree the division of the contents of the property we will abide by the decision of the district judge in the local county court, acting under the small claims procedure (even if the contents are worth more than the small claims limit).

Note about the surveyor appointed under clause 5

6. 'Surveyor' is used in clause 5 to mean a chartered surveyor who is a principal or employee of the nearest estate agency which is able and willing to act.

7. The surveyor will act as an expert.

8. If either of us wishes, the estate agency appointed under paragraph 5(3) will be disqualified from acting under 5(6).

. . . .

[*date*]

Explanatory note

We suggest the note at **www.gov.uk/joint-property-ownership/overview**.

C5   EXPLANATION TO INTENDED OCCUPIERS, AND DISCLAIMER

Disclaimer of rights by occupiers
Important notes
To Jesse and Karen Longword from [*name of solicitor*]

Address of the house to be bought   18 Beresford Road, London SW3 6BY

Intended owners   Erin and Erica Longword

Intended occupiers   Jesse and Karen Longword

As the house is being bought with the help of a mortgage, the building society want you to sign the enclosed consent form.

It says that their rights to the house come before yours. They need this to get a court order to evict you – so that the property can be sold – if your parents fall behind with the payments or break some other important condition of the mortgage.

You should not sign the form unless you understand it, and are sure you are not giving away rights you may have and which you want to keep. If in doubt, ask: you may want to get legal advice from a solicitor of your own, or you might prefer a Citizens Advice Bureau.

You should only sign if you are sure that you are not selling yourselves short. You will need someone from outside the household to witness your signatures. You can sign separately or both at once, with the same or different witnesses, whichever is more convenient.

If you decide not to sign, please let me know as soon as possible. Otherwise, please return the signed form to me.

C6   NOTICE OF SALE AND CHARGE

Notice of sale and charge

given to landlord of leasehold premises

23 Belsize Mansions, Fleet Road, London NW3 2HY

To: Mr B.B. Woolf

The Big House

Peckham Road

London SE5 8UB

On 17 April 2017
Jane Doe
assigned her lease to
Eric Scissorman
who charged it to
Dorking Building Society
of Queens Park Road, Bristol BS1 2JJ (A/c 6059 2876).
The lease is dated 13 December 2003 and runs for 125 years from 28 November 1998.

I enclose:
- a certified copy of the transfer
- a copy of this notice for receipting (please), and
- my cheque for £20.

Please arrange for the building society's interest to be noted on the insurance policy.

17 April 2017

Elizabeth Laws

G.N.G. Din & Co

5 Mill Lane

Dorking

RH4 3JN

Tel: 01306 741055

Solicitor for the new tenant and the mortgagee

Received by Mr B.B. Woolf [*date*] April 2017

Bibliography

Articles and reports

Adler, Mark (1991) 'Bamboozling the public', *New Law Journal* (26 July); reprinted in *The Scribes Journal of Legal Writing* (Vol.9, 2003–04); and at **www.adler.demon.co.uk/pub.htm**.

— (1993) 'British lawyers' attitudes to plain English', *Clarity* 28 (Aug); and at **www.adler.demon.co.uk/pub.htm**.

— (1993) 'Alphabet soup', *Law Society Gazette* (Nov); and at **www.adler.demon.co.uk/pub.htm**.

— (1994) 'The folly of euphemism', *Clarity* 31 (Oct).

— (1996) 'Tried and tested: the myth behind the cliché', *Clarity* 34 (Jan); and at **www.adler.demon.co.uk/pub.htm**.

— (2008) 'In support of plain law: an answer to Francis Bennion', *The Loophole* (Aug); and at **www.adler.demon.co.uk/bennion.htm**.

— (2011) (Feb) 'What is plain language when there's more than one egg on the wall' at **www.adler.demon.co.uk/plain.htm**.

— (2011) (Mar) 'Judging styles' at **www.adler.demon.co.uk/judging.htm**.

— (2011) (May–Jun) 'Professionalizing plain language' at **www.adler.demon.co.uk/professionalism1.htm**.

— (2013) (Mar) 'Full disclosure: the truth, the whole truth, and nothing but the truth' at **www.adler.demon.co.uk/disclosure.htm**.

— (2013–15) 'Legal style through the ages' at **www.adler.demon.co.uk/history.htm**.

Arden, Dame Mary (Lady Justice) (2008) 'The impact of judicial interpretation on legislative drafting', *The Loophole* (Aug) p.6. This article reproduces Dame Mary's keynote address to the Commonwealth Association of Legislative Counsel's biennial conference (Nairobi, 2007). The quotation on p.118 comes from p.13 of *The Loophole*.

Armstrong, Stephen V. and Terrell, Timothy P. (2015) 'The art and architecture of paragraphs: Focus, flow, and emphasis', *Perspectives: Teaching Legal Research & Writing* (Vol.23, No.2).

Assy, Rabeea (2011) 'Can the law speak directly to its subjects? The limitation of plain language', *Journal of Law and Society* (Vol.38, No.3, Sep) pp.376–404.

Bennion, Francis (2007) 'Confusion over plain language law', *The Commonwealth Lawyer* (16) pp.63–68.

Benson, Robert W. and Kessler, Joan B. (1987) 'Legalese v. plain English: An empirical study of persuasion and credibility in appellate brief writing', *Loyola LA Law Review* (Vol.20).

Berk-Seligson, Susan (2016) 'Linguistic issues in courtroom interpretation' in Tiersma and Solan (2015).

Bertlin, Alison (2014) 'What works best for the reader? A study on drafting and presenting legislation', *The Loophole* (May) at **calc.ngo/sites/default/files/loophole/may-2014.pdf**.

Bowman, Sir Geoffrey QC (2006) 'The art of legislative drafting', *Amicus Curiae* (issue 64, March/April) pp.2–9, at **journals.sas.ac.uk/amicus/article/view/1117**.

Cheek, Annetta (2010) 'Defining plain language', *Clarity* 64 (Nov).

Child, Barbara (1992) 'What does "plain meaning" mean these days?', *Clarity* 26 (Dec).

Clark, Paul (2015) 'A model lease?' in *The Conveyancer and Property Lawyer* (Conv.2015, 4, 291–300).

Corsellis, Ann and Clement, Amanda (2006) 'Interpreters and translators in the criminal legal process' in Heaton-Armstrong, Anthony, Shepherd, Eric, Gudjonsson, Gisli, and Wolchover, David (eds.) *Witness Testimony*, Oxford University Press.

Eades, Diana (2002) '"Evidence given in unequivocal terms": Gaining consent of Aboriginal young people in court' in Cotterill, Janet (ed.) *Language in the Legal Process*, Palgrave Macmillan.

Eagleson, Robert (and others) (1996) 'A singular use of "they"', *Clarity* 34 (Jan).

Elliott, David (1990) 'Gender-neutral drafting in Canada', *Clarity* 16 (Mar).

— (1993) 'The arguments in favour of using examples in legislation', *Clarity* 28 (Aug).

Fraser, Helen, Stevenson, Bruce, and Marks, Tony (2011) 'Interpretation of a crisis call: persistence of a primed perception of a disputed utterance' in *The International Journal of Speech, Language and the Law* (Vol.18.2) and at **helenfraser.com.au/wp-content/uploads/Fraser-Stevenson-Marks-crisis-call. pdf**.

Garner, Bryan (2009) 'The importance of other eyes' in *Garner on Language and Writing*, American Bar Association, p.415.

— (2010) 'Interviews with United States Supreme Court Justices' in *Scribes Journal of Legal Writing* (Vol.13).

Grice, Paul (1975) 'Logic and conversation' in Cole, P. & Morgan, J., *Syntax and semantics (3. Speech acts)*, Academic Press, pp.41–58.

Goldstein, Naomi, and others (2012) 'Potential impact of juvenile suspects' linguistic abilities on *Miranda* understanding and appreciation' in Tiersma & Solan (2015).

Hart, H.L.A (1958) 'Positivism and the separation of law and morals', *Harvard Law Review*, 593, 71(4), pp.593–629.

Henderson, Gordon D. (1989) 'Controlling hyperlexis – The most important "law and …"', *The Tax Lawyer* (Vol.36, No.1, fall) pp.177–99.

Heydon, Georgina (2013) 'From legislation to the courts' in Heffer, Rock, and Conley (2013).

HM Courts & Tribunals Service (2016) *Chancery Guide* (see **www.gov.uk/ government/uploads/system/uploads/attachment_data/file/644051/ Chancery_Guide_updated_0917.pdf**).

Independent Online, The (2007) 'Endless new criminal laws that lead to injustice' (31 October).

Kavanagh, Eileen (2005–06) 'Robert Traver as Justice Voelker – The novelist as judge', *Scribes Journal of Legal Writing* (Vol.10).

Kuhn, Deanna, Weinstock, Michael, and Flaton, Robin (1994) 'How well do jurors reason? Competence dimensions of individual variation in a juror reasoning task', *Psychological Science* (Vol.5, No.5, Sep) pp.289–96.

Law Reform Commission of Victoria (1987) *Plain English and the Law.*

Lee, Jieun (2011) 'Translatability of speech style in court interpreting', *Speech, Language, and the Law* (Vol.18.1).

Mackay, A.J.G. (1887) 'Introduction to an essay on the art of legal composition commonly called drafting', *Law Quarterly Review*, 3:326.

Manning, Bayless (1982) 'Hyperlexis and the law of conservation of ambiguity: Thoughts on section 385', *The Tax Lawyer* (Vol.36, No.1, fall) pp.9–15. The quotations on p.26 are from pp.9 and 14.

New Zealand Law Commission (with Parliamentary Counsel Office) (2007) *Presentation of New Zealand Statute Law* (see **www.lawcom.govt.nz/sites/default/files/ projectAvailableFormats/NZLC%20R104.pdf**).

Oerton, Richard (1993) 'The split infinitive' (letter to the editor in *Clarity* 29 (Dec)).

Orwell, George (1946) 'Politics and the English language', *Horizon* (April); reprinted in *Inside the Whale and other essays* (Penguin, 1962).

Rix LJ (2006) 'Plain language in legal agreements: is it safe?', *Clarity* 56 (Nov) p.47.

Rock, Frances (2016) 'The caution in England and Wales' in Tiersma & Solan (2015).

Russell, Bertrand (1905) 'On denoting', *Mind* (Vol.14, No.56, pp.479–493).

Russell, Sonia (2000) '"Let me put it simply…": The case for a standard translation of the police caution and its explanation', *Forensic Linguistics* (7(1):26–48).

Sarcevic, Susan (2015) 'Challenges to the legal translator' in Tiersma & Solan (2015).

Schroth, Peter W. (1986) 'Legal translation', *American Journal of Comparative Law* (Vol.34). The extract on p.212 is quoted in Sarcevic (2015).

Solan, Lawrence M. (2004) 'Pernicious ambiguity in contracts and statutes', *Chicago-Kent Law Review* (Vol.79) p.859 (see **ssrn.com/abstract=500543**).

Staughton, Sir Christopher (1987) 'Courtly language', *Counsel* 50.

Stumpff, Andrew Morrison (2013) 'The law is a fractal: The attempt to anticipate everything', 44 Loy.U.Chi.L.J.649. See **lawecommons.luc.edu/luclj/vol44/iss3/2**.

Sumption, Jonathan (Lord) (2017) 'A question of taste: The Supreme Court and the interpretation of contracts' (see **www.supremecourt.uk/docs/speech-170508.pdf**).

Torbert, Preston M. (2007) 'Globalizing legal drafting: What the Chinese can teach us about *eiusdem generis* and all that', *The Scribes Journal of Legal Writing* (Vol.11).

UK Public Accounts Committee report: **www.publications.parliament.uk/pa/ cm200910/cmselect/cmpubacc/389/389.pdf**, para.14, Q14 of the attached evidence.

Volokh, Alexander (1998) 'n guilty men' (**scholarship.law.upenn.edu/cgi/ viewcontent.cgi?article=3427&context=penn_law_review**).

Waller, Rob (2015) 'Layout for legislation' (Apr), at **www.simplificationcentre. org.uk/download-a-document/?h=c446b8cf045833690c7f150fd208cc20**.

Williams, Martin J. Bourgeois and Croyle, Robert T. (1993) 'The effects of stealing thunder in criminal and civil trials' in *Law and Human Behavior* (Vol.17, No.6, Dec) pp.597–609.

Wolchover, David and Heaton-Armstrong, Anthony (2010) 'Audio recording witness statements – No further excuses, please!', 174 *Criminal Law & Justice Weekly* (No.23, Jun 5) pp.341–44.

— (2010) 'Reasonable doubt', 174 *Criminal Law & Justice Weekly* (No.32, Aug 7) pp.484–489.

Wren, Christopher G. (2002) 'E-Prime, briefly: A lawyer's experiment with writing in E-Prime', *Clarity* (Dec).

Books

Bingham, Tom (2010) *The Rule of Law*, Penguin Books.

Blackstone, William (1765) *Commentaries on the Laws of England*, Clarendon Press.

Butt, Peter and Castle, Richard (2013) *Modern Legal Drafting*, Cambridge University Press (3rd edition revised by Peter Butt alone).

Child, Barbara (1992) *Drafting Legal Documents*, 2nd edn, West. The *swimming pool* definitions are at pp.182–3.

Cutts, Martin (2000) *Lucid Law*, 2nd edn, Plain Language Commission.

Dawkins, Richard (1989) *The Extended Phenotype: The Long Reach of the Gene*, Oxford University Press.

Denning (Lord) (1979) *The Discipline of Law*, Butterworths.
Doyle, Margaret (1995) *A–Z of Non-Sexist Language*, The Women's Press.
Driedger, Elmer (1974) *The Construction of Statutes*, Butterworths.
DuBay, William (2004) *The Principles of Readability*, Impact Information (**www.impact-information.com/impactinfo/readability02.pdf**).
Duckworth, Mark and Spyrou, Arthur (eds) (1995) *Law Words: 30 Essays on Legal Words & Phrases*, published by the Centre for Plain Legal Language, Sydney. It is now out of print but is downloadable without charge from **www.clarity-international.net**.
Eagleman, David (2015) *The Brain: The Story of You*, Canongate Books.
Eagleson, Robert (1990) *Writing in Plain English*, Australian Government Publishing Service. The quotation on p.42 comes from p.4 of his book.
Felker, Daniel, and others (1981) *Guidelines for Document Designers*, American Institutes for Research.
Flesch, Rudolf (1979) *How to Write Plain English*, HarperCollins Publishers.
Fowler, H.W. (1926) *A Dictionary of Modern English Usage*, 1st edn, Oxford.
Garner, Bryan A. (1999) *The Winning Brief*, Oxford University Press. One hundred tips on persuasive brief-writing in US trial courts. The quotation on p.157 is taken from §84. (British readers should bear in mind that a US brief is a written argument to the court, not the solicitor's instructions to trial counsel.)
— (2011) *Garner's Dictionary of Legal Usage*, 3rd edn, Oxford University Press. A legal dictionary and style guide from a plain language perspective.
Good, C. Edward (1989) *Mightier than the Sword*, Blue Jeans Press.
Gowers, Sir Ernest (1987) *The Complete Plain Words*, 3rd edn, Penguin.
— (1965) Fowler's *Modern English Usage*, 2nd edn, Oxford; by Sir Ernest Gowers.
Grice, H.P. (1989) *Studies in the Way of Words*, Harvard University Press.
Grove, Trevor (1998) *The Juryman's Tale*, Bloomsbury Publishing plc.
Heffer, Chris, Rock, Frances, and Conley, John (eds) (2013) *Legal-Lay Communication*, Oxford University Press.
Humphries, Carolyn (2003) *Really Simple English Grammar Essentials*, Foulsham.
Kimble, Joseph (2006) *Lifting the Fog of Legalese*, Carolina Academic Press.
— (2012) *Writing for Dollars, Writing to Please*, Carolina Academic Press.
Mattila, Heiki E.S. (2013) *Comparative Legal Linguistics*, 2nd edn, Ashgate.
McArthur, Tom (ed) (1992) *The Oxford Companion to the English Language*, Oxford University Press.
Mellinkoff, David (1963) *The Language of the Law*, Little, Brown & Co.
— (1992) *Dictionary of American Legal Usage*, West Publishing Co.
Miller, Casey, and Swift, Kate (1995) *The Handbook of Non-Sexist Writing*, 3rd edn, The Women's Press.
Mowat, Christine (2015) *A Plain Language Handbook for Legal Writers*, 2nd edn; Carswell.
Ostler, Nicholas (2005) *Empires of the Word*, HarperCollins.
Piesse, E.L. (1995) *The Elements of Drafting*, 9th edn, Law Book Co (ed J.K. Aitken).
Pinker, Steven (1994) *The Language Instinct*, Penguin Books. The *Time flies like an arrow* example of ambiguity on p.195 is taken from his p.209.
— (1998) *How the Mind Works*, Allen Lane, The Penguin Press. The Borges quotation is on his p.307.
Tiersma, Peter (1999) *Legal Language*, University of Chicago Press. A linguist's view of legal language (though the author was also professor of law at Loyola Law School, Los Angeles.
— (2010) *Parchment, Paper, Pixels*, University of Chicago Press.
Tiersma, Peter, and Solan, Lawrence (2015) *The Oxford Handbook of Language and Law*, Oxford University Press.

Weiner, E.S.C. and Delahunty, Andrew (1994) *The Oxford Guide to English Usage*, 2nd edn. The quotation on p.141 is taken from their p.212.

Periodicals

Clarity – The journal of Clarity, the principal international body promoting plain legal language. For membership information, and recent back numbers, visit **www.clarity-international.net**.

The Loophole – The journal of the Commonwealth Association of Legislative Counsel (CALC), available at **calc.ngo/sites/default/files/loophole/aug-2008.pdf**.

The Scribes Journal of Legal Writing – The journal of Scribes, an association of published legal writers. Its main goal is to promote better legal writing. For membership information, visit **www.scribes.org**.

Index of cases

Alghussein Establishment v. *Eton College* [1988] 1 WLR 587.
Ambatielos v. *Anton Jurgens Margarine Works* [1923] AC 175.
Anglo Continental Educational Group (GB) Ltd v. *Capital Homes (Southern) Ltd* [2009] EWCA Civ 218; *Anglo Continental Educational Group (GB) Ltd* v. *ASN Capital Investments Ltd, (formerly) Capital Homes (Southern) Ltd* [2010] EWHC 2649 (Ch).
Aquarius Financial Enterprises Inc v. *Lloyd's Underwriters (The Delphine)* [2001] Lloyd's Law Reports, Vol 2, p.542.
Agarkov v. *Tinkoff Credit Systems* (Russian case reported online, see, e.g., The Independent Online (9 August 2013)).
Arnold v. *Britton* [2015] UKSC 36.
Associated Artists Ltd v. *Inland Revenue Commissioners* [1956] 1 WLR 752.
Ayling v. *Wade* [1961] 2 QB 228.
In the matter of B (a child) [2016] UKSC 4.
Bairstow Eves (Securities) Ltd v. *Ripley* [1993] 65 P&CR 220.
Balogun v. *Boyes Sutton and Perry* [2017] EWCA Civ 75.
Bank of Credit and Commerce International SA v. *Munawar Ali & others* [2001] UKHL 8.
Ben Nevis (Holdings) Ltd v. *HMRC* [2013] EWCA Civ 578.
Berton v. *Alliance Economic Investment Co Ltd* [1922] 1 KB 742.
Beswick v. *Beswick* [1966] Ch 538.
Beyers v. *Secretary of State for Environment, Transport and Regions and Uttlesford District Council* [2000] EWHC 387 (Admin).
Bradshaw v. *Boynton Beach Mall and Simon Property Group* Florida's 4th district Court of Appeal, 10 April 2013, 4D11-4242.
BOC Group Plc v. *Centeon Llc* [1999] EWCA Civ 1293.
Bronston v. *The United States* 409 US 352 (1973).
Burford UK Properties Ltd v. *Forte Hotels (UK) Ltd* [2003] EWCA Civ 1800.
Burgess v. *Rawnsley* [1975] Ch 429.
Caisse populaire Desjardins de Val-Brillant v. *Blouin* 2003 SCC 31.
Cambridge Antibody Technology v. *Abbott Biotechnology Ltd* [2004] EWHC 2974 (Pat).
Chase International Corporation v. *Oliver* [1978], unreported.
Collier v. *Williams* and other appeals [2006] EWCA Civ 20.
Commercial Management (Investments) Ltd v. *Mitchell Design and Construct Ltd* [2016] EWHC 76 (TCC).
Cornish v. *Accident Insurance Co* (1889) 23 QBD 453 at p.456.
Cosco Bulk Carrier Co Ltd v. *Team-Up Owning Co Ltd (The Saldanha)* [2010] EWHC 1340 (Comm).
Daventry District Council v. *Daventry & District Housing Ltd* [2011] EWCA Civ 1153.
Davies v. *Meadwestvaco Calmar Ltd* [2008] EWCA Civ 8. The 'elsewhere' to which we refer on mentioning this case was Arden LJ's article 'The impact of judicial interpretation on legislative drafting', listed above.
Dawson v. *R* (1961) 106 CLR 1.
Doherty v. *Birmingham City Council* [2008] UKHL 57.
Evans v. *Davis* (1878) 10 ChD 747.

Index